Big Brother

Also by Jonathan Bignell

AN INTRODUCTION TO TELEVISION STUDIES

BRITISH TELEVISION DRAMA: Past Present and Future (*coeditor*)

MEDIA SEMIOTICS: An Introduction

POPULAR TELEVISION DRAMA: Critical Perspectives (*coeditor*)

POSTMODERN MEDIA CULTURE

THE TELEVISION HANDBOOK, THIRD EDITION (*co-author*)

TERRY NATION (*co-author*)

WRITING AND CINEMA (*editor*)

Big Brother

Reality TV in the
Twenty-first Century

Jonathan Bignell

First published in 2005 by
PALGRAVE MACMILLAN
Houndmills, Basingstoke, Hampshire RG21 6XS and
175 Fifth Avenue, New York, N.Y. 10010
Companies and representatives throughout the world.

PALGRAVE MACMILLAN is the global academic imprint of the Palgrave
Macmillan division of St. Martin's Press, LLC and of Palgrave Macmillan Ltd.
Macmillan® is a registered trademark in the United States, United Kingdom
and other countries. Palgrave is a registered trademark in the European
Union and other countries.

ISBN-13: 978–1–4039–1684–6 hardback
ISBN-10: 1–4039–1684–5   hardback
ISBN-13: 978–1–4039–1685–3 paperback
ISBN-10: 1–4039–1685–3   paperback

This book is printed on paper suitable for recycling and made from fully
managed and sustained forest sources.

A catalogue record for this book is available from the British Library.

Library of Congress Cataloging-in-Publication Data is available from the
Library of Congress.

10 9 8 7 6 5 4 3
14 13 12 11 10 09 08 07 06

Printed and bound in Great Britain by
Antony Rowe Ltd, Chippenham and Eastbourne

Contents

Preface and Acknowledgements

I am grateful to the students on the 'Television and Documentary' course at the University of Reading in 2004–05: Helen Dunworth, Jessica Garland, Rozzie Hughes, Alexandra Lishman, Alex Papadakis, Caroline Reed and Amy Tucker. Their ideas about Reality TV helped to shape my own, and their contribution has added valuable insights to this book. I am especially grateful to Alexandra Lishman, whose careful notes on our discussions reminded me of ideas that would otherwise have been lost in the to and fro of argument. My friend David Kail has made important comments and corrections to my ideas about the institutional position of Reality TV as a result of his experience of working in the television industry, and I am grateful for his insights. I presented some of the conceptual issues outlined in this book at the conference 'Reality TV: Contexts, Debates, Futures' at the University of Surrey, Roehampton in May 2004, where contributions from the participants have aided my work. Some of the work on the aesthetics of surveillance in Chapter 5 was suggested by John Gibbs's detailed studies of style and meaning in cinema, and I am pleased to be able to acknowledge the importance of his work on mise-en-scene to my analyses of programmes in this book. I have also been influenced by the approach of Sarah Cardwell to the specifics of television textuality that have modified some of my ideas on the subject despite some fundamental disagreements between us that still remain. My former colleague Helen Wheatley assisted by providing videotape copies of some programmes that I had missed and contributing to the stimulating research culture in the Department of Film, Theatre and Television at the University of Reading. An important component of that culture is the Centre for Television Drama Studies, and while the topic of this book is not exactly within its remit my colleagues and postgraduate students working in the Centre have given valuable intellectual stimulus. In that context, my colleague Derek Paget's expertise in factual television has been formative in shaping my thinking about Reality TV and its relationships with documentary traditions. This book has taken much longer to complete than I originally intended, and I am grateful to the editorial staff at Palgrave for initially suggesting that I write it, and for their continuing forbearance as deadlines came and went. As always, Lib Taylor deserves my profound thanks for her encouragement, support and love.

Introduction

At some time around the end of 2002, I needed to come up with a very short definition of Reality TV. It had to be short and simple because it was going to go in the glossary of key terms in my book *An Introduction to Television Studies*. Even though I was in a rush to finish the book, I took a long time trying to define Reality TV in about ten words. The definition that I came up with was not very satisfactory. It was 'programmes where the unscripted behaviour of "ordinary people" is the focus of interest' (Bignell 2004a: 313). Clearly this definition is problematic because it could apply to all kinds of programmes that might not normally be considered under the label of Reality TV, so one of the subjects of this book is what both academic discourse and ordinary conversation is referring to when using that term. A second issue follows from that, which is what the use of the term 'Reality TV' makes possible. Once some kinds of programme are grouped by the term, patterns of continuity among them become discernible at the level of their production, the aesthetic qualities of the programmes as audio-visual texts and in terms of their reception by audiences. By adopting the designation Reality TV, television phenomena once thought to be discrete can be brought together in new ways, which can be productive for analysis and debate. However, the necessary consequence of adopting such a terminological label must also be that disputes will arise about its boundaries, the history of this phenomenon and its possible directions or future consequences. The internal stability of Reality TV as a consistent and uniform entity is necessarily posed by the activity of naming it, but the term also raises questions about its purchase and significance. It is these matters of grouping, development of a television form, patterns of reception and cultural significance that this book addresses. Reality TV is a contested term and a focus of debate, so this book is less concerned

1

to find a single definition than to explore the kinds of critical argument that are enabled by it, the relationships between those arguments and the examples that can be used to support them. While I have debated these theoretical issues in earlier work on television drama (Bignell 2005), this is my first substantial attempt to consider them in relation to factual television.

Because of the diversity of the programmes that have been grouped together under the label of Reality TV, this book focuses on a range of examples and also discusses how critical arguments can be erected on the basis of some examples rather than others. Theoretical propositions, including those in this book, cite objects of analysis (usually programmes) in order to outline a notion of what Reality TV might be. In all writing about television, programmes interact with theoretical understandings of television culture, creating a feedback loop. Both critical academic discourse and the media culture that it addresses are constructed in this way, through making selections and citing an aspect of one to illuminate the other. So the citation of a programme example might help to construct the identity of Reality TV as programme type, for instance, or a theory of the cultural significance of Reality TV will lead to a certain approach to analysing selected programmes. Theories and examples gain a status and inflection in critical discourse that is obtained from the uses they make of each other. In academic writing about Reality TV, there is still a paucity of close analysis of examples, and this is unfortunate since examples function as indicators or evidential grounds on which a theory can be erected. As critical work on television genre has shown (see Creeber 2001), examples are never random, and do more than represent the larger class to which they belong. As I have debated in relation to media examples in an earlier book (Bignell 2000b), each example brings with it an implicit claim to stand in the place of a larger number of equivalent objects, while also containing within itself the potential to represent not only the features of its class but also a particularity rendering it worthy of selection. This makes the choice of examples important to definitions of Reality TV, and makes the theorization of Reality TV dependent on its choice of examples.

With regard to the choices of methodology that could be brought to bear on Reality TV, there are two possible responses to this problem of critical positioning. One alternative is to begin with the 'texts' of media culture, whether that text is a body of information about the technologies and institutions that produce programmes, the screened programme itself or the responses of viewers to programmes or programme types, for instance. When analysing production, this could involve discussion of the availability of new cameras and editing technologies, the outsourcing of production from national broadcasting institutions like the BBC to independent producers, the framework of regulation and law relating to the shooting of private individuals for television programmes and the assumptions about good taste and public decency that affect how programme participants can be shown. Each of these sources of information can be regarded as a 'text' whose implications can be interpreted on the basis of written documentation, spoken testimony by the people involved or reports and analyses conducted by previous scholars. Similarly, television study has a long tradition of interpretive work on programmes as screened, critiquing their structures and meanings using the methods of detailed textual analysis adapted from literary and film criticism and based on the close analysis of audio-visual detail. The study of audiences' reception of programmes draws on both the statistical information gathered by broadcasters about audience share and ratings and also the interpretation of viewers' own comment about programmes that can be gathered by methods such as questionnaire, interview, monitoring programme websites and fan discussion forums. Here too, the analytical process is interpretive, since audience research is based on a textual corpus of raw data that requires the critic to organize, shape and explain it.

From this textual perspective, Reality TV is unpacked by an operation in which the critic or analyst submits himself or herself to the operations of the text or texts that have been chosen as the raw research data. The aim is to produce a sensitive reading, which discovers the functioning of the text and its specific effects in shaping the meanings of Reality TV. The potential danger in this procedure is that the text itself becomes a subject which 'reads' the critic as its object. What is discovered in the analysis is not a truth about the text as such, on its own terms, but the production of the critic's discourse and the text's discourse together as interdependent entities. The textual examples chosen reward their critic by producing him or her as a 'knowing subject' whose apparent mastery of their significance was always already there in a potential form among the research data. It just took the work of the critic to reveal the underlying significance that makes sense of what the text has to say when addressed and interpreted in the right way. Research into textual examples is a form of unmasking, clarification or revelation that aims to make plain what Reality TV is and what it means, by synthesizing conclusions out of the particular details of the chosen material. This is an effective method that this book uses in different ways in each of its chapters, but the conclusions it leads to are dependent on the examples selected for analysis and are always open to challenge when relevant examples can be found which lead to different conclusions.

The other alternative to the problem of how to make arguments about Reality TV that explain its meaning and significance is to adopt a premise first and test it against a range of evidence. One such assumption that is discussed and tested in the chapters that follow is that Reality TV's emergence is evidence of changed social relationships between individual and society that are mediated and encouraged by television. From this perspective, the designation 'Reality TV' is a way of alerting readers to a cultural phenomenon by identifying it at work across a range of different programmes. Once this phenomenon has been named, it can be shown that Reality TV programming has quickly become common in television schedules around the world and gained significant audience ratings. There are various individual programmes or programme types that can be claimed as the origin of this process, and once it is diagnosed, contrasting evaluations of it can be made. For example, Reality TV could be understood as a programme type based on offering a voyeuristic gaze to its viewers and promoting exhibitionism in its participants (Dunkley 2002). On the other hand, it might represent a new kind of access to, and interest in, ordinary people on television that can air important issues about identity and community in contemporary society. Whatever the direction of these arguments towards a negative or positive evaluation, recognizing Reality TV as a category is the first step in the analytical process. Once named, the sheer visibility of Reality TV provides ready evidence for a cultural shift, since both British and US television, for instance, have developed a range of unscripted programmes that have occupied prime-time schedule positions formerly taken by more established genres like sitcom. Some of these programmes are shown in several countries, using formats adapted for country-specific versions such as *Big Brother, Survivor, Temptation Island, Pop Idol* and *The Bachelor*. The reports and analyses of Reality TV programmes in both academic and journalistic sources contest over their status as either new kinds of insight into social behaviour or tedious and manipulative kinds of cheap television. Whatever the value given to Reality TV, however, the crux of this argument is that the growth of Reality TV as an identifiable programme type must in itself prove that it has cultural, social and political significance.

Chapter 1 discusses ways of constructing the origins of Reality TV in some detail, but a brief and partial version of a history here can help to explain how a conclusion about Reality TV as socially significant rests on assumptions about it as a much more widespread and extreme version of trends that were already under way. The term 'reality television' was first applied to the combination of surveillance footage, crime reconstruction, voice-over narration and on-screen presentation in programmes such as *Crimewatch UK* (1984–). The term was extended to include constructed factual programmes such as *Castaway* (2000) where situations were devised for the purpose of shooting them, and docu-soaps like *Airport* (1996) which impose on real events the conventions of soap opera including editing techniques of parallel montage, character-focused narrative structure and basis in a single, geographical space and community. Looking at Reality TV in this way as a programming history that increasingly diverges from documentary results in the argument that Reality TV loses the authenticity and explanation of documentary, and develops instead towards a spectacle of the everyday that emphasizes its participants' performance of identity. For instance, the distinguished writer on documentary, Bill Nicholls (1994), argues that Reality TV exhibits a strategy of deterrence that distances the television audience from reality, rather than seeking to represent and interpret it. Nicholls demonstrates that the Americans series *Cops*, which began in 1989, was one of the first Reality TV programmes, and uses it as evidence for the argument that this emergent television form seeks to narrativize and police the real rather than observing and investigating it. Looking in detail at the way the camera is used in *Cops*, Nicholls shows that the programme recuperates the excess and disorder of reality by aligning the camera with the police, who represent an agency that can cope with and normalize crime and criminals. For the audience, the threatening is made banal, and the abnormality and danger of the real is contained within the programme by the police and within television conventions by the capacity of the camera and the narration to make sense of it. In this argument, Reality TV domesticates reality and acts as a force of deterrence that holds its anxiety-producing potential at bay.

Whereas the first methodology for studying Reality TV selected examples and followed the logics of meaning underpinning them in order to produce generalizable conclusions, the second proposes a general historical and social process and finds evidence for it in selected examples. The drawbacks of the first approach are its dependence on the choices of example, and on the vital role of the critic as the skilled interpreter who, like a palm reader, appears to know more about the subject he or she is interpreting than the subject does, by virtue of specialized skills in reading clues that have been unknowingly made available. The second approach has the disadvantage that having set up a general thesis about the relationship between cultural change and changes in television programming, specific examples play a supporting and subservient role in grounding the thesis in evidence and can all too easily lose their particularity. Here, the critic plays the role of a magician, this time pulling the rabbit of significance out of the hat in which it was already hidden. The second kind of approach to working on Reality TV is also valuable however, since it has a capacity to synthesize and bring together ideas and can be very effective (as Nicholls' own study is) in proposing value judgements about a wide range of texts and phenomena. Like the first approach, aspects of this methodology appear across this book as histories, genre groupings and social implications are constructed and debated.

The foregoing discussion of methodology will, I hope, draw readers' attention to the productive tensions that should make this book most effective as a contribution to academic studies of Reality TV. Since the chapters have self-explanatory titles, there should be no need to outline their content here. The book is a wide-ranging analysis of the so far most-noted television phenomenon of the early twenty-first century: Reality TV. It explores Reality TV as a location from which to propose synthesizing and generalizing cultural and political arguments that engage with television and society and discusses some of the competing versions of the genesis of the form and its relationship to contemporary television production. It considers how Reality TV connects with, and breaks away from, television factual and fictional conventions seen in the texts of a variety of related and apparently unrelated programmes. Reality TV connects with many television genres. Constructed situations and environments (like the *Big Brother* house) are like those of sitcom. Reality TV is obviously like documentary in that it observes non-actors. It is also like drama in its sequential flow based around detailed exploration of character. In many of its forms, it is like the game show in being structured by competition. It is like the talk show in being about the ventilation of social issues and dwelling on its participants' personal confession. It is like lifestyle television in its emphasis on making and changing the persona and showing that social relations are changeable too. The book also explores Reality TV's relationships with surveillance, celebrity and media culture in television and outside it. Since Reality TV has been hugely popular in some of its manifestations, the book includes lengthy discussion of its significance for viewers and the ways in which they have been studied. At the end of the book, I return again to the tensions inherent in approaching Reality TV as a single unifying topic and discuss the resources the book offers (and does not offer) for an appraisal of the directions that television culture is taking in the new century.

As well as drawing on academic writing across the lengthening history of television and media analysis, this book also selectively discusses the insights of some of the recent spate of academic studies specifically addressing Reality TV. As a whole, however, the book does not claim to offer a summative account of previous writers' arguments and conclusions. Instead it takes up an eclectic range of critical questions and programme examples and brings them together in ways that will sometimes seem uncontroversial but also in ways that might appear surprising. These methods of study range from institutional studies of the production context of Reality TV to discussions of empirical audience research. The book works outwards from a close analysis of selected Reality TV programmes and also inwards towards specific programmes from theoretical issues such as globalization, genre, performance and format. The critical concepts and approaches deployed in the book therefore range across the discipline of television studies and the broader study of media culture.

Reality TV matters to the academic discipline of television studies because it forms a focus for critical enquiry and the ways that it functions as such a focus are discussed at intervals throughout this book. Reality TV has an organizing function, almost in an anthropological sense of being a totem whose various and multiple meanings crystallize and set off certain kinds of activity and discourse. Working on these questions suggests that the definition of Reality TV and the issue of how to evaluate it relate closely to each other, because if Reality TV functions as the focus or motivating force for academic activity, then obviously Reality TV has some kind of identity or agency. Reality TV is the subject, as it were, of a grammatical structure in which events are caused to happen like the publication of books and the development of university courses. There is a certain unity or coherence therefore to a notion of Reality TV as a stimulus or occasion. If Reality TV has this identity, unity or coherence, there is an assumption that those who use the term know what they are talking about when they refer to it. But I would also like to suggest that no one really knows what they are talking about in the sense that it is not possible to stabilize what the term Reality TV means. An important part of the analysis of Reality TV should consist of debate about the processes of how Reality TV comes to be an object of study, and this book combines those two activities of defining its topic and also considering how the process of definition bears on what Reality TV might mean.

1
Genesis

Introduction

This chapter discusses the ways that Reality TV represents both a development of television documentary forms and also a departure from their conventions. The argument that can be made in these terms is based on a model of development that addresses changes in technologies, television institutions, the cultural role of the medium and the relationships between television and its audiences. From this perspective, Reality TV is a recent form of factual programming emerging from the established mode of television documentary. The historical trajectory that leads to Reality TV has a wider scope than its reference to factual programmes, and suggests that documentary has changed because television has changed. Television documentary emerged during the era of scarcity (Ellis 1999a) in British broadcasting when there was initially one, then two, then three, four and five terrestrial channels, supplemented at the end of the twentieth century by satellite, cable and interactive broadcasting. The function of television as public service that was set in place from the beginnings of the medium in Britain has included the aim to draw together a nation and its constituent cultures, social classes and regions by showing to audiences how other people live. This resulted in the imperative to record the lives of others, but not simply to document places, occupations, social groups and classes but also to analyse their characteristic perceptions of themselves and their environment, in relation to home, work and leisure, for example. These perceptions, as well as being presented for themselves, would be analysed and subjected to the professional knowledge and potential intervention of powerful individuals and institutions who might be able to change them and the material circumstances from which they emerged. So documentary could be an important contribution to the public sphere of rational debate and democratic participation by enabling the exchange of information and the possibility of vicarious experience for separated viewers, separated by place, class, education and political outlook. Documentary, therefore, had an anthropological and political agenda, and this affected the textual form of documentary programmes for television and their address to the viewer.

In a contemporary multi-channel environment, the purpose of television and of television documentary has changed. There are still residual impulses to use factual television as a means of informing diverse audiences about the ways of life and outlook of people different to themselves. There are still factual programmes that investigate social problems and propose solutions and explanations that may be taken up by institutions, especially political parties and government agencies. But in the context of a widespread disillusionment with the ability of institutions to make essential improvements in national life, where barely more than half of the population votes in general elections and where continual attempts to address the problems of major institutions such as the National Health Service or the education system are seen to fail repeatedly, the ambition of documentary to connect with these large-scale ideological strategies has become significantly less important.

As well as the fact that individual documentaries have less impact because they are surrounded by many more competing programmes and channels than before, thus splitting their audience, television institutions have a different relationship with their audiences than they did in the era of scarcity. While it has always been the case that broadcasters and programme makers are interested in the reactions of their viewers and in the size of the audiences drawn to their programmes, the role of the audience has become less that of a client and more that of a market. Television channels need to sustain substantial audiences in order to generate advertising revenue and in the case of the BBC to justify the claim for a compulsory licence fee. Individual television programmes occupy their schedule position by virtue of their success in attracting either an audience of significant size or an audience which is composed of valuable consumers. Since television can be regarded as a buyer's market, where institutions act as the gatekeepers controlling access to the airwaves, programme producers attempt to construct programmes that are attractive to those institutions because they will attract audiences to them rather than their competitor. The attractions of risky activities, controversy, entertainment, excitement and identification have become increasingly significant in comparison to information, argument or specialist knowledge. The criterion of relevance to the supposed audience's interests is expressed in the assumption that factual programmes about other nations and unfamiliar cultures will be less interesting than programmes about ordinary people who are recognizable in the context of the generality of British life. Since audiences are imagined as seekers of entertainment and distraction, programmes are also designed to be relevant to the supposed need for relaxation, diversion and fascination. This historical narrative, then, explains the emergence of Reality TV as the result of a complex of factors. While this history allows the opportunity to critique the situation it explains, showing how alternative histories may have been possible, it is primarily a descriptive and diagnostic discourse.

The documentary heritage

Many writers (see for instance Corner 1995) have explored the development of Reality TV from the tradition of documentary that assumes social responsibility and adopts a mode of explanation and argument, exemplified by the work of John Grierson. Grierson was one of a team of film directors now referred to as the British Documentary Cinema movement, working in the 1930s, making films for institutions such as the Empire Marketing Board, the G.P.O. Film Unit and the Crown Film Unit. Some of their most significant films included *Song of Ceylon* (1933), *Coalface* (1935), *Housing Problems* (1935) and *Night Mail* (1936). This group was interested in developing the language of cinema, not simply as a means of recording reality in some unmediated way, but to explore how the creative interpretation of subjects drawn from real life could result in an art cinema that would reveal society to itself and provide resources for the democratic improvement of British society. The aim was, therefore, not only to expose audiences to fragments of the world around them that they might or might not already know about, but also to involve them in an understanding of industrial mass society so that they could participate in decision-making about it. Britain was regarded as a complex and interdependent organism in which work, family, private life and the organization of labour all contributed to the efficient functioning of the nation. Community and the obstacles to the formation of community were significant in the approach to representing people and their ordinary lives in the films that the group produced. Because of this agenda to inform and educate, the British Documentary movement's participants were willing to make persuasive films that matched the agenda of the bodies that funded them, whether governmental or private institutions. John Corner (1995: 82) summarizes the tensions that this generated: 'Realist in general philosophy yet also interested in modernist "experiment", ethnographically exploratory yet didactic, democratic yet propagandist, egalitarian yet often condescending, analytic yet often celebratory' are some of the terms that he suggests for understanding the complex aesthetic of the films.

A more recent and more influential heritage for Reality TV has been claimed by noting its connections with the French tradition of cinema verité and the American documentary filmmakers who developed the mode of direct cinema (Barnfield 2002, Brenton and Cohen 2003, Dovey 2000). These French and American documentary forms are more observational than argumentative, and their aim to produce the impression of intimacy and immediacy resonates with an understanding of television as, by nature, an intimate and immediate medium. These characteristics are evident in the attempts to capture the real as it unfolds, together with the inevitable lapses in technique, accidents and surprising juxtapositions that such attempts can include. The spontaneity of these American and French documentary traditions suits the characteristic presentation of time in Reality TV as potentially the tedious coverage of minor incidents as they unfold in real time or the efforts to capture the unexpected and surprising as documentary subjects go about their business. American direct cinema largely did away with analysis and argument, aiming instead to reveal individual and social truths through the camera's witnessing of a situation. Its most prominent practitioners included Richard Leacock, Robert Drew, Don Pennebaker and Frederick Wiseman. Having been given apparently unmediated evidence, the audience is invited to draw its own conclusions. Since they are necessarily unscripted, direct cinema films use the juxtaposition of editing to energize a sequence of shots into a revelatory and dramatic structure. While the conventions of documentary suggest that the role of the film is to become a document that records actuality, the American direct cinema film makers sought to produce narrative and involvement with their subjects by shaping their films to provide pace, a narrative arc and a sense of development across the period of time that the subject was filmed (Winston 1995: 149–69). The French tradition of cinema verité much more openly admitted the role of the filmmakers in constructing the film as an object and shaping the behaviour of the documentary subject. The ordinary people who they filmed were seen interacting with the filmmakers, being asked questions or interrupted as they spoke and sometimes filmed as they looked at the rough cuts that had been produced. Whereas the American direct cinema filmmakers attempted to bracket themselves out of the situation they observed, French verité filmmakers saw themselves as participant observers, like anthropologists (and verité's most prominent exponent, Jean Rouch, was himself an anthropologist), taking part in the situation and putting pressure on it and its participants in order to reveal what they saw as a deeper truth.

These two related but very different traditions of factual filmmaking, emerging and having their greatest impact on the documentary tradition in the 1960s and 1970s, exemplify two important components of contemporary Reality TV. The first concerns the subjects of the programmes, who are in general ordinary people, or celebrities who are observed as if they were ordinary, and are either witnessed as if the camera makes no intervention into their situation (as in American direct cinema) or are put into situations explicitly set up by the filmmaker or the agency of production, and subsequently pressurized, manipulated or invited to interact with the situation and the production team (as in the French verité tradition). The second key component from these traditions that can be seen at work in Reality TV is the purpose of the programme. Both the French and American traditions emphasize moments of crisis or transformation seeking to allow the audience to reflect on the forces impacting on individuals and how individuals respond to those forces. They also aim to enable the documentary subject himself or herself to have a space in which to speak about personal transformation.

In British television, this autonomy for the programme's subject developed into the BBC series *Video Nation*, for example, made between 1995 and 2000. Its producers were keen to bring to television the heritage from the 1930s of the Mass Observation project, which collected the comments and personal accounts of a large number of people who kept diaries of their everyday lives and commented on the social and political events of the time. *Video Diaries* continued this interest in ordinary people and the concept of collecting reports from a wide range of social classes and regions of Britain. But instead of providing a picture of social and political attitudes, it focused on the detail of people's everyday lives, their work and leisure, worries and attitudes. In the last 20 years, in *Video Diaries* and many other programmes featuring ordinary people, the video diary format has been introduced as a component of both conventional documentary (where both the subjects of the programme and also its makers might produce video diary recordings) and created Reality TV formats (like *Big Brother* and its diary room). Participants speak privately to camera about themselves, knowing that this private speech will become public when the programme is broadcast.

In contemporary television, the boundaries between private and public are blurred by the video confessional. Furthermore, the notion of the makeover and the ideology of self improvement are implicit in both American direct cinema and French cinema verité and are crucial to contemporary Reality TV formats. What people say to the video diary camera is often based on their feelings about themselves and how these are changing over time as part of a learning experience. While some residue of the aim of the earlier documentary forms to place their projects within a social dimension remains, Reality TV blurs the distinction between private and public, and the relationships between a personal experience that might reveal something about an individual and a more broadly conceived public world involving work, institutions or communities.

The possibilities of production technologies

When television increasingly took on the role of the primary mass broadcasting medium in the 1950s, people associated with the British Documentary Cinema movement and its successors among the film-makers who produced propaganda and informational films during the Second World War moved into television production. Developments in recording technology enabled television documentary makers to record sound synchronized with the image and drew on the achievements of BBC radio's features department in basing programmes around interviews conducted on location and recording the ordinary speech of non-actors. While the shaping of documentary programmes remained the province of directors and production teams distanced from their subject by their class status, expertise and membership of professional broadcasting institutions, the speech of ordinary people reflecting on their own experience and attitudes became an increasing feature of television factual programming. This notion of the access of ordinary people to the representations of their own lives has become progressively more significant in television documentary, and can be seen in Reality TV as the participants are not always just a resource for the programme maker but their very presence affects the possibilities for programme construction available to the producing team.

The organization of television programmes into series during the 1950s, with a consistent format, duration and a regular presenter who might appear on screen rather than being just a disembodied voice, shifted documentary and other forms of factual programme such as current affairs towards increasing recognition of the apparent demands of the audience. The regularity of a format under a consistent title, appearing week after week, with some consistency in its approach to subjects and presentation, allowed for the establishment of programme brands and viewer relationships with them. As a domestic medium viewed in the home, the mode of address to the audience in television factual programming became less formal and more intimate, moving towards a blend of documentary's traditional sobriety with the recognition of audience demands for entertainment. Filming technology contributed to this change and made its characteristic forms possible. When light-weight 16 millimetre (mm) cameras became available to the makers of factual television in the 1960s, the possibilities for extended work on location following the activities of ordinary people became greater and innovations in documentary became possible. Although the recording of actuality was made easier by lightweight equipment, it also gave a measure of creative control to the programme makers on the ground. Documentary could not simply report the real, but intervened in it as it was being recorded and subsequently shaped it through editing. The two most significant forces in this respect were the American direct cinema movement and the French cinema verité movement, each of which made use of the greater possibilities for location work that light-weight equipment brought and also represented important aesthetic experimentation that would affect the expectations of filmmakers and thus audiences about what television factual programming could be.

A famous exponent of this use of lightweight equipment for location shooting, producing a string of significant programmes in this history of documentary development, is the British programme maker Paul Watson. He made the observational (or 'fly-on-the-wall') documentary series *The Family* for television in 1974, following the lives and relationships of the Wilkins family from Reading. It was regarded as a landmark programme, as was the preceding US series *An American Family*, made in 1972, because of the detail of ordinary speech and interaction traced by witnessing the conversations in the family home at a level of realistic observation previously absent in documentary. The 'bad language' used by the family attracted attention and controversy but added to the claim of the visual style to document interpersonal relationships realistically. The factual form dealt with a working-class family, followed verbal exchanges rather than physical action and the family was headed by a strong matriarchal figure, Mrs Wilkins. These factors made *The Family* similar to the social realist dramatic fictions that have occupied British television in the form of soap opera (like *Coronation Street*) and drama documentary, as well as factual television's emphasis on the public representation of the private lives of the working class. In 1992, Watson made *Sylvania Waters*, named after the well-to-do Sidney suburb in which it was set. As in the case of *The Family*, the dominant figure was the middle-aged matriarch of the household, Noelene Donaher, a divorced woman living with her new partner. The daily routines of family life were dominated (as a result of the editorial selection of moments by Watson) by conflict between its members, often caused by their materialistic ambitions. The series was controversial both in Britain and when shown in Australia, mainly because it seemed to expose the day-to-day racism and sexism of apparently ordinary people. Rather than presenting its subjects as victims in need of the kinds of public policy improvement that might be taken on by middle-class professionals and institutions, Watson seemed simply to document everyday life. By suspending the functions of documentary to make an argument on behalf of an apparently excluded or powerless group, these documentary series offered both the fascination of detail and also the opportunity to stigmatize or make fun of their subjects. And very significantly for the labelling of these programmes as docusoap, both *The Family* and *Sylvania Waters* were serials, with each week's episode containing an opening update on the story so far, and continuing the real-life storylines across a run of programmes.

New possibilities for this kind of intimate tracking of ordinary life became possible in the 1990s. Lightweight digital video cameras and high-capacity editing suites for assembling programmes using computer software coincided with what John Ellis (2005) has described as a crisis of public confidence in the inherited conventions of television documentary. In the 1995–97 period lightweight digital video cameras and high-speed digital editing suites became available. The first digital video cameras were introduced by Sony as a consumer format, rather than a professional one. But when equipped with professional standard microphones, these cameras could produce footage suitable for television, at much higher visual quality than analogue video. As the capacity of Avid editing suites increased, in the same period it became possible to load the digital footage from these cameras into computer memory and assemble programmes with software that could handle sufficient data to edit a one-hour episode. Television documentary producers were thus able to make the cuts in their films relatively quickly and have greater flexibility in manipulating the layers of sound that would accompany the image. The recording of the everyday, using natural light and recording synchronized sound, became much cheaper and more convenient, and the resulting footage could be manipulated quickly to produce complete programmes.

At the end of the 1990s, *Big Brother* arrived on television screens, first in Holland and subsequently in other countries around the world (see Chapter 2). Technologically, it combined the digital production system of cameras producing easily manipulable images with the use of radio microphones attached to the contestants' clothing and used the high-speed high-capacity editing software that had become the industry standard. It became possible to edit footage very quickly for evening compilation programmes showing the highlights of a day's events in the *Big Brother* house. In addition, the workflow from raw images to finished programmes was becoming increasingly based on all-digital technology that made it easier to broadcast over the Internet as well as by conventional television transmitters. Almost-live streaming of images and sound could be done along the phone lines that carry broadband data to personal computers, as well as in the form of digital broadcast signals that can be received by owners of interactive television sets. *Big Brother* and other specially devised Reality TV formats require complete environments to be built in which the contestants will be sequestered for the duration of the programme and where the camera and sound crews and the production staff working on direction, editing and planning can be accommodated in the same large facility. In this respect, they are like complete mini television studios where production and action are set up to suit each other. But the same kinds of portable radio microphones and digital cameras can also be used on location to make Reality TV programmes that follow action in a location that has not been designed by the production team. In *Airport, Wife Swap* or *How Clean is Your House*, large amounts of tape footage and recorded sound can be easily gathered in locations with cramped conditions and low available light, then quickly edited and shaped into complete programmes.

Television institutions

BBC Producers Guidelines (2003) include this general principle, which is an important component of the tradition of Public Service Broadcasting: 'The BBC has a responsibility to serve all sections of society in the United Kingdom. Its domestic services should aim to reflect and represent the composition of the nation.' Reality TV programmes claim to reveal insights into human behaviour, in general, and attitudes among specific groups linked by age, sex or workplace location, for instance. This claim of representativeness is enhanced by the use of newly developed techniques of live broadcasting and viewer interaction, as mentioned earlier. *Big Brother*, for example, uses the medium's capacity to relay events live or almost live, and this has been one of the distinctive attractions of the medium since its invention. Television as a medium has always placed great emphasis on the moment of the now, partly because live broadcasting has been so significant throughout its development. British writers in the 1930s who predicted the future of television emphasized its ability to relay events (like sporting events, Royal events and General Elections) live across the country, thus keeping people in touch with what happened beyond their immediate experience and neighbourhood. It was felt that television would not compete with cinema as entertainment because of the placement of the television set in the home and the consequent lack of a sense of occasion and would therefore focus on information. The legacy of these predictions is the continuing preoccupation with kinds of realism in television (see Chapter 3), a relentless commitment to what is new (and the forgetting of television's own past) and sensitivity about allowing disturbing or controversial programmes to intrude into the home. Reality TV develops these factors through its shooting of domestic spaces (like the houses of *Wife Swap*) or creation of spaces that place obstacles in the way of the formation of domesticity (like *Survivor*'s desert island). Some Reality TV programmes are live, and others are based on the recorded observation of ordinary lived time. The institutional role of factual television (especially documentary and its Reality TV variants) not only corresponds to this emphasis on representativeness and the interest in the present moment but also raises problems in relation to it.

By 1999, public and press confidence in the veracity of documentary was challenged by a series of controversies about 'faked' footage and manipulation in factual programmes (Ellis 2005). The emergent television form deriving from both documentary conventions and drama, the docusoap, provided a ready way out of this crisis for television institutions. Docusoaps never aspired to the same sober respect for actuality as conventional documentary and were less subject to criticism for that reason. The lessening ability of documentary makers to gain access to locations like workplaces, because once there they might cause trouble for the hotels, hospitals or other institutions they featured, meant that conventional documentary was becoming more difficult to make. If situations were constructed by the programme maker, these problems of access were much less significant. The arrival of *Big Brother* in Britain from 2000, in which the artifice of the format is central to its structure and appeal, added another impetus for factual programming to rely on material under the control of the programme maker, rather than subject to the constraints of found subjects or locations. But before *Big Brother*, it was the BBC docusoap *Driving School*, originally produced under the aegis of the BBC's Education department, that brought the format to significant public attention. The series was planned to focus on the driving instructors rather than their pupils, but in the process of making the programme, the pupils were more interesting and the emphasis of the programme changed. Docusoaps like *Driving School* 'offered new subjects, new relationships with those subjects, a new visual system (both framing and editing), new forms of narrative construction and a novel place in the schedules. It is not surprising, then, that the nature of factual television was suddenly thrown into question, especially as it happened alongside other developments like the enfranchisement of everyday argument and opinionated speech in daytime talk shows' (Ellis 2005: 346). Programme makers accustomed to working in inherited documentary forms had good reasons to shift their activity towards the more easily produced, more easily defended and more audience-pleasing form of the docusoap. For example, Chris Terrill, maker of the BBC docusoap *The Cruise*, had first made observational documentary such as the BBC series *HMS Brilliant* (1995) but achieved remarkable success as *The Cruise* audience rose to a peak of 11 million, approaching the maximum audience for *Driving School* of 12.5 million.

The fact that Reality TV in its docusoap form, with its emphasis on personal stories and relaxed attitude to documentary's claim of veracity, seems to be based around entertainment rather than the sobriety of documentary is not in itself a reason to devalue it as a television form. Its blending and blurring of genres and its dramatization of the real can be just as effective for the working through of the stakes of social life and its strictures as the sobriety of conventional documentary. What is different, and this is a significant rider to that point, is Reality TV's lack of acknowledgement of itself as social commentary except in the most basic ways. Once the docusoap had proven its ability to gather very large audiences throughout the 1990s, broadcasters developed a bandwagon mentality that led to the BBC, for example, putting 12 docusoap formats into production by 1999. The ethos of early documentary filmmakers such as John Grierson in the 1930s was grounded in an attempt to enlighten the audience about their society, aiming to produce change driven forward by the state after the public ventilation of knowledge that pointed to a need for social betterment. The historicizing comparison between this documentary tradition and its Reality TV successors enables several derogatory evaluations of the more recent formats to be made. *I'm A Celebrity, Big Brother, Survivor, Fear Factor, Fame Academy* and *Temptation Island* are premised on a controlled environment, which is rendered free of poverty or other social determinants, and therefore sidesteps the agenda that Grierson set for British documentary.

However, this argument neglects the evolution of genres and the historic lineage it proposes is only partially accurate. Reality TV formats may have drawn on some of the generic components of documentary, but they occupy a schedule position and audience address associated with entertainment more than documentary. So it is invidious to compare them with something to which they are related but from which they are distinct. In some of their manifestations, Reality TV shows stage elaborate stunts, are presented by established television personalities and have much larger budgets than documentary programmes. The schedule positions they occupy have been in many cases vacated by entertainment and variety formats which are perceived by the industry and by audiences as dated and tired. Documentary films such as Five's *9.11: The Tale of Two Towers* and the BBC2 series of speculative documentary dramatizations *If ...* retain the engagement with social issues and critique of state policy in the Griersonian tradition. Multi-channel television, including genre-specific satellite and digital channels have given greater opportunity for traditional documentary to be screened, though it tends to appear at later times in the evening schedule and on minority channels such as the History Channel, BBC2 or Channel 4. The prime-time slots in the 8.00 pm–10.00 pm period on terrestrial television are more likely to be filled by docusoaps, gamedocs or Reality TV programmes about ordinary people placed in contrived situations.

The changes in the ecology of television in Britain place pressure on major television institutions to outsource production of a significant proportion of their programmes to independent producers, and the small crews, lightweight and relatively cheap equipment and location shooting of many Reality TV programmes makes them an attractive programme type to buy in rather than produce in-house. For example, the BBC reduced its staff by 7000 between 1986 and 1990, and since the 1980s the use of temporary contracts, the outsourcing of production to independent producers and the introduction of an internal market at the BBC shifted decision-making powers from programme makers to schedulers and commissioners and made the career paths of programme makers much more unstable. The BBC sold off many of its programme production and technical facilities in the early 1990s, and increased the proportion of programmes commissioned from independent producers. It increasingly resembles Channel 4 as a commissioning rather than programme-making organisation. The setting up in 1982 of Channel 4, was the result of a combination of inherited and traditional views of broadcasting with the new imperatives of the 1979 Conservative government and its allies. From the past came a commitment to public service, to educational and cultural programmes and to programmes for minority audiences. But Conservative policies in the 1980s attempted to introduce the principles of the market into all aspects of British life. So Channel 4 bought programmes from independent programme makers who were forced to compete with each other for commissions, and Channel 4 itself made no significant investment in production facilities or training. The channel's funding derived from advertising revenue through a levy on the ITV companies which sold advertising time on Channel 4 in their regions and was therefore reliant on the buoyancy of the British economy. The Broadcasting Act of 1980 which established Channel 4 required it to 'encourage innovation and experiment in the form and content of programmes' and to provide 'a distinctive service'. Channel 4 introduced significant changes to several programme forms, as well as opening up the independent production sector in Britain. It was empowered in 1993 to sell its own advertising slots, freeing it from ITV but encouraging it to compete with other channels more fiercely for audiences of sizes and types which are attractive to advertisers. The channel was intended to have a social responsibility, providing an out-let for non-mainstream programmes and airing unconventional ideas, thus extending the public service remit of television in Britain since its inception. This mix of a commitment to innovation and a dependence on attracting valuable audiences set the stage for Channel 4's acquisi-tion of the *Big Brother* format, which promised to fulfil each of these two imperatives.

Risking Reality TV

Historically, the fact that Reality TV formats make economic or institu-tional sense for the channels that commission them or buy them in from outside does not explain their success as a television form, nor predict which examples of Reality TV will be perceived as successful. For instance, *Big Brother* was a risky proposition in its early days, because no directly equivalent programme had been made. It was a huge risk for Channel 4 to strip *Big Brother* across the week in one-hour prime-time slots before they knew whether British audiences would like it. For a programme like *Big Brother* which is acquired as a format from else-where, and made at great expense by its British purchaser, the manage-ment of financial risk is crucial and is carefully specified in the contracts that govern the transaction. The buyer of the format is responsible for capital costs (like building the *Big Brother* house) and production costs, and is thus investing a lot of money, especially in a relatively expensive case like *Big Brother* where considerable resources of equipment, settings and personnel are involved. On the other hand, the buyer of the format gets the income from the merchandising, tie-ins, charges for telephone voting and advertising slots sold during the broadcast. The seller of the format does very well because they do not have any of the on-the-ground costs of making the programme, and are in effect selling the future profitability of an idea. In this respect it is important for format sellers to build up a brand reputation for themselves that can raise the prices they charge on the basis of their success with certain kinds of programme. In the Reality TV market, companies such as Endemol (devisers of *Big Brother*) and RDF Media (makers of *Wife Swap*) are established brands, and the risk of buying a new format is to some extent offset by the track record of its deviser.

For the creators of a Reality TV format, there is a significant risk that it will be imitated by a competing business, and of course the presence of very similar programmes in the schedules that are passed off as different might dilute audience interest in the original and threaten the programme brand that format devisers have invested in creating. *Survivor* was the first Reality TV format to be a must-see prime-time programme, beginning in the United States. After the success of *Big Brother* in Europe, the owners of the *Survivor* format initiated a legal case against Endemol, arguing that it infringed the *Survivor* format. While ideas cannot be placed under copyright, formats are regarded as property and can be owned and therefore their ownership can be legally defended. The key components of the *Survivor* and *Big Brother* formats are certainly similar. They consist of a group of contestants who are strangers to each other and are drawn from among the ordinary public. The series takes the form of a game or competition in which there is a winner and a prize. Periodically during the run of the series trials and challenges are set for the contestants, who are rewarded or penalized accordingly. Continuous 24-hour observation of the contestants is undertaken, and episodes consist of edited selections from that material. The programme is shot in a restricted location that the contestants are unable to leave and into which outsiders cannot penetrate. The series are time limited, and the aim of the contestants is to win by surviving the complete run of the series.

A similar situation occurred over the allegedly derivative premise of *I'm a Celebrity*. In the American court case brought by the CBS network against its competitor ABC, CBS claimed that *I'm a Celebrity* infringed the copyright of *Survivor* and sought an injunction to stop ABC screening the US version of *I'm a Celebrity* in February 2003. However, ABC successfully argued that *I'm a Celebrity* was original. The court battle was significant because ABC had spent about $15 million on *I'm a Celebrity* and had made provision for 17 hours of programming in its schedule (Lamont 2003). Copyright law does not explicitly protect a format itself, but instead there is copyright in the work of the people who devised it. Charlie Parsons, the owner of the rights to *Survivor*, said in court that he had begun work on the programme in 1992, pitched it unsuccessfully to ABC in 1994 and sold the programme to CBS subsequently. Expert witnesses watched the programme and identified similarities between *I'm a Celebrity* and *Survivor*, such as the challenges in which contestants ate live worms. However, James Allen, one of the people behind *I'm a Celebrity* at Granada television claimed he thought of the idea for the programme in 1996 after watching a documentary where Joanna Lumley was stranded on a desert island for nine days. These disputes are clearly pursued more vigorously when large amounts of investment are at stake and where major corporations are involved. But expensive formats like *Big Brother* or *Survivor* are not the only way of making Reality TV. The time from pitching an idea to a commissioning producer to shooting a Reality TV programme can be very short. It could be possible to make this period as short as about five weeks, since a programme about householders competing over their interior decorating, for example, could use volunteers with existing houses, a small crew of only a handful of people, no script, no stars and no capital costs. This makes some kinds of Reality TV programming a very useful way of responding to sudden ups and downs in television markets, audience interests or competition environments and much easier to plan than drama or another scripted format.

For the producers of the more elaborate and costly Reality TV programmes, the opportunities to make money not only arise from fees paid by broadcasters to the production companies. Supplementary services also add value to the programme in economic terms through phone lines, spin-off products, tie-in books and DVDs, mobile phone text updates and sponsorship of programmes. One of the advantages of an elaborate competition format like *Pop Idol* is that a whole range of branded products can be created, all of which are owned and controlled by the television institution. *Pop Idol* is a programme that can attract audiences and also make money through spin-offs and licensing agreements to third-party companies, who might create a range of chocolate bars, soft drinks, tee shirts and other products. The merchandise associated with the first series of *Pop Idol* included predictable products such as a tee shirt, book, video and a cover for a mobile phone. The second series had a much larger range of branded products including a song book, a game for the Playstation 2, an interactive recording studio and a perfume. Interactive services included voting by text message and downloads of songs from the programme. In Britain, retail sales generated by licensed products of all kinds was worth £3 billion in 2002, and across the world, the licensing business as a whole generated £110 billion (Bulkley 2003). In the case of *Big Brother*, nearly 30 per cent of the revenue to Endemol comes from the merchandising and licensing of branded products associated with the programme.

The *Pop Idol* format is owned by the production company Fremantle, which had sold it to 20 countries by 2003. Fremantle predicted that up to half of the company's total revenue would derive from income from licenses and merchandising by 2006. The entry of merchandising and licensing into the television business, as opposed to Hollywood films, for example, was marked in 1998 with *Who Wants to Be a Millionaire*, when revenue from merchandise exceeded the value of sales of the programme format itself. The Millionaire board game sold one million units in its first two years, and the personal computer version of the game sold the same number in only seven weeks, becoming the biggest selling game in Britain. *Pop Idol* has the obvious attraction of a core audience of 16–34-year-old men and women, who comprised 72 per cent of the 14 million viewers of the final programme in the first series. The programme's sponsor, the food company Nestlé, was able not only to feature its name at the opening and closing of the programme and of its individual segments, but also created animated chocolate characters representing pop singers performing songs in the advertising breaks. Viewers could vote for their favourite chocolate pop idol, merging the audience's relationship with the sponsor's products into the format of the programme as a whole. Although it is not yet the case that television programmes have budgets based on the future income expected from merchandising and licensing, as is the case in the film industry, this development may happen in the near future as Reality TV formats pose the programme as a loss leader whose profitability depends on the brand extensions and spin-offs it may generate. In the case of *Pop Idol*, the very structure of the competition ensures that it will produce a person-commodity of one or more pop stars who has at least a partly guaranteed market appeal and the prospect of getting to number one in the charts and achieving major record sales. However, there is a significant risk of consumer exhaustion with such a blanket product range, so when one of these series becomes a hit the companies rush into producing the next one, sometimes straight after or just a few months later, so the ball can be kept rolling for as long as the series has a prospect of being profitable. That is why there are so many quickly appearing sequels like the various series of *Pop Idol* and *American Idol*, for example, because the format can only maintain momentum for a limited time. New variations on the Reality competition format have to be created to refresh the market.

In the more costly staged Reality TV series, production risk is ever-present during shooting because of the multitude of things that can go wrong. The scale of productions such as *I'm A Celebrity ... Get Me Out of Here*, first shown on ITV in 2002, 'involve a level of ambition and scale more at home in the movies than television', according to the executive producer of the fourth series, Alexander Gardiner (2004). The crew of *I'm a Celebrity* amounted to about 400 people including the transport, catering and security teams that supported the people behind and in front of the cameras. The on-site edit suites worked around the clock, and there were about 40 preview screens showing the output of the various cameras that almost continuously recorded the behaviour of the contestants. An art department was needed, responsible, among other things, for the bushtucker trials where contestants were enclosed in tanks of cockroaches, for example. The hosts, Ant and Dec, had a big responsibility for linking and presenting the programme, and this extended not only to the conventional smoothness of professional programme presentation but also to humorously deflating any problems caused by technical errors or unexpected contestant behaviour. This unexpectedness is crucial to the planning of Reality TV programmes and also to their appeal, since the continual possibility of their collapse due to some kind of catastrophe is always potentially present in the minds of their viewers. Contestants on the second series of *I'm a Celebrity*, led by the chef Antony Worrall Thompson, rebelled against the production team because of late and insufficient food. With eight episodes to go, they threatened to leave all together as a group, which would stop the series. They confronted the producers on camera and were rewarded by being given steak. In another example of this risk that Reality TV formats involve, the Irish series *Cabin Fever* involved participants sailing a boat around Ireland, and placed amateurs together on the boat sailing into a storm, putting them in great danger. The boat later ran aground and broke up, and the contestant-crew had to be rescued by helicopter.

For the fourth series of *I'm a Celebrity*, Alexander Gardiner (2004) reported that the health and safety team on the series had to deal with a surge in the mosquito population that made simple preventives like citronella candles ineffective. The institutional requirement to protect the celebrity contestants (known as the 'talent') and follow regulations meant that different and more complex problems occurred than would be the case for holidaymakers, trekkers or other non-professional people going into the series' jungle setting. Members of the production team had been breeding rats to take part in some of the challenges the contestants would face, but their population got out of control and the males had to be separated from the females. Like a scientific experiment gone wild, the breeding of the animals for this purpose needed to be managed and controlled just like the management of the contestants for the programme and the management of the crew. In each of these anecdotes, the governing narrative form is one of a conflict between control and excess. There were too many mosquitoes, too many rats and an overall impression that the risks and problems in producing the series were parallel and equivalent to the challenges that drew audiences to the series.

Reality TV as the end of documentary history

Television institutions, programme makers, audiences and commentators arrived at this moment of interest in Reality TV out of a past comprising other moments and different kinds of television. This raises the question of Reality TV's place in television history. From American programmes based on footage from the emergency services, the term Reality TV then referred to docusoap as a more widely used and public term for serial programmes about ordinary people that gained large audiences throughout the 1990s. Reality TV has gradually emerged as a designation that describes programmes characterized by a controlled environment, lacking documentary's heritage of interest in social action. It is closer to entertainment and increasingly replaces entertainment in the schedules. Before the advent of Reality TV as a significant programme type in its currently accepted form, John Corner (1996: 55) noted that: 'It remains to be seen what further modifications will, or can, be made to the vérité approach as documentary attempts, within an increasingly competitive context, to renovate itself both as "good viewing" and as "socially significant television" '. The question of whether documentary even had the possibility to renovate itself opens up the issue of whether documentary was playing a dangerous game with its own death, putting some kind of end to its distinguished twentieth-century history.

The advent of Reality TV has been an occasion for commentators to lament the death or terminal illness of several television forms and traditions. These include the death of variety where in the past a programme form comprising a mix of performances from comedians, singers, magicians and dancers and anchored by a celebrity such as Cilla Black or Bruce Forsyth would form the core of an evening schedule. The argument here is that Reality TV supplants light entertainment programmes in prime-time schedules and fills those prime-time slots with light factual programmes. Reality TV has also been claimed to signal the death of documentary, killing off a great tradition of observational and socially concerned programme-making. The arguments about Reality TV as the end of documentary are part of a larger postmodernist argument that Western society is in a condition in which history ceases to move forward in a progressive way (Bignell 2000b) with the consequent impossibility of improvement of social conditions by the rational means which the documentary tradition has espoused. As in Fredric Jameson's (1984) conception of postmodernity, the present is supposedly an epoch in which representations, forms and aesthetic codes from the past are perpetually reworked, with their distinctiveness and cultural contributions blunted. For factual television, this would mean that the Reality TV of the present absorbs the programme formats of the past and that documentary's discourses of social and historical analysis are relativized and disempowered, with the consequent loss of an authoritative means for television to contribute to social betterment.

The theoretical discourse about the present as an end of history is most well-known from Jameson's influential essay 'Postmodernism, or the cultural logic of late capitalism' (1984: 53), which begins with the assertion that the late twentieth century was characterized by 'an inverted millenarianism, in which premonitions of the future, catastrophic or redemptive, have been replaced by senses of the end of this or that'. In this formulation of the end of history, contemporary culture has ceased to innovate or move forward. An especially conservative version of the end of history thesis was articulated by Francis Fukuyama (1989). His 1989 essay and his subsequent book argued that events were still occurring, 'but History, that is, history understood as a single, coherent, evolutionary process' has concluded (1992: xii). Fukuyama argued that ideological conflict is now outdated, and the idealisation of a different model of social organization than consumer capitalism is impossible. Consumer capitalism is the model towards which all societies aspire, he argued, because capitalism promises the attainment of material desires, and utopia can be practically attained through the accumulation of commodities. But the resulting culture of consumption, although it offers the attainment of material desires, has its own inherent dangers. The 'Last Men', which it produces, are in danger of becoming secure, self-regarding and passive, with little incentive for productive effort. So the end of history threatens to be an end of masculinity, and 'Last Men' become feminized both by lack (lack of masculine productiveness) and by their compensatory activities (shopping, gazing and other forms of consumer behaviour). This seems to amount to a feminization of society, in the sense that shopping, consuming and passivity or non-productivity are practices and identities conventionally attributed to women. The positive feature of this situation is the possibility of play with and in identity, measured against what are regarded as former monolithic identities (like stereotypes of masculinity). In watching Reality TV, for example, with its apparent lack of a rational project of social betterment and mastery over a reality that can be understood and mediated by documentary conventions, audiences are getting pleasures previously understood as feminine. The implication is that constructions of masculinity or femininity as ways of characterizing television forms and the pleasures of television audiences may therefore become less fixed. The case study which follows analyses *Wife Swap*, which is concerned directly with gender roles as its subject. But furthermore, the programme also offers pleasures of judgement that might be assimilated into a masculine discourse of rational evaluation, together with a focus on appearance, style and emotional dynamics that conforms to conventional definitions of the feminine. *Wife Swap* is a suitable location to consider whether Reality TV might enact the end of (masculine) documentary at the same time as it participates in the transformation of documentary into (feminine) lifestyle programming.

The function of arguing that Reality TV has put an end to something that came before it is to establish a sense of historical progression and to stabilize the thing that Reality TV is being contrasted with. As part of the same process, contrasting Reality TV to the tradition that goes before also has the function of drawing boundaries or giving a focus to the sense of what Reality TV itself is. So the creation of a history in which Reality TV sits is also the creation of an identity for Reality TV. One reason for writing this book was to respond to the assumption that Reality TV matters as a distinctively new twist in programme-making, and that the emergence of this new phenomenon needs academic attention. However, on the other hand, Reality TV can also be seen as a probably short-lived digression from a larger tradition, perhaps of documentary or factual television. From that point of view, Reality TV is not something distinctively different, but an elaboration on something that remains essentially the same and that has a persistence through time into a future beyond the current moment. There are persuasive arguments on each side of this question, namely that Reality TV is both new and also that it marks a continuity with earlier conventions and traditions, particularly in factual television. If television history is understood as this kind of evolving process, it becomes possible to define the present in distinction and contrast to the past. The moments that have gone before become apparently stable objects for discussion against which the present can be contrasted, and the present also starts to look like a stable object. Historicization establishes a past that enables the production of a present as a distinct development from or contrast to it. However, this means that the past is defined in terms of the present, and the present in terms of the past. Each of them is dependent on the other, but when closely considering anything in historical terms it does not emerge as the stable entity it might appear. As this chapter shows, Reality TV is not an entity but a rather loose and distinctly debatable collection of possible convergences. This line of argument matches the point made by John Corner (1996: 55) that Reality TV has 'staple and converging elements' or 'ingredients' that have been mixed up into 'a new and eclectic symbolic economy, where the very assumptions carried by the idea of a "mixed form" might quickly come to seem naively inappropriate'. The case study that follows analyses an example of this kind of convergence, and leads to the chapter's conclusion.

Case Study: *Wife Swap*

Whereas the first phase of Reality TV used found footage provided by the emergency services or by camera operators following policemen, ambulance drivers or firefighters, more recent programmes have shifted their focus from the observation of action in public space and towards an interior and private dramatic world. This corresponds to the increased significance of home decor programmes, programmes about property and gardening, and makeovers of individuals' dress, makeup or personal fitness (Piper 2004). The combination of a focus on the family, and especially central women in it, with questions of class and lifestyle that formed the foundation for comparisons of participants who viewers could find both fascinating and repellent, was the basis of *Wife Swap*, first shown in Britain in 2003. In contrast to earlier observational documentary programmes such as Paul Watson's *The Family* or *Sylvania Waters*, *Wife Swap* added a competition structure where one wife was transplanted from her own family to one with very different cultural and class expectations, to see whether she would be able to change her new family or would be remodelled by it herself. The wives exchanged places for two weeks, and attempted to lay down rules for their new family in the second week, after living according to the expectations of the new family in the first week. Editing was crucial to the format, since each one hour programme had to condense the results of observation of two families for two weeks, as well as brief introductory information about the participants and a concluding segment in which each family (but primarily the wives) could confront and comment on each other. Across the episodes, it was obvious that the women carried out the vast majority of domestic work, and that different families lived by strongly contrasting rules of schedule and hygiene. While a conventional documentary treatment might use this material as the basis for arguments about gender roles in contemporary Britain, and about the effects of differences of income, class status and educational expectations on private life, *Wife Swap* focused its interest on individuals, and the power struggles between the transplanted wives and their unfamiliar family environments. In this way, the strength of character of the wives and the families, and the competitiveness involved in attempts to change other people by persuasion, negotiation or tantrums took the place of analysis of the politics of either public or private space. While the programme had value in ventilating the surprisingly great differences between ways of living in contemporary British family life, it withdrew from evaluating or commenting on these differences, appearing simply to present them as personal challenges.

Wife Swap was made by the independent production company RDF. Its director of programmes, Stephen Lambert, was trained as a documentary producer at BBC and made the critically acclaimed documentary series *Modern Times* for BBC2. RDF is the second largest independent production company in Britain, with an annual turnover of £53 million. The genesis of the series was at a creative meeting at RDF's headquarters, as Lambert explained: 'We were looking at an article in the *Daily Mail* about how a nurse on £15,000 lived, compared with a barrister on £200,000. What about them swapping lives, then what about a wife swap?' (Brown 2004a: 10). Lambert rejected the criticisms from within and outside the television industry that Reality TV 'dumbs down' society, and also the view expressed by Paul Watson that his closely observed documentaries presented actuality whereas contemporary Reality TV is artificial. Lambert argued that there were good and bad examples of all genres, including Reality TV: 'As a genre, reality television is one way of telling us stories about human nature and in many ways it is more honest than observational documentary.' His evidence for this view was that Reality TV does not pretend that it is observational, and thus comes clean about its manipulation, whereas observational documentary does not: 'look at how people's nature is revealed because of the situation we've put them in'. He drew attention to the pleasures of Reality TV formats for audiences because of their basis in a narrative structure that makes satisfying viewing, in contrast to the less obviously narrativized observational documentary form. Referring to RDF's *Faking It* and *Wife Swap*, he argued that these 'are formats that give you those narrative structures, but there's still an enormous variety and unpredictability about what will happen in them'.

Episodes of *Wife Swap* usually set up the conventional domestic routine of each household, then follow the difficulties encountered as each woman deals with the differences between her expected routines and those of the partner family. As tensions and crises build up across the period of filming, an established pattern of paralleling segments shot in each house builds towards the return of the women to their original homes and discussions among the members of each household about what they have loved and hated, learned or repudiated from their experience. As Helen Piper (2004) has shown, much emphasis is placed on the details of the mise-en-scene in each house, as revealing evidence of the class and cultural expectations of the participants. The kinds of furnishing, level of cleanliness and tidiness, and the repertoire of items kept in the fridge and in kitchen cupboards become key signs of definition for the two households and shorthand ways for the programme producers to indicate potential contrasts and differences between them. Having established this visual evidence of what each household is like, the dialogue between the new entrant into the household and its existing inhabitants focuses on what the household norms might be, according to the explanations that each person gives. There are many opportunities for statements to the camera or statements made by one participant to another to be confirmed or undercut by the evidence that the visual representation of the house provides.

The narrative pace of *Wife Swap* can vary extremely, notably from the very short montage of shots introducing the participants and their houses at the beginning, to the often lengthy conversations, usually in the kitchen, between the newly arrived woman and her new family. Occasionally music cues are used to sharpen a dramatic incident, but both sound and voice-over more usually allow action to speak for itself or simply frame an incident. This places the opportunity to identify with the participants and to judge them squarely with the audience. Since the programme has identified the houses and the people both through what they say and how they look, social codes of behaviour and class and cultural codes of homemaking are made readily available for the audience to use as its criteria. As Piper (2004: 281) points out: 'The text incorporates a tacit invitation for the audience to judge, not what is necessarily best for the participants, but the degree to which their relationship measures up to a societal ideal, and *ergo* it presumes society's right to know.' Nevertheless, the degree of detail presented even in a single episode about the attitudes and lives of the different families makes it difficult to establish preferred ideological standards for individuals or families. Although *Wife Swap* assumes the possibility and even the desirability of television's intervention into the home and the family, Piper shows that 'the text collapses together ethical choices (the division of roles, childcare) with matters of taste and consumer preference' (2004: 281), so that an easy identification of a norm becomes impossible. So *Wife Swap* offers a concrete example of a format devised by an independent production company, which combines an observational style with highly controlled and structured episode form. It does not make an argument about its subject, though it does invite its audience to evaluate its participants and might offer resources for comparing the viewer's gendered and familial roles with those on the screen. It draws on video diary form, a kind of competition, and an emphasis on lifestyle and consumer choices about food and décor, for example. In many ways, *Wife Swap* instantiates the conjunction of historic traditions of television and the blurring of boundaries between genres, gender roles and modes of address to the audience that this chapter has considered.

Conclusion

Placing Reality TV in a historical narrative that emphasizes its divergence from documentary leads to the conclusion that it threatens a loss of the seductive mastery over the matter of reality that the documentary tradition posed through documentary's relationships between programme makers as subjects of knowledge and the objects of knowledge that featured in their programmes. In terms of the internal structure of recent Reality TV texts, audiences are not offered a viewing position that moves progressively towards the resolution of an explicitly posed social problem, and programmes are not structured by the multiplication of arguments and a process of investigation which invites both the programme's investigative look and its audience into an adventure of understanding. This tension between documentary's claim of mastery and the apparent incoherence of Reality TV as a television form that does not take on the role of a social agent of change can be read as a destabilization of documentary's masculine discourse. The anxiety about Reality TV as putting an end to documentary includes the assertion that contemporary television inhabits a perpetual state of being at the end, without the revelation or judgement about the world that documentary is seen to have involved, and therefore without hope for the fixing of meaning. This argument for an apocalyptic end of television history is dependent on comparing Reality TV to documentary's past but differentiates Reality TV from that past and makes it seem like a separate development. And yet, because Reality TV continues to focus on the moment of the present and on recognizably actual people, places and events, sometimes through live or nearly live transmission, it is also relentlessly in the here-and-now. Unlike earlier kinds of documentary, Reality TV is not a form that attempts to mould the future by intervening explicitly in the world of its viewers. In these respects, Reality TV seems to float free of history, existing in a continuous present, and thus looks to its critics like an irresponsible television form. However, these value judgements can only operate on the basis of the comparative and developmental narratives that this chapter has explored. The remaining chapters in this book focus on different ways of conceptualizing Reality TV, in order to argue that it should instead be understood as a nodal point or conjunction of the temporally shifting traditions in television production, perceived audience demands and in critical discourse. The argument developed in subsequent chapters is that Reality TV is a space where influences and needs converge and diverge, producing an understanding of Reality TV as dynamic and contingent.

2
The World is Watching

Introduction

Television programming's ability to cross national and cultural borders has long been acknowledged, and this chapter considers the reasons for broadcasters' desire to produce versions of Reality TV formats around the world. The chapter discusses the critical frameworks and assumptions that make different kinds of sense of the international popularity of this form of programming. The first requirement for Reality TV programmes to be watched in different nations and cultures is the availability of television sets on which to watch them. The global spread of television sets and television distribution systems across the developed world appear at first sight to provide evidence for postmodernist theories of contemporary media culture which emphasize homogeneity (Bignell 2000b). From the middle of the 1980s transnational television flows have increased due to the use of distribution technologies including cable and satellite and the increase in the variety of distribution systems that can deliver programmes such as live streaming over the Internet. Writers on the phenomenon of modernity have argued that modernity reorganizes time, space and social agency, and that the mass media are crucial to this process (Thompson 1995; Giddens 1995). Material production, social control and cultural activity can be acted out independently of local times and space. Communications and transport globalize and relativize the division of labour in time and space, computers centralize the administration of organizations and institutions away from their local base and television enables the seeing of the same events in many different places and local time zones. Such an analysis provides the possibility of arguing that the boundaries of space and time have been radically transformed, with Reality TV programmes as an important contemporary example of this phenomenon.

Reality TV and theories of globalization

It was the international music channel MTV which is sometimes credited with inventing the Reality TV form in its programme *The Real World*, so it is useful to begin a discussion of Reality TV as a phenomenon of globalization with a brief consideration of MTV as a global broadcast organization. MTV can be regarded as an American-owned capitalist enterprise which aims to bring non-American music to the American market, and to stimulate desires for American products outside the United States. The media institution of MTV could then function as an example of corporate global media culture for the channel is available across diverse cultures and markets. It is not only concerned with disseminating American or Western programmes and musical styles, since it sometimes screens videos originated outside Western pop culture, but its address to a youth culture with supposed shared concerns and consumer desires would support the argument that its overall effect is one of homogenization. MTV's own self-promoting advertising seems to support this, with such early slogans as, 'One world, one image, one channel: MTV', which celebrate the effacement of difference by global consumerism. More recently, however, MTV has diversified into regional and sometimes national channels directed at more specific audience groups, and not all of its programmes are available everywhere.

MTV's programmes (which should be distinguished from its music video sequences) were developed after the channel's initial focus almost exclusively on screening chart videos. Its Reality TV series *The Osbournes* has been the biggest earning success for MTV in its history, gaining 8 million viewers in the United States and 500,000 in Britain, for example (Plunkett 2005a). The programme's producer, Greg Johnson, initially intended to shoot the episodes on location at the Osbourne family's Beverley Hills home for three weeks, but the appeal of the programme led to over three years of production. Despite the fact that *The Osbournes* is produced and structured as a factual series adopting the conventions of many other docusoaps, it retains both historical and textual connections with the international pop music culture that MTV promotes. Ozzy Osbourne had been the subject of MTV's house tour series *Cribs*, in which cameras are shown around the usually luxurious homes of pop stars, and this led to the commissioning of *The Osbournes* by MTV's US controllers. As the singer and frontman of the heavy rock band

Black Sabbath, Ozzy had an established reputation in Britain, Unit States and elsewhere as a pop music performer, though the high-point of his career had occurred in the mid 1970s. Ozzy, who is originally British and from Birmingham, had first appeared on factual television in a British programme, as the subject of a Channel Five documentary *Ozzy Osbourne Uncut*, made by September Films in 1998. MTV's managing director in the United Kingdom and Ireland, Michiel Bakker, credited *The Osbournes* as the programme that 'elevated us out of the music TV niche and into a bigger league' (Plunkett 2005a). Bakker is referring here to twin achievements of *The Osbournes* as an international Reality TV success. First, *The Osbournes* gained press coverage, public profile and large audiences when shown originally on MTV in the United States, demonstrating that series programming in the docusoap format had a continuing potential to draw the predominantly youth audiences that MTV already targeted with its music video programming. But Bakker is also referring to the success of *The Osbournes* as an internationally traded programme, whose already established brand as a result of its screening on MTV made its appearance on terrestrial television on Channel 4 in Britain a relatively predictable hit for the channel.

Inasmuch as *The Osbournes* works as an example of an internationally traded programme property that can transfer from the culture in which it was produced and initially screened to other television cultures and markets, it is one piece of evidence for the homogeneity in contemporary television culture that has been criticized for decades. This argument is by no means new and is not dependent on the specific features of Reality TV as a programme type. Globalization theses by Herbert Schiller (1969, 1976), for example, have argued that the globalization of communication in the second half of the twentieth century was determined by the commercial interests of US corporations, working in parallel with political and military interests. This discourse connects cultural imperialism with the dynamics of colonialism, arguing that the colonial empires of Britain or France have been replaced by commercial empires. Traditional local cultures are said to be eroded by dependencies on media products, with their attendant ideologies derived from the United States, with the effect of globalizing consumer culture across regions and populations which become constrained to adapt to its logics and desires, despite the lack in some of these regions (in the developing world) of resources to participate in them. This cultural imperialism thesis, developed in the 1950s and 1960s, pays scant regard to local and national specificities in media organization or consumption, nor to regional flows of media products, based for instance on the legacy of imperial languages like Spanish in Latin America. Not only do regional media flows run across global ones, but they also provide the basis for a reversal of media flows from Latin America to Europe, where the export of telenovelas among Latin American cultures and to Europe is a well-known example. Institutionally, the synergy between the separated realms of hardware manufacturing, content providers and transmission or broadcasting corporations appears to provide market dominance to a few major companies, mainly American and Japanese (like Time-Warner or Sony), so that the assumption that globalization is the same as Americanization has been modified to stress the power of corporate, rather than national, control over media.

Big Brother Africa ran for 106 days and was broadcast across Africa in 2003, drawing an audience of over 30 million (about two-thirds of the continent's 900 million population saw the programme in total). The suggestion that the series represented African unity and produced a sense of shared identity is complicated by the fact that it was accessible primarily to English-speaking Africans. Its audiences consisted not only of individual viewers but also of communal groups watching in bars or in the homes of the 4 per cent of the continent's population who own television sets. But led by South Africa-based satellite television company M-Net, which co-produced *Big Brother Africa* and broadcast to more than 40 African countries, the number of Africans with satellite television has been growing by around 10 per cent each year although most of these are people living in South Africa. The programme types attracting those wealthy enough to subscribe to M-Net consist of formats familiar to audiences in the developed world such as soap operas, football and African versions of Reality TV series including *Big Brother* and *Pop Idol*. *Big Brother Africa* was also broadcast in early-evening terrestrial highlights episodes, in a similar way to its dual scheduling in Britain. It seems likely that for Africans the appeal of this kind of programme mix, and of *Big Brother* in particular, was that it represented an African-originated programme whose focus was not on the international news agenda's usual list of representations of the continent, which centres on war and natural disasters. Because of African nations' underfunded domestic production base, programming has consisted largely of imported Western and mainly American content, and the African housemates of *Big Brother Africa* combine with a known international format to bring these domestic and globalized forces together. *Big Brother Africa* in 2003 was the first pan-continental version, following two earlier series that contained only South African contestants and where the winners of each series were white men. *Big Brother Africa* in 2003 included contestants from Angola, Botswana, Ghana, Kenya, Malawi, Namibia, South Africa, Tanzania, Uganda, Zambia and Zimbabwe. The series began with an equal number of male and female contestants, and was won by a 24-year-old Zambian woman who collected the $100,000 prize. She met the South African president Nelson Mandela and together with fellow contestants became a celebrity. As in other versions worldwide, the housemates secured contracts as endorsers of products in advertising, as actors and as television presenters.

The series achieved a significant fan base, organized in some cities into semi-formal clubs. But among the political elites of some African countries, *Big Brother Africa* raised moral and political questions. The parliament in Malawi banned the series for two weeks until the high court declared this unconstitutional and required the national broadcaster to carry it again. President Sam Nujoma of Namibia asked the state-owned Namibian Broadcasting Corporation to cease broadcasting the programme, though Namibian audiences were largely heedless of his intervention. In Uganda, religious and women's groups, members of parliament and commentators denounced the series for immorality but it continued to be shown. Similarly in Zambia, *Big Brother Africa* was declared immoral by a pressure-group of Zambian churches, though they failed in their attempt to have it taken off air. The Nigerian media regulator sought legal grounds for prosecuting the channels broadcasting *Big Brother Africa* but failed to pursue a case successfully. These controversies were not confined to Africa, however, since the Arabian version of *Big Brother* was suspended after two weeks because of its alleged un-Islamic content, and in Italy, the channel broadcasting *Big Brother*, Canale 5, was fined for infringing standards of taste and decency. In Africa, the attempts at intervention arose because of what was perceived as non-African, Western immorality among the contestants, who were as a group relatively educated and liberal. After only 29 days of broadcasting two housemates had sex quite openly. *Big Brother Africa* demonstrated the shared standards of personal ethics prevalent among younger educated Africans from the participating nations, thus drawing public attention to generational differences between 'traditional' and 'liberal' social groups, and the impact of Western culture as one of the causes of that social change across the continent. Thus, *Big Brother Africa* demonstrated the hybridity of contemporary African culture, both in terms of the mixing of different national contestants and the use of the format in itself as a Western one made specific to its region of broadcast. The visits by non-Africans to the house, notably a housemate from the British version of *Big Brother* and the exchange programme whereby one African housemate went to Britain's *Big Brother* house in return, drew attention to the negotiation of national, regional and global difference. Reality TV claimed itself as a public space in which these homogeneities and differences could be played out by ordinary people.

What happens in the discourse of globalization is a shift from arguments for the homogeneity of media culture to arguments for the homogeneity of the political economy of the media, despite regional and local differences in the cultural forms which the media take. MTV's successful export of *The Osbournes* and the example of *Big Brother Africa* have aspects that suit the direction of each of these two kinds of argument. MTV itself is an international media institution whose economic structures and functions are similar in each of the markets where it operates, so it offers evidence for the theory that the political economy of contemporary media has become increasingly homogenized. But since the programme text of *The Osbournes* can also be screened on mainstream terrestrial channels (as it was in Britain) in multiple television cultures, it also supports the view that media content can function in similar ways in different broadcasting territories, as *Big Brother Africa* did. Such an argument is more difficult to make in the case of Reality TV programmes that are exported as formats rather than completed programmes such as *Big Brother*, although differences in this respect are less important than similarities.

International programmes and formats from Britain

British factual formats that have made significant impacts on the US television schedules include *Supernanny*, made by Ricochet, and *Wife Swap*, made by RDF Media. Factual formats developed in the US or UK programmes converted into US versions such as *The Apprentice, Pop Idol* and *The Biggest Loser* have changed the culture of programme commissioning in the United States and brought not only British-originated formats but also British staff to the central location for American television production, which is in Los Angeles. British producer Conrad Green moved from the BBC in London to Los Angeles to become executive producer on *Pop Idol*, for example, and RDF Media's Los Angeles office is run by former ITV production executive Joe Houlihan (Rogers 2005). RDF began its sale of formats to US television with a version of *Scrapheap Challenge*, commissioned by the cable channel TLC. The cable channel ABC Family acquired RDF's Reality TV format *Perfect Match*, where volunteers allow their friends to choose appropriate partners for them, and the male oriented cable channel Spike bought the company's makeover series *Ultimate Batchelor Pad* (Wells 2003). US television executives have until recently been inexperienced in producing Reality TV series, and the influx of British programmes and staff has led to something of a reversal in the direction of television innovation, which is usually understood as moving from the United States eastwards, rather than westwards from Britain to America. *Pop Idol* and its subsequent American version *American Idol* were created by Simon Fuller, the British former manager of the pop groups S Club 7 and The Spice Girls. The second series of *American Idol* ran twice a week from January to May 2003, with 34 million viewers watching the final programme on Fox (Jones 2003). This audience was the third biggest of the year, beaten only by the final of the American football final, the Superbowl, and the last episode of the Reality TV series *Joe Millionaire*. The same schedule slot that was occupied by *American Idol*, from 9 to 10 pm on Mondays and Wednesdays, was then occupied by the British-designed Reality TV series *Paradise Hotel*, made by Television Corporation, the makers of the British gameshow *Robot Wars*. There is plenty of evidence for what could be called a reverse colonization of US television by British programmes and producers in the Reality TV arena.

As Chapter 1 explained, the independent production company RDF Media is the maker of *Wife Swap*, which was first aired in the United Kingdom in 2003. RDF had their Reality TV makeover series *Faking It* commissioned for the US cable channel TLC in an American version, as well as developing *Wife Swap* for a US version on the national ABC network. The US *Wife Swap* previewed there at the end of October 2004 on a Sunday, gaining 10.9 million viewers (Brown 2004a: 10). The US version of this British Reality TV series launched with a first regular Wednesday night episode that attracted 11.1 million viewers. It achieved the same share of 18–49-year-old viewers as the established US police drama *Law and Order* and gained the highest share of 18–34-year-old women, the most valuable audience sector to US television advertisers. A similar format had already been tried by the Fox network in summer 2004, *Trading Spouses*, but *Wife Swap* beat it in the ratings. The order for the first US *Wife Swap* series was for 20 shows, and Lambert hoped for an extension to 30 shows. In the US version, Stephen Lambert was one of the three executive producers, and the programme was edited in London rather than in Los Angeles as might be expected. Producers were American whereas the directors were from the United Kingdom, since there is little tradition of observational television in the United States.

The American television networks divide their production into news (mainly on the East coast) and scripted drama (sitcom and filmed drama, mainly on the West coast), with no significant production departments making factual programmes as happens in Europe. The factual US production teams make factual specials and cover one-off events like awards ceremonies, and in recent years have diversified into high-budget Reality TV like *Survivor* that use specially adapted location environments, although *Survivor* was designed by a British company, Castaway. One of the appeals of *Wife Swap* to US television institutions was that it is filmed in people's houses and emphasizes spontaneity and authentic behaviour, unlike the factual entertainment that American producers have been accustomed to. While US networks avoided this spontaneous docusoap format because it could not be planned in advance and thus its predicted audiences and appeal could not be established, they recognized that *Wife Swap* had enough continuity of format and structure to deliver some of the predictability that they need.

The production of the US version has affected the way that the British version is now made. The US version is broken into seven segments (for commercials), the last of which is an update on how the couples have changed since the end of initial filming. It also uses more music to underscore tone and narrative form. The return visit to the couples and an increased use of music became part of the British version for its Autumn 2004 series, at Channel 4's request, thus making the show seem faster paced. However the British version is still much cheaper, at £150,000 per episode, than the $750,000 US version, partly because of larger pre-production costs in vetting contestants and arranging legal protections in the American context. Nevertheless, despite these differences, the example of *Wife Swap* in the United States is a significant one in its demonstration of a flow of programme ideas and personnel from Europe to America.

The globalization of privacy publicized

The focus on personal confession, modification, testing and the perfectability of the self in Reality TV has become transnational. The programmes themselves make public these dramas of the personal and bring the ideologies of privacy publicized into new relationships with the negotiated meanings they derive from their particular local and regional television contexts. This kind of programme focus can be abbreviated by the term 'makeover TV' and can be regarded as an instance of new transnational practices of body regulation, configurations of subjectivity and functions of television as a medium. This genre of programme both develops new conceptions of the public and private spheres and also draws on discourses of body and self that have already been in circulation in such spheres as popular magazine journalism, elective medical procedures (especially plastic surgery) and lifestyle-interview television programmes. The cultural citizenship that these programmes respond to and shape displays a problematic negotiation between the project of the perfectability of the self and the institutions, socio-economic constraints and networks of familial and social relations that border it. The circulation of makeover formats in factual television places a new emphasis on ideological currents that have specific and problematic relationships with consumerism, laws and state apparatuses and notions of community. Established television genres have already dwelt on the negotiations of body, sexuality and emotion in their relationship with kinship, community and generational identity. Television soap operas routinely focus on the sexual relationships of their now predominantly youthful characters, even though sexual activity itself cannot be shown in the prime-time slots in which the soap episodes are broadcast. Instead, the focus has been on the emotional and social significance of sexuality in making and breaking interpersonal relationships with partners, and the consequent disturbances of relationships with parents, friends, previous and potential partners and colleagues. These melodramas already prepared the ground for makeover TV by establishing the personal as the terrain of moral and civic drama, set within an extended fictional world that represents community and society in microcosmic and symbolic forms.

By adding the lure of the factual to melodramatic explorations of the personal and social, makeover TV in Reality TV formats has rendered this concern much more public by stressing its verisimilitude and its social extension beyond the fictional microcosm. In particular, television programmes have been preoccupied with the ability of television to bear witness to the varieties of ordinary people's lives, and its ability to become a forum for the public airing of confessions and revelations that seem unable to be shared with a person's intimate circle. The special circumstances of the staged factual series are designed to develop this to an extreme degree and to focus it on the body and ethics of bodily exchange for public broadcast circulation. *Big Brother* is a notable example of this trend, in which well-honed youthful bodies are routinely paraded on screen (the presence of a Jacuzzi and cameras in the bedrooms of the contestants have been well-publicized means of achieving this), and where the question of how far the contestants will go in their intimate relationships with each other is a large part of their fascination for audiences. Clearly, the transnational circulation of this combination of the private body and self and public and communal ethical challenges and tests, is the vehicle for economic activity inasmuch as the television formats involved are traded goods, and the attraction of audiences promotes economic well-being for television institutions in a variety of ways (through advertising, sponsorship or brand extensions into spin-off consumer products, for example). Youth audiences have been addressed by this combination of elements because they watch relatively little television but are very valuable to advertisers because of their disposable income. *Big Brother* was designed to be successful with this audience, and proved to be so in many of the television cultures around the world in which it was shown, though not all. The case study at the end of this chapter discusses the circulation of *Big Brother*, and the effects of the format on the institutions of television where it was broadcast. Matters of audience address, local difference within global television culture and the economics of television, are therefore important to consider, because they comprise the framework for the dissemination of ideologies of body and self, community and society.

Reality TV and television scheduling

The first 'people shows' or Reality TV formats in the United States were driven by institutional concerns about audiences, as the schedules of the major television networks saw their high ratings eroded by new ways of delivering programmes to audiences. In the United States in the 1980s, the competition between four networks, cable channels and the attractions of home video led to smaller sectors or 'niches' of the audience being targeted by programme makers and schedulers, defined either by age-group, interest (such as sport) or social class. This was when MTV began – the channel that introduced perhaps the first observational Reality TV format in its series *The Real World*. The same problems and opportunities as those that enabled Reality TV to come to prominence in the United States emerged in the United Kingdom during the 1990s as new channels, cable and satellite began to erode and segment traditional audiences, leading to the perception of a threat to scheduling as the means to gather and control high ratings. The purpose of programme scheduling is to organize elevision viewing time offering programmes that will raise ratings at particular times of day (such as mid-evening prime-time or early in the evening as adults return home from work).

In a broadcasting culture with multiple channels, the schedule enables channels to compete with each other for audiences by scheduling their own programmes with regard to what their competitors will be showing. Reality TV programmes are only profitable and successful if they continue to justify their costs and attract returning viewers over a relatively long run. The promise that a continuing series or serial has of holding onto an audience for the duration of the programme's run offers the prospect of a consistent audience whose demographic appeal and/or large size may be attractive to advertisers and can raise the broadcasting channel's public profile.

The power to commission new programmes is in the hands of the executives at broadcasting channels, but schedulers have an important role to play in identifying programmes which are likely to gain audiences based on information schedulers have about what audiences have watched in the past. So schedulers provide recommendations to commissioning executives and thus have an important influence on which programmes are made. The scheduling of *Big Brother* in the summer has been successful for Channel 4, since television programming in summer is usually made at lower cost per hour and involves numerous repeats, because people are expected to be outdoors and going out more than at other times of year. *Big Brother* was initially shown in the late evening, but was shifted to an earlier timeslot once the audience had sampled it and word of mouth began to increase the numbers of people interested in the programme. According to BARB figures published in an article by Maggie Brown (2003: 2), Channel 4's top ten rated programmes in 2003 were headed by Reality TV series. *Big Brother* topped the list at 7.2 million viewers followed by *Wife Swap* (5.9 million) and *How Clean is Your House* (5 million). While the sitcom *Friends* was the fourth highest rated programme for the channel at 5 million viewers, the property-themed Reality TV formats *Property Ladder* and *Grand Designs* were eighth and ninth with 4.6 million viewers each. As head of Channel 4, Mark Thompson's aim, subsequently realized, was to retain *Big Brother* as a core programme aimed at 16–34-year-old viewers, but to diversify the Reality TV offering into programmes that would use the components of the form in different ways for different audiences. Thus *Operatunity* was aimed at more upmarket ABC1 audiences, while *The Salon* and *Wife Swap* attempted to develop ongoing factual storylines and one-off series episodes in different ways for viewers seeking light entertainment. This illuminates matters of development of formats, schedules, patterns of viewing and programmes' address to, and creation of, audience constituencies in relation to planning by national television broadcasters.

US network schedules used to be organized around sitcoms such as *Friends*, *Sex and the City* and *Frasier*, which were the most popular 'tentpole' programmes that held the audience ratings up at their highest level. In the early years of the twenty-first century it proved difficult for the networks to find equally successful sitcoms to continue this. By contrast, however, HBO and other cable channels managed to find some sitcoms which were perceived as rather controversial and gained much higher profile than the main networks' competing programmes. For example, the relatively adult content (in US terms) of the sitcom *Will and Grace*, which features a household comprising a young gay man and a straight woman, or *Sex and the City*, which frequently contained scenes of sexual activity and 'bad language', addressed relatively young and affluent audiences, especially women. Cable channels were also quite successful with drama series, such as *The Sopranos*, which contained levels of violence that were significantly greater than network practice. The reason for network conservatism of this kind is that they find it hard to commission programmes that might disturb the conservative outlook of their big advertisers such as Coca-Cola and Proctor & Gamble. Rather than being primarily a matter of institutional culture and inertia (though these factors are important), the major advertisers are concerned that programmes do not offend any sizeable proportion of the audience. In response to this problem of reliable and long-running 'banker shows' not being created in the established sitcom genre, networks have tried to import successful formats from abroad. Two British examples are the sitcoms *The Office* and *Coupling*, which were bought as formats and were developed into US versions. However, each of these programmes, and the imported sitcom formats in general, enjoyed limited success. But the programme format that has worked for the networks is Reality TV. The big four networks have produced large numbers of Reality TV formats either of their own such as *Joe Millionaire* (subsequently sold to foreign television markets for domestic remakes) or which they have imported and made into US versions. In the early years of the twenty-first century the US schedule is tentpoled with the remaining high-profile drama series and sitcoms of an earlier generation (such as the long-running hospital drama *ER*), with Reality TV series all around them. These series are cheap to make, have good penetration into both male and female audiences and into different demographic groups defined by age or race, for example.

The highest-rated night of the week in the United States is Thursdays (when *ER* and *Will and Grace* have been shown) because this is when advertisers want to place ads for products that people may go out to buy on Saturdays when they are away from work (people go out on Fridays so this is not such an attractive evening for placing advertisements). The comparative value of sitcoms and Reality TV in the US network environment can be seen by direct comparisons between examples from each genre. In 2004, the NBC network launched its new sitcom, *Joey*, starring Matt LeBlanc as Joey Tribbiani, the same character he played in 11 series of *Friends*. The series was designed to plug the gap in NBC's Thursday evening schedule that was left after *Friends* and *Frasier* finished. In Britain too, Five has paid £450,000 per episode for *Joey*, using it to anchor a 'comedy night' strip of programmes. Jason Deans (2005a: 2) refers to figures published in *Variety* that report that there were only 33 comedies on US network TV in autumn 2004 compared to a peak of 62 in 1997. It is Reality TV series that have taken the place of sitcom in the US evening schedule. When *Joey* was launched by NBC in September 2004, scheduled in the same Thursday slot previously occupied by *Friends*, it gained 18 million viewers, but its ratings subsequently fell in competition with the Reality TV gamedoc *Survivor* on the CBS network. Once *Survivor* finished its run in January 2005, *Joey*'s ratings rose again to 12.5 million, placing it as the highest-rated sitcom launched in the autumn 2004 season, but weak in ratings terms by comparison with the audiences of 20 million attracted by some Reality TV programmes. On the Fox network, for example, 60 per cent of prime-time programming in autumn 2004 was Reality TV. The final of *American Idol* attracted 23 million viewers, the highest non-sports audience for the Fox network in over ten years. The winner was a Texas cocktail waitress, Kelly Clarkson, who got a contract with RCA records and was signed up to endorse numerous products after running the gauntlet of the judges, who were headed by the British impresario and nemesis Simon Cowell.

The television producer Kevin S. Bright, who was one of the creators of *Friends* and subsequently executive producer of *Joey*, commented: 'Sitcoms are very expensive if they fail. You probably spend less than half the money if a reality show fails' (Deans 2005a: 3). The cost of sitcoms has always been recouped by syndication sales where prime-time sitcoms were sold on to be repeated in early evening and daytime slots around the regions of the United States and abroad. But this market has been declining, so the high upfront cost of sitcoms looks much less attractive as an investment compared to the lower production costs of most Reality TV formats. Furthermore, comedy has become more the province of US cable channels, especially HBO and Comedy Central, where the studio-shot sitcom has been successfully replaced by variations on the format such as *Sex and the City* or *South Park*, leaving the networks' production system of studio shooting and syndication eclipsed by the different funding models of subscriber cable. On these subscription channels, viewers pay directly for their monthly connection charge to the channel, whereas the apparently 'free' television offered by the networks is funded by the charges advertisers pay to screen commercials.

The screening of *Big Brother* on Channel 4 in Britain enabled it both to compete with the other terrestrial channels by offering a potentially high-rated programme, but also to continue its focus on distinctively different and experimental formats, and its address to particular audience sectors. As in the case of the worries over audience ratings for channels supported by advertising revenue in the United States, Channel 4 had concerns about its competitive position in relation to competing terrestrial channels, and also the effect of new delivery systems like digital multi-channel television on its share of the most lucrative sector of the audience, young people. Channel 4 scheduled a group of new sitcoms and dramas in 2004 with this audience in mind and had also been pursuing it by screening Reality TV formats, especially *Big Brother*. As Tess Alps (2004), chair of the marketing company PHD Group UK explains, advertisers ready to invest in television commercials want involved viewers who are likely to pay attention to ads or the sponsorship sequences attached to the programme content in programmes that viewers watch intensely such as the drama serial *Sex Traffic* and the sitcom *Green Wing*. These programmes may have relatively small audiences, but they encourage attentive viewing and are perceived as 'quality' television. Alps commented: 'Advertisers loved these programmes too; they paid a premium because of their demographic profile and their light viewer content.' Light viewers are those who watch relatively little television overall and mainly consist of young adults. Because of their propensity to do other things than watch television, such as going out, using the Internet or playing computer games, they are sometimes referred to as Elusive Light Viewers (ELVs) because they are difficult for channels and advertisers to target. The rewards are potentially great, however, for programmes such as *Big Brother* that become popular with this group, as Alps notes: 'a few programmes like those can transform the whole schedule, enhance perceptions of the brand and hence maintain Channel 4's healthy average pricing'. The average pricing she refers to here is the level of the charges that can be levied on advertisers, for whom the value of commercial slots is dependent on the size and composition (in terms of age or social class, for example) of the audience expected to view at a particular time. In the unstable commercial world of Western television cultures, Reality TV has been a welcome innovation for television institutions.

The globalization of institutional forms

The possibility of Reality TV being traded and consumed transnationally depends on the configurations of television institutions and how these have converged or diverged such that appropriate markets, audiences and production systems exist in which these formats and programmes can be circulated. This is particularly significant in television cultures where state-licensed or state-controlled television institutions have been challenged or displaced by commercial television. In Britain, the 1970s marked the beginnings of the notion that some channels would direct their resources to some types of programme more than others, leaving viewers to choose for themselves the programmes which catered to their existing tastes. Television is increasingly considered as a market in which providers of programmes give their public what they seem to want. With multiple channels it no longer seems necessary for each channel to expose the audience to the full range of both 'accessible' and 'difficult' programmes. This change can justly be seen as one where television institutions are perceived both internally and externally as shifting from a paternalistic notion of the viewer as a member of a collective national audience to the notion of the viewer as increasingly an individual consumer, offered multiple choices of television content by a proliferating number of channels. Rather than supervising the viewer's cultural education towards 'better' taste and informed citizenship, as Britain's public service broadcasting culture has aimed to do, television institutions increasingly offer either mixed programme schedules, which attempt to satisfy perceived desires and capture large audiences through entertainment, or diversify their offerings into themed channels, which offer related programme types to smaller niche audiences.

The parallel between choice and democratic empowerment is of course a false one, although in principle there is no reason to regard choice as antagonistic to democracy. If viewers in newly commercialized television cultures, where consumer capitalism takes over from state control or paternalistic regulation, choose to watch makeover formats and other kinds of Reality TV programming, this can be seen both as an embrace of the new culture of selfhood, as a project of secular perfectability and also as a testing or ventilation of social anxieties about the processes of the commodification of the self and the body as things to be worked on, improved, modified and shown off. The pain involved in the exposure, testing, risking and failure of the self thus shown under construction are as much at stake as the pleasures of watching and identifying with contestants engaged in projects of self-improvement and self-analysis. The episodic serial process of pressuring, testing, exposing and judging selves and bodies in *Big Brother* can be seen as an opportunity for questioning the shift to body/self projects of perfectability as well as a celebration of it.

The use of television as a medium in which makeover TV is translated and exchanged across different local and regional spaces draws attention to the temptation to take television as a causal agent of local and regional social change based on the specific form it takes in the United States. This is partly for the pragmatic reason that theories of television are readily available from US academics and theorists. It is also the result of the assumption that the model of television institutional organization in the United States is the historic destiny of television in all contemporary societies. For example, the de-differentiation of space and time in transnational makeover TV forms and formats relates interestingly to theoretical work on the medium (based on its US forms) in the work of Margaret Morse. She argues that television is parallel to the freeway and the shopping mall, noting first the flow and movement in which billboards are driven past on an American freeway and second the segmentation and multiplicity of products in the self-contained and privatized space of the shopping mall. For Morse (1990: 197) television, the freeway and the mall are 'derealized or *nonspace*'. Television can take the viewer anywhere in time and simulate the past (like the artificial village square of the shopping mall) and can also shift the viewer in space by offering visions of distant places that are rendered the same as each other as they rush past in an evening's viewing (like the infinite horizon and endless journey of the freeway). This produces a mobile subjectivity and an experience of distraction which is dislocated from traditional spaces and times at the same time as it simulates and commodifies them, turning them into products offered for the audience to choose. As in many theoretical accounts of the specific aesthetics and politics of the television medium, the metaphors used to analyse it connect television to America, postmodernism and feminization in their connection with consumption, the erosion of boundaries and the liquidity of flow. So the argument is that makeover TV abstracts the people who are transformed from their specific spaces and times of existence, making each made-over self and body equivalent to all the others that are subjected to Reality TV's weekly transformations. Some Reality TV formats are adapted to particular localized cultures and the expectations about identity, private space and the role of television in different societies. However, the fact of transnational export of formats in itself represents an erosion of local particularity, and the adoption of television modes of address to viewers about identities and bodies that derive from Western models. *Looking Good* and *All New Plastic Surgery Live* may be distinct in many ways, but their assumption that people can be changed psychologically, socially and physically by interventions made possible by Reality TV programmes is based on a shared ideology.

Local regulatory cultures

Within a few years of its first broadcast on Dutch television in 1999, *Big Brother* had been adopted with some nationally specific variations in diverse television territories. The antics of its contestants varied, as did the reaction of the programme's broadcasters to content that could be considered offensive or potentially challenging to the norms expected of television in different nations. For example, the first British series of *Big Brother* included contestants stripping off their clothes, covering themselves with paint and creating imprints of themselves on the walls of the house. By contrast, the American *Big Brother* contestants talked a lot about sex and relationships, but remained modestly clothed and no sexual liaisons took place. In Holland the contestants were more uninhibited than in Britain, and there was some sexual activity, but the programme was not permitted to be screened at all in some Muslim nations. These differences cannot be explained by simply drawing on national stereotypes, and are instead the result of two main forces. One of them is the regulatory environment for television in different countries, where some words or images could not be broadcast (though live streaming over the Internet had lower thresholds in this respect), and the other is the internalization of norms of privacy in social life in particular cultures, inflected by the fact that the contestants knew they were on television and therefore must have modified their behaviour in relation to what they expected that television could and should show. What look like national differences between individuals in Reality TV must in fact be national differences between how people who know they are on television adapt themselves to what they think television is and can do.

Factual programmes have always aimed both to reflect society to itself and also to inform and educate the audience about the society in which they live. Reality TV, as a factual form, can claim some justification in these terms. But as an entertainment form which is set up and planned to include some of the appeal of drama and game shows, it can also fall foul of accusations of deliberately courting offence and controversy. The tensions that can arise in this hybrid form with hybrid aims and relations to Britain's Public Service Broadcasting traditions, can be seen at work in the BBC Producer's Guidelines (2003) in the section on 'Taste and Decency' that attempts to offer balanced advice covering all genres: 'The right to challenge audience expectations in surprising and innovative ways, when circumstances justify, must also be safeguarded. Comedy, drama, and the arts will sometimes seek to question existing assumptions about taste. Programmes which question these assumptions should seek to tell the truth about the human experience, including its darker side, but should not set out to demean, brutalise or celebrate cruelty.' However, these rules were originally designed when comedy, arts and drama consisted entirely or almost entirely of scripted programmes, and these were recorded rather than live. This underlying assumption of producer control, and the possibility of controlling programmes by executives' and broadcasting managers' oversight of writers and performers can also be seen reflected in the language of the ITC Programme Code (2002) in its reference to taste and decency: 'Much great fiction and drama have been concerned with love and passion which can shock and disturb. Popular entertainment and comedy have always relied to some extent on sexual innuendo and suggestive behaviour but gratuitous offence should be avoided.' The genres being referred to as examples of how to deal with offensive material here are all scripted and recorded television formats, as opposed to Reality TV in its recorded or live forms.

Since Reality TV programmes are popular and aimed at young people, they tend also to feature young people whose use of 'bad' language, expectations about sexual behaviour and rebelliousness could conflict with some norms of taste and decency. This may be one reason why the commercial ITV channel exploited the controversial potential of Reality TV the most in the years when it first developed, because of a historic rise in the average age of ITV viewers and the channel's intention to attract younger audiences. BBC Producer Guidelines (2003) state: 'Game shows, people shows and light entertainment can be both popular and enjoyable without breaching standards on taste and decency. Crudeness is unacceptable; language and sexual innuendo have to be judged according to the scheduling and the likely audience at home. Be careful not to promote sexual, racial or other stereotypes. Game shows and People shows are the points where the BBC most evidently comes into contact with its mass audience. It is important that these programmes set the standard for the way the BBC treats people. We must not patronise them or exploit them, nor be seen to humiliate them.' This is an extension of a legal requirement which also affects commercial terrestrial broadcasters, and is referred to explicitly in a similar statement on taste and decency in the ITC Programme Code (2002): 'Section 6(1) of the Broadcasting Act 1990 requires that the ITC does all it can to secure that every licensed service includes nothing in its programmes which offends against good taste or decency or is likely to encourage or incite to crime or lead to disorder or be offensive to public feeling.' Specifically in relation to bad language, Channel 4 introduced a short delay between the occurrence of events on *Big Brother*'s live late-evening broadcast and the transmission of the programme, since the delay could allow for the bleeping-out of offensive dialogue. This follows the ITC Programme Code's (2002) guideline: 'There is no absolute ban on the use of bad language. But many people are offended, some of them deeply, by the use of bad language, including expletives with a religious (and not only Christian) association. Offence is most likely if the language is contrary to audience expectation. Bad language must be defensible in terms of context and scheduling with warnings where appropriate. The most offensive language must not be used before the watershed and bad language of any sort must not be a frequent feature before then.' The key phrase in this statement is 'audience expectation'. Channel 4's expected audience was young, and that audience's expectation could be for customarily scatological or sexual language and blasphemy. But the channel had to balance this against the much wider audience drawn to the programme and the high public and media profile which it had gained.

The issue of taste and decency is closely connected to the imagining of television audiences and the mechanisms by which programmes are delivered to audiences through the schedule. The BBC Producers Guidelines (2003) recognize this when they state in the 'Taste and Decency' section: 'Context is everything: scheduling can be vital to audiences accepting difficult material. It is vital to consider the expectations that audiences have of particular programmes and timeslots. The widespread availability of material in other media, or on other broadcasters is not reason enough to judge it acceptable.' In this statement, it is worth noting that a 'me too' argument is not regarded as a justification for causing offence to some audiences. The fact that an ITV company or Channel 4 might broadcast a challenging or offensive Reality TV programme is not regarded as a justification for BBC to follow suit in one of its own formats or in an acquired programme.

Big Brother was a means to attract audiences to Channel 4's new paid cable, satellite and digital channel E4. Different regulations affect the scheduling of programmes on these channels, as well as different strategies developed by broadcasting institutions to use them as add-ons, supplements, alternatives or groundbreakers for their terrestrial free-to-air services. The additional coverage of Reality TV programmes in non-free-to-air channels is not subject to same watershed rules that are enshrined in the guidelines on Taste and Decency. The ITC Programme Code (2002) states: 'The decision to subscribe to a specialist channel available only to those who have specifically chosen it, carries with it an acceptance of a greater share of responsibility by parents for what is viewed and the watershed on such channels is set at 8pm rather than 9pm.' This allows E4 to broadcast more, and less controlled, coverage than on the parent channel. But in June 2004, Michelle and Emma, two *Big Brother* contestants who had been evicted and then placed in an annexe where they were able to watch a video feed of events inside the house, were returned to their fellow contestants. This departure from the programme's former structure occurred in response to criticisms of the 2003 *Big Brother* for being dull and boring, leading to the production team's decision to introduce greater stress on the contestants, paraphrased as 'Big Brother gets evil'. During their time away, the pair were criticized roundly by their housemates, and when they reappeared in the living area of the *Big Brother* house an aggressive confrontation occurred. Emma confronted Victor, shouting obscenities at him and vowing to kill him after he threw wine over her and appeared to spit in her face. Other contestants shouted at each other and attempted to pull apart the arguing housemates. Three security guards were sent into the house to break up the argument. More than 6 million people were watching at the time, and five viewers who saw the programme called the police and two officers visited the house. The media regulator Ofcom received 12 complaints and began an investigation. Live footage was being screened on the digital channel E4 at the time of the incident and was withdrawn for about one hour. Members of the production team and the programme's psychologists talked to each of the contestants about the events and their feelings about them. While the confrontation took place, Channel 4 replaced the live footage of the house with shots of its exterior accompanied by recordings of bird song. Clearly, the national regulatory cultures where Reality TV programmes are shown have a significant impact on what can be broadcast, at least over terrestrial transmission systems. The case study that follows considers the different impact of *Big Brother*, in particular, on the fortunes of its broadcasters in different nations.

Case Study: *Big Brother* as a transnational property

Gamedocs have been traded around the world as international formats that are locally produced, and this had previously been a distribution model adopted by the owners of more conventional game show formats like *The Price is Right* or *Who Wants to be a Millionaire*. The documentary aspect is new to the game show trade around the world. As Chapter 1 outlined, the pre-designed and tested formats of Reality TV cost less to produce than wholly new programme ideas devised for specific national channels and reduce the risk that new programmes face in finding the right audience and becoming popular. Annette Hill's work (2002: 325–6) on the different national audiences for *Big Brother* forms the basis for some mainly statistical comparison in this section. The emphasis here is on the comparative success of *Big Brother* in different countries, not only in terms of the ratings and audience shares that the programme achieved, but also in terms of its role as means to define the brand identity of its channel and to raise the profile of that channel.

The first ever version of *Big Brother* was produced in Holland by John de Mol Productions for the Veronica channel. De Mol's company Endemol in the United Kingdom is the market leader of independent production companies, and is owned by Dutch Endemol, which is in turn owned by Spanish media company Telefonica. The programme formats that Endemol has devised include a range of Reality TV variants such as *Fame Academy, Changing Rooms, Fear Factor* and *The Salon*. In Holland, the first *Big Brother* series peaked at 6 million viewers when two contestants enjoyed a moment of physical intimacy whose exact nature has been disputed but was certainly sexual. The healthy ratings for the programme assisted in making the format an attractive prospect for broadcasters in other countries, but perhaps equally important was the profile of the programme as evidenced by press and television coverage, which supported a rapidly growing public culture of talk, consisting largely of speculation about the contestants and the outcome of the competition. This word-of-mouth circulation of information about the programme has been a key aspect of *Big Brother*'s success internationally (see Chapter 6), and has the spin-off benefit of drawing viewers to the channel broadcasting the series and potentially keeping them watching it for other programmes in its schedule.

In Germany, *Big Brother* was produced by Endemol Entertainment for the RTL2 and RTL channels. Its success meant that a second series was commissioned during the summer run of the first series, so that a second series could begin in Autumn 2000 as soon as the first one finished. RTL2 was a small broadcaster with an average 3.9 per cent share of the audience in *Big Brother*'s timeslot, and the channel increased this to 15 per cent for the second *Big Brother* series. Then a third series was commissioned for the post-Christmas season (finishing in May 2001) but the ratings did not equal those of its predecessor. The opportunity to raise a minority channel's audience share was more dramatically demonstrated in Portugal, where TVI screened *Big Brother* (produced by Endemol Entertainment) from September to December 2000, gaining an average share over this period of 61 per cent in contrast to its normal average share of 9 per cent, and a peak share of 74 per cent in the series' final week. Similar success followed when a second *Big Brother* series was screened by the same channel. *Big Brother* in Spain was broadcast by Tele 5 (produced by Zeppelin Television) in April–July 2000. Tele 5 had a normal average share of 21 per cent, and although at the start of the *Big Brother* series the channel's initial share was 13.7 per cent this rose to 30 per cent with a peak for the final episode of 70 per cent, when the ratings for this climactic end to the competition overtook those of the Champions League soccer semi-final. *Big Brother* in Belgium was on Kanal 2 (produced by Endemol Entertainment) from September to December 2000, and the channel's average share rose from 9 per cent to a peak of almost 50 per cent. Similarly, *Big Brother* in Switzerland was on TV3 (produced by B&B Endemol) in Autumn 2000 and increased the channel's share from an average of only 2.5 per cent to 30 per cent. In Argentina, *Big Brother* was first shown from March to July of 2001 on Telefe, a privately owned channel, and its audience share peaked at 20 per cent for the eviction programmes. Telefe commissioned a second series to begin one month after the end of the first series, starting in August 2001.

To provide a little more detail about the production of overseas versions of *Big Brother*, focusing on another of the successful national variants, it is useful to look more closely than in the examples above at the Australian version (referring to research by Jane Roscoe, 2004) before considering the most significant case where the format did not have such an impact on the fortunes of its parent channel. *Big Brother* in Australia was produced by Southern Star Endemol for Channel 10, where it attracted a 50 per cent share of 19–39 year olds, which was the target audience group for the channel. *Big Brother* Australia facilitated Southern Star's move from being a producer of drama into making factual and light entertainment programmes. The *Big Brother* house and the production offices were at the Dreamworld theme park on Queensland's

Gold Coast, forming the nucleus of a production centre that could be used for future *Big Brother* series and also exploited by Dreamworld itself for broadcasting its own productions. The space surrounding these facilities in the theme park also provided public space in which the public could gather to witness live eviction shows broadcast on Sundays. The Australian version utilized over 170 staff, 25 cameras and 36 microphones. The raw material produced by this setup resulted in 96 hours of video material per day, used for daily broadcasts, the Thursday programme *Big Brother Uncut, The Saturday Show* and the live eviction, plus the possibility to stream footage live on the Internet. *Big Brother* Australia was the most expensive programme ever to be made there, costing something between 13 and 16 million Australian dollars.

In concurrence with other international versions of *Big Brother*, the Australian house emphasized an outdoor lifestyle, which matched Australian perceptions of its own local culture. A swimming pool and barbecue facilitated outdoor living, and a culture of personal fitness among young Australians was matched by the participants engaging in yoga, jogging and other kinds of physical training. Roscoe (2004) reports that among the producers, there was a sense that the Australian participants were much less interested in their individual or collective success in the tasks set by Big Brother, in contrast to the emotion and conflict produced by tasks in other national versions. She suggests that the emphasis on leisure, matey bonding and having fun that are reputed to characterize Australian culture was reflected in the behaviour of the people in the house. Like the British and other international versions of *Big Brother*, the Australian version featured psychologists who were involved in the selection process of the housemates and in periodic evaluations of their behaviour in the television episodes. This adoption of a scientific discourse both prompted the gradual construction of character typologies for individual participants and also legitimated the programme's emphasis on gossip and comparative discussion that could be shared between viewers. Roscoe notes that this suggests similarities between audience interest in *Big Brother*, especially among older women and the prominence of gossip and information exchange in soap opera. She quotes the executive producer Peter Abbott saying that the production team 'try and emulate the pace and the grammar of the soap opera much more than anyone else has done. We are using voice over to truncate, we're editing to truncate' (Roscoe 2004: 316). She quotes one of the producers, Dave English, saying: 'roughly speaking there are four breaks, five segments, each with maybe two-three stories in each, so you're talking about 12–15 brief story lines per episode' (Roscoe 2004: 316).

The vocabulary of pace, scenes and storylines draws attention to the parallels between *Big Brother* and soap opera, and the serial continuity of the programme is reinforced by opening trails of highlights of the day's events and closing previews. This structure of continuing drama is of course a key resource for continuing viewer involvement across the run of the series.

The executive producer Peter Abbott discussed the casting process in which over 10,000 people were whittled down to 40 potential participants. Rather than casting to look for potential conflicts, Abbott explained that he saw the programme as more like inviting people to a dinner party: 'You might invite somebody to be provocative, but you would have to assume that the party was still going to be a pleasant experience for everybody ... It was a failure in the American *Big Brother* that they cast too much for conflict and there was no sense of group' (Roscoe 2004: 317). Participation was made possible in several ways in addition to television viewing. The location at Dreamworld enabled members of the public to come and witness the comings and goings associated with the programme, especially its eviction evenings. Fans of the programme were allowed to go behind the scenes and see aspects of its production. The production area became a visitor attraction, where it was possible to see the control room, a mock up of the diary room where visitors could be photographed, and giant screens in the outdoor area around the house showed live footage. Fans were required to buy tickets for 20 Australian dollars each to be present at the production location and were encouraged to dress up as their favourite housemates with the opportunity to win a prize of 20,000 Australian dollars worth of entertainment prizes. As in other national versions, the Australian *Big Brother* website offers live video streams, updates, chat rooms, and background features on the participants, the house and the programme. Merchandising opportunities for programme related products appeared on the website, and users could vote online. National TV ratings for the week of 24–30 June 2001 showed the Australian *Big Brother Live* on Channel 10 at number one, ahead of *Friends* on Channel 9 and *National Nine News*. The Australian version was presented by Gretel Killeen, and the programme aired on weeknights from 7.00 to 7.30, Saturdays from 8.30 to 9.30, with the eviction show on Sunday from 7.30 to 8.30.

In contrast to the Australian experience, *Big Brother* in Sweden did not get high ratings or audience share, but achieved high levels of publicity and profile for its broadcaster. The series was on Kanal 5 (produced by Metronome Television) in Autumn 2000, and the channel's 10 per cent share remained steady during the run. However, the media profile of

Big Brother in Sweden was a significant factor in Kanal 5's decision to commission a second series with a modified format. The most celebrated case of *Big Brother* failing to achieve the ratings or profile that it did in other nations was when it was made in the United States. *Big Brother* US was screened on the CBS network (produced by Evolution Film and Tape) from July to December 2000. The first episode achieved a 23 per cent share but the average share for the series was only 12 per cent. Nevertheless, CBS commissioned a second series with a modified format and took the view that one reason for the low rating was the competing Reality TV format *Survivor* which was very popular and drew audiences away from *Big Brother*. In the American version of *Big Brother* in 2003, the evicted contestants were grouped together in a secret location to decide on who would win the half million dollar prize. Three of the contestants, Jun, Alison and Erika, were known as the Angel Alliance, whereas an opposing group known as the Dream Team, finally comprised only Robert, but previously included Jee and Nathan too. The evicted contestants had a chance to ask questions of the final four, leading to a greater emphasis in the main broadcast of the American version on contestants' self-reflection and evaluation of their experience as a learning opportunity.

In Britain, *Big Brother* was produced by GMG Endemol Entertainment for Channel 4 and gave the channel its best ever Friday evening ratings gained for the regular eviction episodes. The first series began with audiences of 3 million and this rose to 10 million for the final episode. The audience share rose to 46 per cent in the week that the contestant 'Nasty' Nick Bateman's plotting against his housemates was uncovered by them and peaked at 56.5 per cent on the last night of the series. Across the first series, the share averaged 26 per cent, and 67 per cent of the UK population watched *Big Brother* on at least one occasion. Over 7 million people telephoned the voting line in the vote for the winner, the highest phone-in participation for a British television programme. The website received 3 million page impressions per day, becoming the most requested webpage in Europe in 2000. On the day when Nick was unmasked, the site received 7.5 million page impressions. The factors of raising channel profile and producing a public culture of talk that have already been discussed were clearly crucial to this outstanding audience awareness, giving the series the characteristics of a television event (inasmuch as a series can qualify as an event). The second series of the British *Big Brother* averaged 4.5 million viewers and was a 70 per cent increase on Channel 4's average audience share. During some moments in the cable and satellite channel E4's live *Big Brother* coverage, the audience size occasionally exceeded the ratings for minority terrestrial channels, which is exceptional in the British context where terrestrial channels routinely outperform all non-terrestrial broadcasting. On Wednesday, 11 July 2001 at 11.00 pm E4 rated 626,000 viewers while Channel 5 had 300,000 viewers and Channel 4 had 400,000 viewers. There were 15.6 million people casting eviction votes using interactive remote controls or telephones. The website received 159 million page impressions and users requested 16.4 million live video streams from the website.

But the difference in success between *Big Brother* and *Survivor* in the United Kingdom and the United States shows that although Reality TV gamedoc formats can attract big audiences and increase the profile of small channels by raising their share and generating publicity, this cannot be guaranteed. The attractiveness of programmes is not simply a property of the programme text or format itself. The British version of *Survivor* was broadcast on the mainstream terrestrial channel ITV during evening prime-time but only gained 6 million viewers for the first episode in June 2001, and this fell to 4 million across the rest of the series. These are very low figures for ITV, whose most consistently popular programme, *Coronation Street*, can be expected to attract about 13 million viewers on a regular basis. International formats are a striking feature of the contemporary television landscape, and Reality TV formats especially so, but as this chapter has shown, the forces of globalization and localization operate interdependently and give rise to situations that are surprisingly different as well as interestingly similar.

Conclusion

In theories of television culture, aspects of globalization theory and more specific work on national television regions can be seen as attempts to address the perceived inadequacies of each other as discursive articulations which both define themselves against each other and also depend on each other. I have argued that this mutual interdependence is part of a discourse which specifies the character of contemporary television culture, and that studying it continues the issues of referentiality and exemplarity that were introduced in the introduction to this book and in the previous chapter. Critical discourses about contemporary television use the evidence of the global dissemination of television's institutional structures and examples of individual programmes that circulate from one television environment to another to argue that the cultures of nations and societies are being decisively altered in the direction of homogenization. However, the global culture of modernity, which this argument assumes, has the effect of covering over some important problems and differences that complicate it, like the relative failure of *Survivor* to attract audiences in Britain and the similar lack of interest in the United States around *Big Brother*. Nevertheless, the ways in which personnel, format ideas, programmes and ways of interacting with television occur in different locations suggest at least the Westernization of ideas about the self, the body and community, and these ideas are discussed from other perspectives in subsequent chapters. But the travelling of Reality TV around the world is certainly not evidence for the Americanization of television in the ways that earlier theories of globalization proposed. This suggests that rather than a homogenous and monolithic notion of contemporary television, Reality TV and, I would argue, television culture in general, exists in a dynamic state where uneven and negotiated processes need to be recognized. This chapter has mainly focused on television institutions and the television industry, discussing programmes only briefly and considering audiences from a statistical point of view. This kind of analysis still leaves unclear the relationship of specific Reality TV programmes to processes of cultural definition, which need to be explored in relation to the generic characteristics of these programmes and the ways that their audiences can be understood through qualitative ethnographic studies of how viewers watch them. The focus on media audiences as heterogeneous, active in their responses to television and involved in the production of temporary and negotiated identities, is the most radical challenge to the often generalizing discourses about globalization and modernity that have appeared in this chapter. The next chapter takes the debate further by considering in detail how Reality TV approaches the real, and the significance of its status as a form of factual television.

3
Reality TV

Introduction

In this chapter and in Chapter 4, I focus on the relationships between Reality TV and other forms and genres of television which may seem either close to it or distant from it. This is part of a larger concern to contribute to debates about 'televisuality', and the understanding of the distinctiveness of television. Television works through reality, processing it and worrying over it in order to define, explain, narrate, render intelligible, marginalize or speculate about reality (Ellis 1999b). This occurs across all of its genres, not only in news and current affairs, but also in chat shows, soap operas, documentary and drama, so that realism becomes a particularly ambiguous term in the analysis of television. One meaning focuses on the referent of what is represented: that actual scenes, places and people are represented rather than imagined or fictional ones. A second meaning refers to television's representation of recognizable and often contemporary experience such as in the representation of characters the audience can believe in or apparently likely chains of events. This meaning of realism relies on the familiarity of the codes which represent a reality. But finally, another meaning of realism would reject the conventions of established realistic forms and look for new and different forms to give access to the real. In each of these meanings, however, realism posits the separation of the text from a real which pre-exists it. Furthermore, the establishment of category distinctions in television, such as between factual and fictional forms, or between drama and documentary, could be seen as increasingly problematic in contemporary television. Reality TV can be thought of as the trying out of forms and modes of address in one genre or form that are adopted from apparently different genres and forms, thus creating connection and distinction simultaneously. Clearly, the question of what reality means for Reality TV, in relation to different forms of realism, is one of the methodological questions about borderlines, identities and categories in television analysis which this book seeks to address as part of its arguments about Reality TV. Genre is partly about stability and unity, but more importantly perhaps, genre is a way of talking about change and the ways that television changes its programmes and its relationships with its audience. Both genre and historicization each fix the identity of something in contrast to something else but also allow for the possibility of blurring, hybridity and mixing between categories or moments that seem to be different from each other. Both genre and historical periodization are not ways of talking about the self-sufficient stability of a group of programmes, but about the temporary, almost momentary stability of an object of discussion against a background of constant change.

Reality TV clearly gains its name through the claim that these television representations of reality maintain an inherent difference from television fictional narrative (and potentially fictional narrative in other media such as cinema). The artificiality of the scenarios in some Reality TV programmes is countered by their use of non-actor participants, no scripts and a temporal progression which is close to the linear unfolding of lived daily time (Andrejevic 2002). As John Corner (1992: 98) notes, realism has been regarded as 'television's defining aesthetic and social project'. The notion of realism operates as a standard of value within television institutions and for audiences, since each of these regard the connection of television programmes with reality as an assumed basis for judging the value of television content. Raymond Williams (1976, 1977) notes that the term 'real' is used in contrast to 'imaginary', to refer to the material existence of something in contrast to an unreal or fantastical world. In a second meaning, Williams points out that 'real' contrasts with the 'apparent', and refers to a hidden truth that might be revealed beneath the surface of what is communicated. The first of these meanings concerns a notion of representation as reflection. The second meaning refers to revelation or analysis, and each of them has a long intellectual history. Nineteenth century notions of representation assumed that the real world could be adequately explained and could be satisfactorily represented. Williams argues that this produces three features in realism: it is contemporary, it is concerned with actions that can be explained and which take place in the material world and third it is socially extended in that it has an ambition to represent ordinary people. As a consequence, a fourth element of realism is its ambition to interpret in relation to a certain political viewpoint in order to produce a claim of understanding. Williams was a literary critic, and he drew on the historical usage of realism as a literary term to point out that while naturalism in literature is a descriptive method that observes the detail of a reality, realism aims to produce the experience of dynamic struggle in order to provide an understanding of contradiction and causality. This chapter discusses Reality TV's relationships with the real with special attention to the tensions and contradictions that these display, and whether they predispose Reality TV to critique or political comment.

Generic conventions and docusoap

Docusoap is a response to economic pressures within the television industry (see Chapter 1) and a waning faith among documentary makers and audiences in the authority and sobriety of its conventional forms. Television always aims to contain and explain the real, especially through the form of narrative, in order to comply with expectations of cultural verisimilitude (adopting realisms grounded in cultural understandings of the real) and generic verisimilitude (in which genre codes legitimate some realisms and not others). The desire to produce unmediated access to the real goes along with, but is contradicted by, the necessity to domesticate and contain the material. Genre is one of the forces that can achieve this domestication and constraint, as well as being a mechanism for creating new hybrid forms. Docusoap combines the observation and interpretation of reality in documentary with the continuing character-centred narrative of soap opera structured by performance and narrative. Generic categories are no longer separate, if they ever were, and such newer formats as docusoaps, gamedocs and reality sitcoms feed off the rich history and audience knowledge of television to mix realism with reflexivity. As well as being constrained by repetition, genre allows for innovation within and between genres, and programmes gain large audiences by manipulating conventions in new ways. In 1998 the ITV docusoap *Airline* achieved a 50 per cent average audience share, with 11.4 million viewers, while BBC1's *The Cruise* (aboard a cruise liner) and *Animal Hospital* attracted 10 million viewers and shares of 40 per cent each. BBC1's first prime-time factual programme, *Airport* (1998) attracted a 44 per cent audience share, and in response ITV moved their competitor, the fire service drama *London's Burning*, to a different placing in the schedule. But docusoaps have been criticized for lacking the depth of insight into character or situation that television documentary has conventionally aimed for. Formally, docusoaps use rapid cutting between scenes and characters to maintain audience interest, and do not adopt the sustained focus on the subject that has signified television documentary's quest for understanding. Perhaps the best-known (and controversial) docusoap of the turn of the twenty-first century has been the BBC's *Driving School*, which was scheduled against the popular ITV police drama *The Bill* yet attracted twice as many viewers, peaking at 12 million.

The rhetoric of realism in television documentary is paradoxically the result of several very unnatural procedures. The documentary subject will almost always be aware that he or she is being recorded, witnessed or even pursued by the camera operator and often also by a sound recordist. Once the footage has been gathered, editing processes aim to produce a coherent argument or a narrative. While the finished programme may acknowledge the presence of the documentary maker, it is often the case that documentaries imply that the subject is behaving 'naturally' or at least representatively. So there is a tension between producing a documentary which is representative and 'accurate' and providing the audience with a programme which conforms to the conventions of argument or storytelling. It is this tension which gives rise to the complaints and occasionally legal cases brought by documentary subjects against documentary makers, where the subject claims that he or she has been misrepresented or made to look foolish. The assumption of accuracy which always accompanies the documentary mode brings with it the danger of claims of misrepresentation. Techniques such as covert filming, or showing the documentary maker on screen developing a relationship with the documentary subject, are two different ways of coping with these problems. Docusoap adopts the latter of these alternatives, recognizing the structuring and sometimes causative role of the programme maker in generating the material that will be shot.

Rather than attempting a representative coverage of a group of subjects, an occupation or an environment, docusoap makes a virtue of metonymy, in which a selected person, small group of main subjects or single workplace location stands in for a broader social fabric. One day in the life of a hotel metonymically stands for any other day. The work of an inner-city social worker stands metonymically for all inner-city social workers. Specific images or sequences, or specific docusoap subjects, have metonymic relationships with the reality of which they are a part. This device is one of the unstated assumptions which enables docusoaps to claim implicitly that they represent society to itself and connect the specific subjects of programmes to larger social contexts.

But metonymic representativeness depends on the relationship between the codes of the programme and the codes available to the audience for interpreting it, a relationship that Richard Kilborn and John Izod (1997: 39) call 'accommodation' in which the programmes' representations accommodate themselves to some extent with ideological assumptions assumed to be held by the audience.

Soap opera claims the authenticity of realism through its apparent reflection of a social world reduced to a microcosm of ordinariness and structured by condensation and narrative progress. Against a background of continuity where time moves slowly and storylines deal with apparently trivial interactions and events, there are very frequent breaking points in relationships between individuals, families and communities (like divorce, birth, death, gossip and antagonism between characters) which generate new storylines. So while the foundations of soap opera reflect ideological norms in being centred on the family, community and regional identity, it is the lack and disturbance of these structures which drives their narrative. Conflicts like these are a principal attraction of docusoap, which adopts them from the soap opera form. But the conflicts themselves serve the function of illuminating character, and this emphasis on character in docusoap is also carried over from soap opera: 'although soap opera narrative may seem to ask "What will happen next?" as its dominant question, the terrain on which this question is posed is determined by a prior question – "What kind of person is this?" And in the ineluctable posing of this question, of all characters, whatever their social position, soap opera poses a potential moral equality of all individuals' (Brunsdon 1981: 36). Soaps and docusoaps are an arena for a mediated debate about morality and social behaviour in modern societies in which questions of realism become displaced onto patterns of personal identity and interpersonal relationships.

Docusoaps have less of the exaggerated melodramatic forms of soap opera narrative, such as their use of comic, grotesque or stereotypical characters, for instance, but the back and forth movement between fiction and fact in their discourses maintains both fact and fiction's separation from each other and shows how interdependent they are, testifying to the unstable border between what is considered 'real' and what is a performance or representation of reality (see Chapter 4). The cross-cutting between storylines using parallel montage in docusoap, which is one of the distinguishing features that sets it apart from conventional documentary, gives access to the differing people and locations that appear in each episode. But whereas soaps represent a community with a regional identity, with a predominantly residential setting, docusoaps are based mainly in workplace environments. However, as in soaps, the docusoap episodes rarely escape from these settings and focus their attention on action within the represented space and the invasion of that space from the outside. Despite that difference, the comments of Sandy Flitterman-Lewis (1992: 195) about camera technique in soap opera have useful purchase on the moulding of space in docusoaps, where the camera does not create a consistent space by alternating establishing shots and shot–reverse shots in order to situate the drama securely for the viewer: 'The quality of viewer involvement, instead, is one of continual, momentary, and constant visual repositioning, in keeping with television's characteristic "glance." ' The movement of the narrative point of view allows the sense of incompletion and future that is necessary to soap opera form because of its continuity as a serial, and this also serves docusoap by suggesting the unpredictable and unplanned movement of time in a real present. Docusoaps are by definition serials, in that continuing characters and storylines develop from week to week, so the fragments of unplanned time and space that comprise their episodes may be interesting and involving in themselves but they are subordinate, finally, to the process of building a familiar cast and setting that can be returned to week after week by the audience.

Docusoap, ordinariness and celebrity

Driving School attracted 12 million viewers when scheduled against the popular continuing police drama *The Bill*, on ITV, which got 6 million viewers. Although *Driving School* was a docusoap featuring real people and *The Bill* was a fictional drama, there were several codes which the two programmes shared. Like a drama serial, *Driving School* focused on people with easily identifiable characteristics and highlighted dramatic incidents and reversals of fortune. The learner driver Maureen and her husband Dave were the most celebrated of these, becoming minor celebrities appearing in television chat shows and tabloid newspaper features. Maureen's difficulties with driving enabled the programme makers to feature scenes in which she nearly hit other cars, broke down in tears when she made mistakes and got into arguments with her long-suffering husband. Thus narrative codes and codes of character drawn from television fiction were available for the viewer to understand and enjoy the programme, like dramatic crises and turning points, conflicts between characters, and moments of comedy or tragedy. The programme was given structural unity by a narrator, who could provide linguistic cues that encouraged the audience to invoke these familiar codes.

The dramatic aspects of *Driving School* led to argument in the media about the ethics of docusoap production. First, it was alleged that some scenes had been 'faked' for the camera, thus breaking the documentary convention that reality is observed without intervention by the programme maker. A scene in which Maureen woke her husband in the middle of the night, for example, was revealed to be a re-enactment of an event which did take place, so it was a fictionalized reconstruction in a similar sense to the reconstructions in *Crimewatch*, for example. Second, the programme was criticized for selecting subjects (including Maureen) who were likely to deliberately display emotion and 'act up for the camera' and were made into public celebrities for the voyeuristic pleasure of the audience. Again, the neutrality, objectivity and representativeness of documentary seemed to have been discarded. These controversies arose because of the programme's mixed fictional and factual coding systems and the resulting confusion about whether its aim was information or entertainment. What is significant for the argument of this chapter, however, is that the realism of *Driving School* rested on precisely this confusion and mixing of television codes.

Docusoaps feature people who television viewers might easily encounter in daily life such as hotel workers, holiday reps, driving instructors and shop assistants. These people operate in 'middle spaces' of society: they are neither members of a powerful elite (such as company directors, judges and aristocrats) nor powerless, excluded people (such as homeless people or asylum-seekers), but in the middle. This choice of subject separates docusoap from the tradition in documentary of investigating a subordinate, usually working class, group who the programme maker considers voiceless, in order to speak for that group and call for its social betterment by witnessing its plight and posing rational arguments about its needs. While documentary might be said to focus on a group of others and demónstrate they are 'just like us' and deserving of their audience's understanding and identification, docusoap features people who are already 'just like us' and demonstrates how familiar but individually distinctive they are. Docusoap therefore intervenes in the expectations of what 'us' might mean in a potentially interesting and important sense. In a contemporary society that was declared classless by Conservative Prime Minister John Major, for example, where commentators have clamed that in Britain we are all middle class now, docusoap starts from an assumption of variety within a greater homogeneity and works on the tension between these. The form was brilliantly parodied and critiqued by the BBC's spoof docusoap *People Like Us* (whose title suggests the issues I have introduced here).

In the series the supposed docusoap subjects were alternately banal and eccentric, both 'like us' and 'unlike us', but the figure most 'unlike us' was the docusoap programme maker himself, played by Chris Langhan, who was utterly incapable of fathoming the ordinariness of the occupational groups (like estate agents) who he aimed to get close to as people. Docusoap characters are also in middle spaces in the sense that they are in middle positions in a hierarchy. They often encounter members of the public to whom they provide services, and they are responsible to authority figures more senior than them. Docusoap programmes often bridge a line which divides the public working lives of these people from their private lives, a line which is also a mediator between two kinds of experience. As a genre of programme docusoap is a middle genre, between documentary and drama. Finally, docusoaps show people who are represented as 'like us', as ordinary as the television viewers watching them, yet being on television in itself makes these people not 'like us', so docusoaps occupy a middle space between ordinariness and celebrity. Graeme Burton (2000: 159) has suggested that docusoap 'stands for a growing use of viewers to entertain the viewers – an approach familiar from the game show genre and the use of studio audiences. It creates the illusion that television recognises its audience and works for its audience'. In docusoap, the dividing lines between television and everyday reality, programme and audience, celebrity and ordinariness, are fine lines which can easily be crossed. The blurring of these boundaries contributes to the confusion of social categories that has marked political culture at the turn of the twenty-first century where Thatcherism appealed to a 'silent majority' and New Labour to a 'middle England' supposedly beyond the class divisions of earlier ideologies. In representing this apparently homogenous middle, docusoap both offers a realism of reflection but also contributes to the poverty of analytical political discourses that might intervene and transform it. The non-analytical immersion of docusoap in the lives of its subjects that was exposed in *People Like Us* draws attention to what Burton calls the 'illusion' that television 'works for its audience' , since it is far from clear what 'work' the docusoap does.

The aesthetics of Reality TV

In the formative period of the socially conscious television documentary, emerging from the British Documentary Cinema movement and migrating to television as it achieved the status of a mass medium in the 1950s, it was accepted that situations that had previously occurred could be reconstructed by the filmmaker (as in the classic documentary *Fires Were Started*). The filmmaker had witnessed the original event's occurrence, or had other credible testimony about its truth. Based on this prior witness, it was routine for filmmakers to fully or partially script documentary films, to reconstruct settings in a studio and to coach participants in repeating actions for the camera. It is misleading to present documentary as a kind of programme making that represents an authentic reality in an unmediated way, perhaps contrasting it with the staged situations common to Reality TV. The making of documentary already includes the likelihood if not the necessity of manipulating the real in order to shoot it. Shooting documentary often requires a programme maker to prompt a documentary subject in some way, for example by asking that an action be undertaken so that it can be clearly seen by the camera. When something goes wrong, a documentary maker might reasonably ask the subject to perform an action again so that it can be recorded. After shooting, the procedures of editing very often involve a level of manipulation. Sequences shot at different times can be linked together to give the impression of continuous action, and cutting between sequences shot at different times gives the impression that they happened at the same moment.

But the guarantee of this kind of documentary's claim to truth was the notion of prior witness that established the film as a repetition of something that had actually occurred. On the other hand, the American direct cinema approach refused the possibility of reconstruction and staging and based its claim to truth on the witnessing in the present of an event as it actually occurred. The filmmaker intervened as little as possible and aimed for the event to speak for itself, with minimal construction through editing, directorial activity or music. The paradox of Reality TV is that it combines these two modes of documentary, using the aspect of each of them that has seemed most questionable to proponents of documentary as a form of social 'work'. The producers of Reality TV programmes create situations that would not have existed, so that observational programme makers can shoot them. This combines the notion of staging from the earlier documentary tradition with the spurious claim of direct cinema that the presence of the camera makes no difference to the behaviour of the subjects it observes. Reality TV demonstrates how the alternative tradition of cinema verité has eclipsed direct cinema in terms of truth claims. The French tradition of cinema verité acknowledges the intervention of the filmmaker, often present in front of the camera as well as behind it, but without the staging that was necessary before the invention of lightweight equipment.

For example, much of *Celebrity Fit Club*, a Reality TV series in which celebrities attempt to lose weight at a health farm to which they have been invited by the programme makers, consists of interview material where the participants respond to an off-camera interviewer asking questions about their experience and their feelings about their level of success. The trainers are also interviewed and provide evaluations of the celebrities. The structure of segments is based on an alternation between observed action, contextualization in which the narrator provides a gloss on what has been witnessed and then explanation of the state of play. This structure derives from documentary conventions in which material from the real world is presented as actuality footage, to be processed and contextualized through the agency of the programme and evaluated either by a narrating voice or by invited experts. But in *Celebrity Fit Club* this structure is not part of a discourse of analysis but instead a dramatic structure of testing and challenge. The situation is staged, interview questions prompt responses to camera and issues of personality and character are probed. But the action is all true, in the sense that sequences are not scripted and all the on-screen participants are 'real people' rather than performers. Discourses of fact are bolstered by inserted sequences where statistical information about the weight of the celebrities is presented in numerical and graphical form, next to 'before and after' shots of the celebrities posed in front of the camera to show their body shapes. Observational footage from the health farm location blends with interview, statistics and voice-over in a mix of aesthetic forms deriving from documentary, sports coverage, game show, makeover and lifestyle programmes, staging the personal and the real.

Big Brother is in effect a studio-shot programme. Since film became the normal medium for drama in the late 1960s, the television studio became the space for low-budget drama, performance staged for television (like variety shows), current affairs and discussion programmes. In drama, audiences have increasingly judged 'quality' and entertainment appeal by referring to their knowledge of the production values, performance style, and location shooting techniques of cinema. In the factual form most evidently claiming access to the real, television news, the programme aesthetic 'has been driven by the demand that it should provide ever more instantaneous material, to the extent that flexible digital video formats plus satellite technology are moving us towards an era of "real-time" news in which we can see events more or less as they happen' (Ellis 1999b: 56). Writers and producers of drama began to look for new uses of the television studio, to deal with psychological and fantasy subjects which benefited from the artificial environments and confined space in the studio as metaphors for internal mental worlds. Part of this effort was to discover an aesthetic for television which was specific to the medium. However, engagement with the intimate and domestic used film documentary as in the beginnings of the fly-on–the-wall documentary such as *The Family* in the 1970s. *Big Brother* combines the aesthetic of observing ordinariness in the film documentary tradition with the staging of action for the purposes of shooting that comes from drama (especially studio drama). It also adds the presence of a live audience at the location of the programme (though the audience is in a separate space outside the house) and the studio commentary and evaluation found in sports programmes. As a live event, its aesthetic draws on sports coverage and news, especially the multi-camera shooting and voice-over commentary used in football or tennis, but used in *Big Brother* to capture a game of much greater duration. In these ways (and even more relationships with factual and fictional forms could be found), Reality TV both multiplies but defers the meanings of the aesthetic codes of its components.

Reality TV and the public sphere

The critical concept of the public sphere was developed by Jürgen Habermas (1989a, 1989b), and denotes the means of access to information that Habermas regarded as the precondition for political knowledge and action, and as a key resource for the creation of citizenship. The function of the public sphere is to mediate between civil society and the state, and it provides a space in which rational debate is possible, productive of a consensus on public affairs. The space of public sphere might be a literal location, such as a town square or a café where informal discussion between people could occur, but it also refers to the virtual spaces of the media such as newspapers and television, where debates and arguments are represented for the audience and on their behalf. Habermas (1989a: 136) wrote in an encyclopaedia article: 'By the "public sphere" we mean first of all a realm of our social life in which something approaching public opinion can be formed. Access is guaranteed to all citizens. A portion of the public sphere comes into being in every conversation in which private individuals assemble to form a public body.' This term most obviously applies to television programmes that explicitly engage with the public political worlds of current affairs, news and political campaigning. But it also suggests ways of understanding other programmes such as dramas or Reality TV series that can be understood to represent issues of public concern, as considerations of the role of the media in relation to public participation in culture in general and political culture in particular. Ib Bondabjerg (1996) argues that the hybrid mixtures of reality genres and access genres in contemporary television represent the democratization of the discourse of public service. Whereas this discourse was monopolized by experts and official language, new hybrid versions of documentary and reality television produce a new kind of public sphere in which shared knowledge and the experience of the everyday take centre stage.

The focus on the everyday is clearly significant to Reality TV programmes set in recognizable and familiar locations such as homes, hotels or airports, and gives these programmes the opportunity to claim a role in the public sphere. However, the elaborately constructed formats of Reality TV formats like *Big Brother* or *Survivor* can also be interpreted as representations of a social microcosm and a way of airing public sphere concerns. *Survivor* uses the conventional alternation between observational footage of tasks, routine interaction and conversation found in other Reality TV programmes, as well as the response to off-screen interviewer questions that are also adopted in Reality TV, sometimes through the video diary format. The contestants in *Survivor* are divided into two groups, called tribes, who are in competition with each other. When they meet in a specially constructed wooden shelter roofed with palm fronds when votes for ejection are made, they arrive in groups at night carrying flaming torches, and as they arrive they are invited to smear war paint on their faces. The atmosphere of a tribal council is created, as the narrator supervises the ritual of voting and asks each participant to take up specific seating positions and follow through the ceremonial process. In a similar way, some tasks are adapted to the jungle environment such as having to eat live insect larvae or work together to ignite a flaming torch. The iconography of the programme borrows from the imagery of William Golding's novel *The Lord of the Flies* and from more recent narratives such as the film *Castaway*. The generic mix of the programme draws on the makeover genre in its staging of challenges, competition and an emphasis on personal achievement. But it also takes up a subtext of violence, betrayal and tribal solidarity from European fictions that use the desert island location as a means to pressurize individuals to reveal the supposed primitive aggression beneath a veneer of civilization. *Survivor* can be claimed as a metaphorical staging of the tensions between individuals and groups in contemporary societies, displaced into an exotic and pressurizing location that makes these social forces reveal themselves.

The title of *Big Brother* is an ironic reference to the organization of mass society, just as the source of the title, George Orwell's novel *Nineteen Eighty-four* was. In the programme, individuals pursue self-interest and (in the first series) tried to win £70,000, but to do this they have to participate in a community which will not eject them. A structure of rules is imposed on the house by the unseen *Big Brother* production team, including the requirement that participants work at set tasks in order to receive essential supplies and to gain rewards. These components of the programme provide evidence for the argument that *Big Brother* is a metaphor for contemporary capitalist society. From this perspective, *Big Brother* substitutes the house for society at large, and sets up the tensions between freedom and restraint, individual and community, and work and pleasure, which characterize contemporary ideology. However, *Big Brother* can also be understood as a reflexive critique of the ideology which it reproduces akin to the approach of textual criticism in the humanities disciplines that reads texts against their grain to argue that programmes both show and conceal, reflect and distort, the realities which they represent. *Big Brother* was initially marketed as a documentary featuring a social experiment that aims to explore the patterns of interaction between people under various kinds of 'natural' and 'artificial' pressures. This latter form of realism was emphasized in the British version by the prominence of inserted sequences featuring the programme's two resident psychologists analyzing and discussing the behaviour of particular participants. This psychological discourse appeared both in the 'serious' form of the commentaries by Professor Beattie and Professor Collett, but also on the *Big Brother* website which alluded to psychometric data presentation in its flirting index, its kissing index and its statistics on who had hugged who. But the documentary mode signalled by these elements also included directive narration, and the following section discusses *Big Brother*'s narration in comparison and contrast to other Reality TV programmes. Reality television, as John Ellis (1999b) argues, aims to make sense of reality by narrativizing it, but the narratives that are produced are inconclusive, and in the present tense. Although explanation remains an aim and a horizon, the security of producing an explanation of the real is no longer easily available.

The passion and revelation of the real

Reality TV reflects on the notion of witnessing as testament to the real in factual television. At its most basic level, the possibility of seeing the real is contingent on its visibility, on the availability of light. In enclosed

Reality TV spaces such as the *Big Brother* house, great trouble is taken to make enough light available for cameras to record the housemates' activities at any time of day or night. Besides fitting lighting inside the house and reflecting it with the two-way mirrors that conceal the programme's cameras, the housemates are not permitted to reduce the minimal amounts of light that are needed for night-time cameras to operate. The production team manage light and make use of technologies such as low-light night vision cameras to be able to record events when the housemates are asleep. In an apparently very different example, the reconstructions of crimes in *Crimewatch* are often introduced by their victims, who are established as such partly through the aesthetics of lighting. Lit from behind, the victims appear to the camera as dark outlines against lighted backgrounds, and there is enough light to distinguish the shapes of their bodies and to perceive their gestures, but not enough to identify their faces. The lack of light in the performance space of the studio where the victim sits is opposite to the well-lit exterior reconstructions of the incidents that happened to them, but the authenticity of that reconstruction is legitimated by the darkness around the victim in the studio. It is darkness in contrast to light which authenticates the truth of what they describe.

As the space of the studio interview area becomes visible in a reconstruction programme like *Crimewatch*, the viewer becomes a witness to what can be seen there. Within the interviews themselves, areas of light are cast onto human figures, enabling them to witness their surroundings and themselves. Speaking figures and the actors who reconstruct the events experienced by the victims bear witness to events that both take place as reconstructions in the present and have taken place in the past. The darkened bodies of the victims bear witness to their experiences so that the lighted bodies of the actors in the reconstruction can re-enact them. The reported events communicated in the dark produce the lighted events in the reconstruction, and each legitimates the other. The two components of this design strategy in *Crimewatch* and other true-crime programmes are ways of bearing witness to something that happened in reality, but which is inaccessible to the camera because there was no camera there at the time to witness it. Instead, the darkened interview and lighted reconstruction witness the event subsequently for the camera. This witnessing has two contrasting meanings. In the first, the witness is an observer who testifies to the presence and reality of what he or she has experienced. Both the television viewer and the victim can occupy this role since each has access to a version of a real event. In another meaning of witnessing, bearing witness is a form of martyrdom in which the presence, speech and suffering of the victim testifies to the actuality of what he or she experienced and witnessed at the time of a crime committed against him or her. In this second meaning, the witnessing martyr creates the reality of what he or she experienced, rather than observing something that occurs in the same present time. The reality of the past event is recreated at a later time in a reconstruction that can only take place once the victim has recounted it, since its detail is unknown until the story is told. As Jacques Derrida (1996) has written, the martyr's witnessing makes the truth. However, inasmuch as the victim of crime's witness narrative may be incomplete or inaccurate, bearing witness after the event or embodying the event in a reconstruction raises further questions of truth and knowledge in relation to perception and vision. Bringing the victim into public visibility to bear witness may be a means of accessing a special truth, but it is also a performance.

There is a range of uses of this motif. In the reconstructions of *999* for example, the performers enter the lighted area to represent the actual behaviour of the speaker who experienced a disaster in the past. Just as the voice bears witness to the past, the actor comes onto the stage of the location where the reconstruction will be shot, into public view, under the light, to make this past experience visible. Both the victim's voice and the actor offer their performance to the viewer, who is another witness asked to confirm the visibility of this apparent truth. A narrating voice may ask the television viewer to witness the reality of the setting, the actors used in the reconstruction and the actions and feelings that the actors carry out. The action seems to confirm the description and interpretation offered by the narrating voice, so that they authenticate one another. But inasmuch as the actor is called into reality (as is the setting) by the victim's voice, the actors in the reconstruction are instruments of the voice, brought to public view in order to undergo a simulated experience. While the actor makes what the voice says true, the actor is also performing under the control of the story being told, necessarily separating the victim's reality in the studio, the actors' reality in the reconstruction and the narrator's reality as a mediator between them. Bringing real events into vision, calling up the witness, and enacting a version of experience, knowledge and truth, make a reality that is present to the viewer but also raise questions about whether that true reality is an enactment, a performance or a simulation.

The devised Reality TV formats of *Big Brother, I'm a Celebrity* or *Survivor* take this dynamic between being, enacting and simulation as their primary motivation. The constraints of the format can be considered as a collective agency that plays the role of a tormentor and the contestants voluntarily become those who are tormented. The purpose of the controlled environment and of its challenges is to make something happen. Both the contestants of the programme and the representatives of the format, such as the presenters or narrators, are active and visible, and they have the power to speak. But the agency of the production team, represented by the presenters and narrators, act as the gatekeepers of the images and sounds that the audience can see and hear. The contestants' own witnessing of their experience, and the ways that what they say reflects on what happens to them and how they feel about it, offers testimony to the audience about their experience but that experience of the real is framed and shaped by the production agency that has made it possible. Narrating voices reflect after the event on the contestants' behaviour, drawing out for the audience the significance that their behaviour authenticated. The subjects of the programme are the 'tormented martyrs' who bear witness both to their own experiences and suffering and also make it real in the very moment that they become visible to the television audience. Martyrs make reality and also bear witness to whatever human and social truths the programme format claims to reveal. The martyrs are both conduits for the reality to which they bear witness and of which they are an example, but that reality is brought into being by their suffering under the constructed constraints and challenges of the format. The result is passion. Passion has the double meaning of both suffering passively and also experiencing active pleasure. Reality TV distributes the meanings of passion among both the contestants and the audience, alternately parcelling out activity and passivity, pleasure and suffering, to the contestants and the audience. The passionate involvement of the audience in the programme is countered by the suffering that is entailed for both the contestants and the audience in waiting, being bored, being enraged or frustrated. The reality of what happens in *Crimewatch*, *999*, the *Big Brother* house or the jungle of *I'm a Celebrity* is the product of the conjunction between witnessing and passion, as a staged process of creating the real as something that can come to light.

Narration and mediation

Non-fiction programmes like wildlife programmes, history programmes like *Time Team*, commercials, cooking programmes and Reality TV programmes like *Big Brother* or *Survivor* have narrators. In each of these examples, the function of the narrator is to establish a link between the audience and the programme narrative, by inviting the viewer to involve himself or herself in the ongoing progress of the programme structure, which is thereby shaped as an argument or story, or both. Documentary as initiated in the film medium and subsequently adapted into television forms was designed to be socially responsible, and to be an art of record in contrast to cinematic fantasy. In television, documentary especially is able to take up the functions of reflecting and creating a public sphere and carrying out the functions of Public Service Broadcasting by focusing with authority on public events. This depends on an ideology of objectivity that comes from the witnessing of actuality and the recording of natural sound or speech. The presence of the camera and the awareness of television's institutional access to the real operates as a guarantee of authenticity since it is obvious that the real has been observed by a machine whose mechanical operation is an indication of its neutrality, whatever human intervention in framing, point of view or editing might be required. However, Reality TV modifies this existing claim for realism by setting the actuality of the real in a much more controllable setting, and also explains and disseminates the real that has been recorded by framing it with a particular explanatory point of view, usually provided by spoken narration. Whereas documentary conventionally makes an argument and centres on evidence, it includes a reliance on narration and interpretation, and these shaping forces are even more significant to Reality TV.

Narration in Reality TV often has an uncertain discursive role. As in conventional documentary, the role of the voice-over is to make a link between the viewer and the material that has been shot. In this sense, the voice-over stands outside what has been recorded in order to explain, contextualize and identify turning points or forthcoming attractions. The implication of this role of the voice-over is to establish it as a framing narration with control over the text. The voice-over would therefore represent the agency of the programme in containing and processing its constituent material. However, narration in Reality TV is closer to the expected audience position of the television viewer. It is normally delivered in a demotic tone of voice that has a close relationship with the everyday discourse expected of its viewers. It is sometimes surprisingly distant from the sober descriptive and evaluative tone of documentary voice-over. Potentially, this difference of tone draws the Reality TV narration further away from the subjects of the programme and closer to the viewer, thus further emphasizing its framing function as part of the programme's own agency. But the degree to which this happens is dependent on the triangular relationship between narrator, the participants in the programme and the expected audience, as can be seen in the brief discussion of some programme examples later.

While the narration has the power of knowledge, knowing the participants, the past of the programme, the exciting moments that may come in the future and the implicit knowledge attributed to the narration because it is part of the production system of the programme itself, in Reality TV its power is also obscured. The merging of the discourse of participants, narration and audience poses the democracy of Reality TV as a mode that evades and puts aside the sobriety associated with class security and institutional power in documentary. It is therefore regarded as lacking in seriousness, as a capitulation to the supposed desires of the audience and as complicit with the agendas of the performers. For example, the news presenter John Humphrys used his McTaggart Lecture at the 2004 Edinburgh Television Festival to claim that Reality TV was vulgar, cheapened the people featured in it and contrasted strongly with the achievements of British television in other forms. However, Humphreys admitted to enjoying the upmarket Reality TV format *Operatunity* and confessed to not owning a television set for five years, thus undercutting the force of his argument that Reality TV is dumb, without purpose and decadent. In any case, the self-conscious tone and delivery of Reality TV narration can be understood as a reflexive recognition of the form's conventions and a potentially critical resource. If Reality TV redresses the ideological work of drama and documentary inasmuch as they conceal their means of production, the self-consciousness of Reality TV draws the attention of the viewer to the non-equivalence of television realisms with reality in both its factual and fictional forms. Reality TV offers the recognition that the televisual mediation of an exterior reality is precisely a mediation between representations and audiences. The very permutation and convergence of codes in Reality TV might draw the viewer's attention to the fact of representation so that the work of the forms through which representation takes place are recognized as not natural but cultural and constructed.

The first episode of the fifth series of *Big Brother* began with an opening sequence before the contestants arrived. In it, the presenter Davina McCall spoke directly to the camera, which followed her using steadycam as she explained the premise of the new series in which prize money could be lost for non-fulfilment of tasks, with the possible consequence that the winner might in the end leave with nothing. She brought the camera operator with her as she entered the fenced compound of the *Big Brother* house and went into the house itself. She gave the viewer a guided tour of the newly redesigned environment, making use of the liveness of the programme to present the tour as a revelation for the audience of what lay in wait for the participants. The fact of liveness put great time pressure on Davina, and the tour of the house was slightly abbreviated. She explained that the car carrying the new contestants was about to arrive, and lifted her hand up to her ear, where a concealed earpiece was evidently relaying instructions from the production team. So although her narration was authoritative, and she noted that she had already been inside the house earlier in the day and thus knew more about it than the viewer did, she was not in control of the live transmission schedule and was under the authority of that planning of time almost as much as the contestants and the viewers were. Access to the actuality of the *Big Brother* house was being controlled by the production team, of which Davina was a part, but her agency as the representative of the programme was shaped by the liveness of the programme and the need for her to conform to its pre-planned structure. Davina was therefore placed in an ambivalent position between the production team, the contestants and the audience. As a narrator, she could articulate an authoritative discourse of knowledge, but was also aligned with the viewers and the contestants as subject to the constraints of the programme format.

Her address to the camera assumed familiarity on the part of the viewer with the *Big Brother* format and the house itself. She showed off new innovations, many of which were designed to make life for the participants more difficult, such as the smaller space within the house, fewer beds than there were contestants and the reduced privacy in the bathrooms and toilet area. Davina invited the viewer to admire the changes made to the house, and to share a thrill of anticipation about the reactions of the housemates to the more difficult circumstances they would suffer. The housemates were being established as victims of a newly aggressive set of format parameters as well as the lucky survivors of the selection process and potential winners of a prize. Davina was positioned close to the expected reaction of the audience, but also with privileged knowledge. Through the selection of features in the house that Davina emphasized, it was clear that there was an expectation of sexual activity. The housemates were provided with massage oils, a massage table, jacuzzi and a treatment room in which they could potentially be private. The tension between claustrophobia and public intimacy was much more explicit than in previous series. There was therefore another parallel between Davina, the contestants and the audience, which links time to space. In this live episode, it was time constraints that pressured Davina and made her modify her behaviour, shortening her tour of the house and making her run across the set to greet the contestants. This restriction of time matched the restrictions of space that she explained when touring the house, linking the limits placed around Davina's narrating agency with the limits to be placed on the housemates. This contrasted with the privileged knowledge that she had about the house's new design, the programme's modified format and the identity of the contestants. The first two of these kinds of knowledge were shared with the television audience, though the third, the identity of the housemates, had yet to be revealed. What this first episode was enacting is an economy of knowledge, where the witnessing and understanding of the programme is controlled, parcelled out and exchanged according to powerful rules. This economy of knowledge about the actuality of *Big Brother* is reflected in the negotiations of authority and access to information that take place between narrator, contestants and audience.

The narrator of the British version of *Survivors* provided both the on-screen and off-screen commentary to the audience, updating viewers on the progress of the participants and drew on his persona as a journalist. In the voice-over narration, each of the journalistic questions that are used in documentary and news to guide discourses of information appeared, namely the questions what, where, who, why and how. The discourse also included metaphor and adjectives that matched the framing of the programme as a challenging and potentially dangerous adventure. The presenter was dressed in the conventional clothing given to explorers in factual and fictional films and television, the khaki safari jackets and boots of an adventurer. The participants exhibited an interesting mix of costume that matched the mixed genres of *Survivor*. Since they were in a hot beachside environment, they were sometimes seen in swimwear or the colourful tee-shirts that might be worn on holiday. But they were also equipped with the military clothing, boots and shorts that matched the mythology of the explorer adopted by the presenter. *Survivor* is presented as both an excursion from normality rather like a holiday, but also a contest and combat between the two groups of contestants and among individuals, thus explaining the military connotations of their costume.

The closeness to the viewer and potential distance from the participants in terms of tone and address is one of the reasons why some viewers regard the constructed situation programmes of Reality TV like *Big Brother* and *Survivor* as the most manipulative kind of factual television (see Chapter 6). It can appear that the subjects of the series become like laboratory animals presented for the pleasure and distraction of the viewer. However, most Reality TV programmes have participants who are also in some sense close to the presumed audience. They are ordinary, speaking and behaving in forms that link them to a notion of the everyday and have an implicit representative quality. Because of the connection between the participants and the audience in these ways, the participants are bound both to the tone and discourse of the voice-over as well as to the audience. This reduces the apparently objectifying function where the participants are separated and subjected by the agency of the programme. Instead, the three positions of audience, narration and participants come together around a representation of ordinariness.

In the Reality TV series *I'm A Celebrity*, the voice-over and introductory material is presented by celebrities, the former children's television performers and presenters Ant and Dec. Since they are themselves in the same band of celebrity as the subjects of the programme, they have a closeness to the participants that follows the same tonal form that I have previously discussed. Their celebrity matches that of the participants and draws them closer to the stars whose behaviour they frame, explain and shape. However, the focus of the programme is on the potential ordinariness of the participants in dealing with interpersonal relationships, the long and slow unfolding of time and routine tasks in the programme and the tensions between them as a result of their closeness to each other. Ant and Dec develop a discourse in which their celebrity is infused with ordinariness in a similar way to the participants. They call the participants by their first names and provide simple insights into their supposed states of mind, problems and achievements. By drawing Ant and Dec close to the participants as celebrities who have become ordinary, both the presenters and the participants are similarly drawn closer to the presumed audience. By choices of discourse, tone and address, the collapse of the poles of mediator, performer and audience is accomplished in the same way as described earlier in programmes with non-celebrity presenters and non-celebrity participants. This has the same effect as before, in depriving *I'm a Celebrity* of the sobriety and pattern of distanciation that is present in conventional documentary.

Case Study: The *House* series: simulation, recreation and education

The *House* series were jointly devised by Wall to Wall and Channel 4 creating *The 1900 House, The 1940s House, The Edwardian Country House* and *Regency House*. The format was adopted by the American PBS network to make *Frontier House* and *Colonial House*. In Germany, an independent copy resulted in *Black Forest House*, featuring a family in nineteenth century costume. The string of Reality TV recreations of historical living conditions shown on Channel 4 borrowed the assumptions of Public Service Broadcasting about the value of history programmes and education. In the living history Reality TV programme, members of the public inhabit a simulated version of the past that derives from the 1980s trend for creating living museums and environments such as schools, railway stations and household interiors. Television programmes have added to this by creating re-enactments of historical events such as battlefield scenarios (*The Trench*, *Bomber Pilot*), drawing on the focus on interpersonal relationships within hierarchies and households that have featured in docusoaps about hotels and airports, for example. The first of these Reality TV recreations was *The 1900 House* in 2000, that legitimated itself by referring to the educational aims of documentary but also set up tests and challenges similar to those found in Reality TV game shows, and allowed possibilities of narrative development as the process of learning and accommodating to new circumstances affected the members of the household. The subsequent programme was *The 1940s House* (2001) which was more explicitly nostalgic in that it drew on a past that was within living memory for many viewers and paid particular attention to the reactions of the children who both represented their own past for some older viewers and also represented partial outsider figures who could represent the audience in general.

The *House* series is necessarily inaccurate about what the reality of existence in a historical past could have been like. Its participants have only marginal training about how they should behave and have few of the skills that they need, to cook for example, or even to wear the constricting clothes of the 1940s or the Edwardian period. What the series shows is how contemporary people behave under these artificially introduced constraints, thus potentially demonstrating how a similar series of constraints must operate in the present in a less material form. The ideologies of the past are simulated with reasonable accuracy, and although the series has no consistent agenda to draw attention to how there must be similar ideologies operating in the present, it provides some resources for a realization of the role of ideology today. The programmes themselves are the centre of a larger network of texts that promote understanding of cultural history with a similar potential for comparative understanding across past and present. There are books based on each programme in the *House* series, and museum exhibitions, for example at the Imperial War Museum, that connect to the recreations of the television version. The programmes are unable to challenge the basic security of their contemporary participants, for example the family in *The 1940s House* know that they are not going to be killed by falling bombs and the family in *The Edwardian Country House* know that they will not be relegated to the workhouse. But each programme supports the critical function of memory. The vogue for tracing family history, preserving artefacts handed down from the past and collecting antiques feeds into the contribution of the *House* series to the enrichment of the present by comparative understanding of the past. This is an interesting variation on the makeover theme that is so prevalent in Reality TV. Challenges posed to the participants bring out both strengths and weaknesses in them and in both video diary sequences within series episodes and in retrospective evaluation at the end of each series, participants almost universally declare that they have learned about themselves and become better people.

The credit sequence of *The 1940s House* shows a set in which a film projector is positioned among various items of the period. The projector throws home movies of the family on to a blank wall consisting of brief segments of the family playfully larking about in their garden. The family members shown are the contemporary participants in the programme, costumed in 1940s clothing. There is no evidence of transformation from the contemporary period to the past in this opening sequence, bringing the audience immediately into the recreation. The set includes recognizable objects from the 1940s, such as a gas mask and tinplate children's toys. There is a contrast between the projector and the objects disposed around the set and the contemporary living room in which most viewers will be watching the programme. The distinction between now and then is immediately established. But a parallel is drawn between the projection of film onto the wall and the viewing situation of watching television today. By making a parallel between the watching of home movies in the 1940s and the viewing of *The 1940s House* in the present, the opening sequence simultaneously bridges the distance in time between history and the moment of the now, as well as establishing their difference. An extended sequence of voice-over narration sets up the premise of the series, and after the first episode provides a recap of the progress of the war so far for this family. The tone of the voice-over has a slightly distanced or even sarcastic tone, but draws attention to the authority of the 'war cabinet' of experts who have control over the challenges that will be posed to the family. Like the voice-over of *The Cruise*, for example, the narration of *The 1940s House* bridges the gap between the viewer and the programme content in a way which opens up possibilities for both identification with the participants and also a critical attitude in which their behaviour can be judged.

The first episode of *The Edwardian Country House* begins with a very personal sequence showing the participant who will become the butler in the country house, as he prepares for his experience. Over this observational footage, his voice-over commentary has a confessional tone. He compares himself to his own father, noting how similar they look, and how his role will offer him the opportunity to live a life something like that of his own parent. This short opening sequence is in effect a mini makeover itself, as he shaves, puts on Edwardian spectacles and changes his clothes, transforming himself as a means to explore his own identity. This is followed by the credit sequence in which the camera appears to descend as if in a lift through the floors of Manderston, the Edwardian country house. Beginning on the roof and moving down through the servants' quarters at the top of the building, through the rooms in which the house's owners will live, and ending in the servants' working areas in the basement, the camera movement explicitly thematizes the idea of hierarchy. Status is mapped physically, drawing on the title of the long running fictional drama *Upstairs, Downstairs* from the 1970s. The images are electronically processed so that they have a sepia tone, connoting the faded photographs that might record an actual past. The first sequence of the first episode shows the arrival of the family by carriage, in costume. The narration over the sequence is neutral and informative but stresses the distinction between the family upstairs and their servants downstairs noting that Edwardian society was the most unequal in British history. On arrival at the house, visual juxtaposition contrasts the sumptuously furnished and well-lit upstairs living areas with the much darker and more restricted space of the servants' dining room and kitchen below. The voice-over of the butler returns, establishing his view of the past as a more secure society in which each person had a place. The opening of this first episode dwells on the positive reactions of the participants to their forthcoming experience, as the family marvel at the beautiful decorations and period recreation of the building and the butler looks forward to the disciplined routines that will govern his life. The ticking of a grandfather clock persists in the soundtrack across these opening explorations of the space, drawing attention to the theme of time and its ordered progression in the recreated past.

The Edwardian Country House places emphasis on questions of status and class. The opportunities for the different participants are visually related to their roles as either owners or workers in the interdependent organism represented by the house itself. In early episodes, it seems that the family playing the role of the owners of the house have a much easier and more enjoyable life, as they are waited on, dressed and cooked for. But it quickly becomes evident that they are almost entirely dependent on the servants who, according to the social roles recreated in the programme, fulfil their needs for food, getting dressed in the morning and maintaining the daily rhythm of activity. The servants are of course dependent on their masters and on the internal structure of authority below stairs that gives the butler the power to discipline and control them. The proposition advanced by *The Edwardian Country House* is that this micro-society is a single organism. For normality to exist, all of the constituent members are required to function together organically. The subtext of the programme is then that contemporary individualism and the pursuit of private fulfilment are certainly very different and perhaps not always preferable to the enforced community that the Edwardian house required. This is dramatized by some of the sequences selected for inclusion in the episodes. For example, Lucy the scullery maid complains about her workload and the restrictions of her position. While this produces some dramatic conflict, its main role is to instantiate the threat to the community that the actions of a single person can present.

Each episode has several storylines, which include, for example, the forbidden love between the hall boy and the scullery maid, arguments between the family and the staff and the developing understanding of the difficulty of the roles played by individual participants. This development of roles and conflicts makes progression possible in storylines comparable to soap opera, added to which the circulation of gossip between groups of participants parallels the giving and withholding of knowledge between participants and viewers that is present in the soap opera form. The servants become irritated with the hall boy and the scullery maid devoting less effort to their jobs because they are engaged in a romance, so the servants plot to remove the screen covering the hall boy's sleeping area and thus deprive him of his privacy. This storyline parallels the plot development of a soap opera, with the camera positioned as an observer as the participants carry out their plan as if the secrecy of their actions is unaffected by the intrusion of the production team. The audience know about these plots and the different perspectives of the participants on each other before the participants carry out their actions, as well as afterwards, so the audience is given privileged knowledge and is encouraged to predict and speculate on how the actions of one participant will affect the others.

There is a diary room at Manderston, and sequences from video diaries provide personal detail about emotional attitudes to the action that the camera has observed. This format is characteristic of docusoap, as Keith Beattie (2004: 199) has noted: 'the docusoap ... drawing on the appeal of television talk shows, provides people with opportunities for people to express their points of view and describe their experiences in reflections which are presented without the mediation of a presenter or interviewer ... The subjects of the docusoap find moments in their daily working lives to reflect on their intimate selves and personal experiences in ways which provide what is, in effect, an interior monologue in counterpoint to the more "objective" voice-over narration of each episode'. The narration of *The Edwardian Country House* is provided by a female voice whose received pronunciation reflects the period of the setting and locates her more closely with the upstairs participants than the servants. It also enables her to represent the authority of the book of rules given to each participant, as the voice-over is used to present these as the participants read them, while also adding commentary to explain the making of programme and the historical context that it deals with. The Channel 4 website accompanied *The Edwardian Country House* with additional historical information and interactive games and had an accompanying book.

Like *The Edwardian Country House*, *The 1940s House* episodes begin in an exterior setting, with a crane shot that moves across a street and suburban gardens towards the frontage of the house. Moving from public space towards the private space of the home, the opening shots establish location and the reality of the setting as a preamble to the introduction of the participants inside the house and the detail of their experience. Each episode has a thematic focus. Whether dwelling on the moment of the Blitz, the role of women in war, or preparations for the victory in Europe, each episode accommodates selected incidents into a narrative supervised by the narration. Rather than simply following the dynamics of family interaction in the temporal sequence of the series (as *I'm a Celebrity* follows the day-to-day development of relationships in the jungle), episodes of the *House* series retain some of the focus on an issue or problem that derives from the basis in documentary and factual history programming. The *House* programmes could be argued to expose their own historical determinants reflexively, providing the grounds for an evaluation both of the programmes as a historicizing discourse and an evaluation of the cultural and political epoch to which it returns. The recreated reality of the past may be highly constructed and mediated by practices of narration and editing, but it opens up viewing positions that reflect on the differences of ideology between then and now, both positively and negatively, and on how the constraints of a television format can expose the ideological constraints of a social world glimpsed in microcosm.

Conclusion

As Andrew Neal (2003) points out, the cultural theorist Fredric Jameson (1992: 158) draws attention to the inherent problems in the term 'representation of reality': 'if realism validates its claim to being a correct or true representation of the world, it thereby ceases to be an *aesthetic* mode of representation and falls out of art altogether. If, on the other hand, the artistic devices and technological equipment whereby it captures that truth of the world are explored and stressed and foregrounded, "realism" will stand unmasked as a mere reality-or-realism *effect*, the reality it purported to deconceal falling at once into the sheerest representation and illusion. Yet no viable conception of realism is possible unless both these demands or claims are honored simultaneously, prolonging and preserving – rather than "resolving" – this constitutive tension and incommensurability'. So realisms are possible inasmuch as they admit that they are objectively false and do not claim to be real. Realist representations are not deceptive appearances or figments of someone's imagination, they take on the issue of realism and confront it without being able to resolve its contradictions. This chapter has argued that Reality TV forms worry at this problem of claiming access to the real, while also making evident their status as constructed texts or what Jameson calls 'art'.

By doing this, they pose important questions about how representation maintains the notion of the real as the material on which it works and which it transforms. This is the case not only with Reality TV representations that are offered to the viewer as occurring in the present, but also when Reality TV formats like the *House* series counterpose a present with a past, each of which has its own claims to reality. For some media theorists, the reality-effect of representations becomes an ideological effect produced by the semiotic codes and conventions used to produce it, so that the 'real world' is evoked by signs in order to make each of them seem separate, but this is an illusion perpetrated in order to reinforce a belief in the reality of the real and the capacity of signs to describe and communicate it (Baudrillard, 1981: 151–2). So as the empire of signs expands, primarily through the media and especially television, everything undergoes a semiological reduction and the conventions of representation eliminate the reality that seems exterior to them so that representations take over from the real. Indeed the real becomes an ideological guarantee, which Jean Baudrillard calls the 'hyperreal'. When all referents that representations refer to, like the real, the social, or nature, are already reproduced in the terms of the conventions of representation, there is no more real at all. For Baudrillard, contemporary media occupy the role of virtual gazes, through which history and authentic experience are re-formed or indeed abolished except inasmuch as they are simulated. While this chapter has not proposed that Reality TV puts an end to the real, the consequence of its discussion is that Reality TV exposes the contradictions and problems experienced by programmes that are very obviously constructed but at the same time claim to present realities. It would be overstating this chapter's case to claim that Reality TV is a form of critical realism, but I have suggested that in some of its variants this critical project exists as a subtext and a possible way of viewing them.

4
Drama

Introduction

This chapter discusses performance, and especially the critical concept of identity as a performance, in the context of Reality TV. Historically, television fiction has been the ultimate realization of the original aims of Naturalist theatre. That nineteenth and twentieth-century form consisted of various kinds of drama in a small enclosed room and showed a small group of characters living out their private experience in distinction to a larger public world but in relation to the pressures and tensions of an unseen public space. This chapter discusses how these issues of space and private identity that have been central to television drama are modulated by their similar and different appearance in Reality TV. Television drama offers a portrait of individuals and promises a kind of individual and often psychological as well as social revelation about them. The offer of drama to its audience is therefore the opportunity for insight into inner desires and the concomitant assumption that each person's experience is centred on individual identity and personal relationships that are both constitutive and open to modification. The arguments about the revelation of the self that have already been introduced in this book are discussed in their derivations from dramatic television programming and tested against the related concerns of Reality TV.

Narrative forms

Docusoap adopts the interwoven narrative strands that it derives from drama via the soap opera form. In one 2002 episode of BBC's *Airport*, for example, the half-hour episode is structured by a playful parallel between incidents. An airport employee is encountered driving across the airport's aircraft stands to the cargo hold of one aeroplane in which an animal has been discovered. It is his role to identify whether the animal may be a source of danger or disease, to assess its condition and provide treatment where necessary, and to keep the animal while decisions are made about what to do with it. This potential hazard is revealed to be a small lizard, a gecko a few inches in length, that has stowed away among a consignment of cargo. The second narrative strand is about the police working at the airport who identify, arrest and investigate illegal immigrants. The camera discovers them in their office as they assemble information ready to carry out a raid on a nearby address. The camera follows them down a street as a group of officers, some wearing bullet-proof clothing, enter a house and begin to interrogate a suspected illegal immigrant and search his possessions. His documents are evidently forged, and he is not the person he claims to be. In this episode, the structuring principle is the parallel between the animal stowaway and the illegal immigrant. Generically, the episode mixes the heartwarming discourses of care and concern associated with *Animal Hospital* with the blue light genre of documentary in which a hand-held camera follows the activities of a police squad but counterposes these so that they reflect on each other. Both the animal worker and the police are treated by the episode as possessors of specialist knowledge and with some responsibility within the bureaucratic procedures of the vast airport staff. There is a legacy here of the attention to the workings of institutions and the questions of hierarchy, responsibility and the effectiveness of bureaucratic systems and the individuals who work within them that derives from conventional documentary. The episode follows a temporal sequence in which an enigma is presented and specialist staff deal with it, leading to a resolution of the storyline at the end of the episode. Again, the narrative structure of enigma, investigation and resolution follows the conventional documentary focus on a problem and its possible solutions. But at the same time, the episode borrows some of the trivial focus on an emotional issue involving animals that is found in early evening variations on the sick pet format. It also draws on the mid-evening factual format using close observation of the police and emergency services that is found in *America's Most Wanted*, as well as the development of storylines that derives from television fiction. This slippage of genres and potentially different attractions for the audience demonstrates how docusoap sits uneasily in its tone and address to the audience. But it also demonstrates how docusoap became so successful, by offering a range of attractions that can draw different kinds of audience interest to the same programme.

Both closed- and open-ended story lines can be accommodated within the docusoap format. In the episode of *Airport*, the story about the gecko is closed at the end of this episode. But the storyline about illegal immigrants and the police team whose job it is to investigate and deal with them is not closed. There are opportunities to place storylines in a hierarchy in which an on-going issue of public importance can be returned to across various episodes, while at the same time less demanding personal and emotional stories can provide the satisfaction of resolution. This kind of satisfaction requires a careful balance in the tone of the programme. The voice-over by John Nettles is crucial to this in *Airport*, since he carries associations drawn from his role as the investigating detective in the drama *Bergerac*, yet also has the familiarity of a long-running television star in a relatively undemanding programme.

The physical and emotional stress of going through the dieting and physical exercise in a contained environment and under observation produces opportunities for dramatic conflict among the celebrities and their trainers in *Celebrity Fit Club*. The format gives trainers the authority to impose demanding tasks and to verbally abuse the celebrity participants. This is in strong contrast to the symbolic power that celebrities normally have in their professional lives whether in the spheres of politics or entertainment. The physical trainer Harvey is established as especially powerful, drawing on a repertoire of physical and verbal expression that is recognizable from the conventional representations of an army sergeant major in television drama, and especially sitcom. The resistance to Harvey in particular but also to the other trainers means that a degree of group solidarity is created among the celebrities. Dramatic high-points occur when these celebrities band together to resist the constraints of the format and the tasks they are required to undertake, setting up oppositional relationships within the vertical hierarchy of authority between trainers and celebrities, as well as horizontal relationships among the celebrities themselves as they decide to form resistant groups which attempt to negotiate with the programme makers and the trainers. It is these conflicts that are emphasized in the opening sequence of the programme, where brief shots of unhappy celebrities attempting to undertake physical exercises are shown, together with shots of Harvey shouting and encouraging them to try harder. The celebrities are battling both against their own capacities and against the constraints of the format and their temporary masters.

The tone of *Celebrity Fit Club* is predominantly humorous, mocking and emphasizes the ways in which the celebrities can become ridiculous. This reinforces conventional social representations of fat people as amusing, but achieves the apparent desired effect of making celebrities seem more normal and more real precisely because they are overweight. The division of the series into episodes that will finally end with a weighing session and an evaluation of the celebrities' success at losing weight produces a narrative progression throughout the series that adds to the dramatic rather than factual emphasis of the programme. Within episodes, the temporal structure follows the progress of a day, with significant ellipses in favour of a sample of dramatic moments. Since the programme is made for commercial television, internal segmentation of episodes is designed to produce points of punctuation at the end of each segment, in which highlights are repeated and upcoming dramatic incidents are trailed. By means of internal segmentation within episodes, the construction of Reality TV formats as hybrids of serial and series television and the 'casting' of participants as both complex and interesting individuals but also representatives of a larger group (such as occupational groups, celebrities or the lovelorn of *Would Like to Meet*), Reality TV uses narrative form to dramatize.

Performance and genre

In Reality TV, the distinction between an ordinary person and a celebrity is manipulated, and one term can turn into the other. Ordinary people become celebrities in some cases through their participation in Reality TV, while celebrities are offered as ordinary in the sense that they are no longer playing their accustomed role. The function of celebrity in Reality TV is primarily to attract audiences. Television has a series of well-known and established figures such as presenters, news readers, weather presenters and actors who become sufficiently familiar and famous to attract attention. A significant measure of their fame, and one that is significant to their appearance in Reality TV programmes, is the dependence of television light entertainment on celebrity in the form of parody and pastiche. Programmes like *Dead Ringers*, and the work of the impressionists Alistair McGowan and Rory Bremner can only function when television celebrities (and celebrities from politics and other media) are recognizable to the audience. Texts outside television have a crucial role in supporting the celebrity culture, through the news and gossip items that appear in magazines and newspapers, for example. There are various reasons why celebrities might agree to participate in a Reality TV programme. These might include an ambition to restart a failing career or to gain increased media coverage and public attention that may lead to further opportunities for employment. Some celebrity Reality TV programmes give celebrities the opportunity to make money either for themselves or for charity. As well as reinforcing an existing public image, celebrities in Reality TV programming can use the opportunity to change the way that they are perceived by the public, as well as to reinforce it. For some celebrities who are dissatisfied with their press and television reputation, participation in a Reality TV format offers the attraction of correcting the public perception of them by behaving in an apparently real manner which may make viewers more sympathetic to them. And like the challenge that attracts many ordinary participants, a celebrity might also simply wish to do something unusual and different, thus posing the Reality TV programme as a make-over opportunity.

The aim in casting these celebrity contestants for Reality TV series is to create instant recognition for potential audiences of the possible attractions of the programme. To gather an audience of reasonable size right at the beginning of the series requires the cast of celebrities to include some well-known names, and equally as important, some celebrities whose careers are perceived as over. In *Celebrity Big Brother*, for example, the comedian Jack Dee had a strong current level of audience recognition, while Anthea Turner and Vanessa Feltz were known to viewers but perceived as stars whose careers were waning. The mixing of people from different aspects of the public world of celebrity such as Royal correspondent Jennie Bond as part of a group including actors and pop personalities aims to hook viewers by raising questions about the tensions that will arise between these people from different backgrounds. When the first series of *Celebrity Big Brother* was being planned by the producer Ruth Wrigley, the initial idea was to bring together recognizable and successful stars who could be procured by the creator of Comic Relief, writer Richard Curtis, to maximize income for the charity. However, Richard Branson, Dawn French and Chris Evans dropped out of the initial lineup, and the resulting mix of celebrities proved surprisingly successful precisely because they were perceived as having different levels of status and reasons for participating. The rivalry that goes along with this difference of self-perception and audience perception supports the game show aspect of the format and produces the competition among participants and opportunity for gossip by viewers that has been so important to Reality TV culture.

Celebrities in Reality TV are open to audience reactions that encompass both aspiration and critique. The viewer is positioned in relation to the celebrity with knowledge from outside the text that encourages audiences to think that they already know the personality they see. Reality TV opens up the distinction between the accustomed role of the celebrity, as a news presenter or actor, for example, and the new role in which they appear as themselves in a programme. This makes available the lure to the viewer that he or she will gain some insight into the real-life personality of someone they recognize in another television format. So a key distinction is between the playing of a role and the apparent reality of the celebrity as an individual. For example, *Jamie's Kitchen* was made for Channel 4 by the independent production company Talkback Thames, who later made the British version of the US business-themed Reality TV format *The Apprentice*. In *Jamie's Kitchen*, TV chef Jamie Oliver attempted to train 15 disadvantaged youths as cooks to work in his own restaurant. As the producer, Peter Moore's most difficult task was to per-suade Jamie Oliver that after the success of his cooking series *The Naked Chef*, viewers were tired of his happy-go-lucky cockney personality and that Oliver should change his television role: 'we did persuade him that he had to be angry, be down as well as up. He couldn't always be posi-tive, bubbly, slightly annoying' (Deans 2005b). The very familiarity of a celebrity persona requires that persona to change and be undercut, in order for Reality TV programmes to attract audiences by promising the possibility of a new perception of it. In Reality TV, key moments are when the performance facade of the contestant falls away. This seems to reveal the real person, since the audience is aware that the rest of the time the contestant is performing the self that they wish to project. The most interesting participants are those who project a big personality and are interesting as characters, but the other side of this is that the audience wants to see those big characters reduced to being 'like us'.

The appeal of celebrity Reality TV, however, does not always succeed in capturing audiences, and seems to rest on the combination of good casting and narrative interest created through editing and unpredictable turns of events. In *I'm a Celebrity*, surprising counterpoints of casting such as former punk pop star John Lydon with Royal correspondent Jennie Bond may have drawn initial audiences to the programme. But subsequently, developing narrative lines such as the flirting between Peter Andre and the model Jordan, Jennie Bond's arguments with Lord Brocket or the increasing personal strength of Kerry McFadden (who eventually won) seem to have produced continuity of audience interest. Although casting is subject to some control, the development of narra-tive lines is much more unpredictable. In 2004, Channel 5 created *Back to Reality*, in which contestants from other Reality TV series such as Jade Goody (*Big Brother*), Rik Waller (*Pop Idol*) and Nick Bateman (*Big Brother*) were brought together for three weeks in a specially built house. Channel 5 had invested £4.7 million in an 80-camera production sponsored by

Heat magazine (Deans 2004a). After the first seven days, *Back to Reality* ratings fell by 1 million from the 1.8 million viewers for the opening Sunday night episode. Although this audience size was comparatively high for Channel 5, it represented a poor investment of the 3 per cent of its programming budget that the channel invested in the programme. The scheduling of *Back to Reality* at 8.00 pm placed it in competition with the highest rating programmes on competing channels, such as *Coronation Street, EastEnders* and *The Bill.* Overall, *Back to Reality* appeared to have been perceived as a derivative version of *I'm a Celebrity* on ITV, whose 2004 series had attracted 14 million viewers for its final episode. The response of Channel 5 was to increase its coverage by an additional 25 hours in the second and third weeks of the series, adding new daily programmes at 9.30 in the morning and 2.30 in the afternoon. Unexpected events proved positive for the programme's profile, as Nick Bateman led a revolt among the contestants which produced a confrontation with the programme editor. The live streams of video went off air, and the row interrupted the end of the 8.00 pm terrestrial highlights programme. The tension between the design of the format and the need for unexpected conflicts and crises is an unstable mixture in Reality TV when broadcast live and demonstrates both the attractiveness of the form and also its dangers. The attraction of celebrity as the guarantee of performance from people the audience may already know, together with the appeal of involuntary performances of authenticity that undercut those celebrity roles, depends not only on that flip-flopping between kinds of performance but also on the development of narrative lines and dramatic character dynamics.

Characters

As earlier chapters have explained, British formats penetrated the US television market after the success of *Who Wants to be a Millionaire* and *Survivor*, which both originated from British companies, leading to interest from US network executives in the possible success of other British factual programmes. According to Stephen Lambert, head of programmes at the independent production company RDF, the legacy of scripted comedy and drama in US television created a reluctance to try programmes based on observation. Even when *Survivor* was made, its contestants were in effect cast by a process of screening applicants after advertisements announced the programme. Instead, RDF's series *Wife Swap* is made by producers finding potential participants themselves. Lambert remembered that 'docusoap was never picked up by anybody in broadcast [network] television in America – they couldn't get their head round the idea that you could just make a show that was just about character' (Wells 2003). The US version of *Wife Swap* contained more intervention into the flow of edited sequences of observational material by inserting segments of interviews to camera where the participants in the previously recorded observational scenes commented on what was going through their minds at the time and also commented with hindsight on their own actions. The effect of these changes was to direct the viewer's interpretation of the action more strongly, rather than allowing the observational footage to be interpreted on the basis of the sequences themselves and their edited counterpoint with each other. The emphasis was, as Lambert mentioned, on character, which is a term most often used to describe the personae of drama. Reality TV as an entertainment form has been most successful when it promises to reveal character in this way, even if its participants and settings are offered to the audience as real rather than cast or coached.

While celebrities offer Reality TV producers a short-cut into dramas revolving around character, because they already seem to have ready-made personas, choosing ordinary participants or contestants offers the audience the pleasure of discovering the character of people who seem like themselves, or at least begin by seeming ordinary. The ordinary people selected for Reality TV programmes often have outgoing and dominant personalities, which creates considerable dramatic conflict between them as well as numerous occasions for performance and display to the cameras. *Hell's Kitchen* is made by Granada for ITV, and in 2004 the programme was a success as celebrity chef Gordon Ramsey exercised his authority over a collection of fellow celebrities including politician Edwina Currie as they struggled to complete the complex task of creating food for customers in a restaurant. Ramsey left the programme after making an exclusive deal with Channel 4 to make another Reality TV series, *Ramsey's Kitchen Nightmares*, and the second series featured another celebrity chef, Gary Rhodes, together with the French chef Jean-Christophe Novelli. Rather than assembling a crew of celebrities to work in the kitchen, the producers enlisted ordinary people divided into two teams headed by each of the professional chefs. The producer, Natalka Znak, got the idea from a rehearsal for the first series: 'At the dry run last year to check the format worked, we put in people who were simply enthusiasts, catering students, amateur chefs. It was amazing, because they cared so much. We thought: this is how we want to make it. On the dry run last week, we had a lad trying to get his soufflé to rise. It sounds boring, but all of life was in that soufflé. Celebs are great but they are never going to work in a kitchen. They don't care about it, they care about themselves' (Brown 2005: 11). The attraction of ordinariness was designed to appeal to viewers' fascination with the challenges posed to ordinary people whose characters could be both tested and exhibited.

The result of this elevation of ordinary people to celebrity status, however, is that they then become celebrities themselves, if only for a short period, thus acquiring both the character of ordinariness and also the added frisson of fame. In Britain, the end of July is a quiet time for news, but at that time in 2001, both *Big Brother* and *Survivor* ended their runs on television. On Wednesday 25 July 2001, five tabloid newspapers produced 15 pages of stories about the participants in these programmes on their news pages alone, with no regard to additional features later in the papers. On that day, a total of 56 pages were taken up by the activities of television, film, music and sport celebrities. Six months after the first edition of *Big Brother*, nine of the ten original contestants were working in the media as radio disc jockeys or reporters, and the tenth became a professional musician. News presenter Nick Clarke (2003) lamented this situation, arguing that it derived from a recent explosion of formats based on real life, and offered programme makers a way of filling extended air time and viewers a realistic chance of getting on television or at least seeing people like themselves on screen. For Clarke, this devalued news and the kinds of reality that have customarily been the subject of media current affairs programming. Its negative effects, he suggested, extended to bad language, an obsession with celebrity and the stigmatization of what had been thought of as the respectable professions of teaching, the law or being a doctor. In an amusing example of a response to that kind of criticism, Reality TV can sometimes seem like a way of redressing the balance and restoring the public profile of those professions that Clarke complains have been devalued by the celebrity effect of the form. In November 2003, my local member of parliament for Reading East, Jane Griffiths, contacted Endemol to suggest a House of Commons version of *Big Brother*. Her idea was to attract greater public interest in politicians, because: 'It really struck me how people were really into *Big Brother* and took time to vote, but are disinclined to vote for us. I don't think they see us politicians as human and this is a fun way of changing ideas and helping to raise money for good causes at the same time. When I approached Endemol I think they thought it was a wind up' (Haque 2003). Helen Clark, fellow Labour MP, was also keen to participate. If Reality TV claims to be a new kind of public sphere (see Chapter 3), it is not surprising that politicians would like to use it to raise both their own celebrity value and public awareness of their activities by promoting themselves as characters who might make suitable subjects for broadcasting, combining their public status with the appeal that the revelation of character through ordinariness seems to have for audiences.

Melodrama

Melodrama emerged in the early nineteenth century as a form that could dramatize the ideological changes and contradictions thrown up by capitalism. Rather than focusing on a surface level of realism, melodrama expressed these tensions by 'pressuring the surface of reality' (Brooks 1985: 15). There was a transition from a spiritual order governed by the institutions of the church and the monarchy into a secular order that replaced these legitimating values by an ethical code that infused the everyday with meaning and significance. This ethical dimension of the everyday, Brooks argues, is repressed by realist narrative, but by contrast the mode of melodrama heightens moral conflict and pushes narrative and style towards excess, thus provoking the revelation of an otherwise buried realm of spirituality and social values. Melodrama symbolically represents social tension by exerting a pressure on the representation of everyday experience, leading to excess and extremity of moral positions. For Brooks, the structure of melodrama is characterized by an initial presentation of virtue as innocence, followed by the introduction of a threat or obstacle that imperils virtue. Under the pressure of this threat, violent action emerges which physically catalyzes this moral struggle and leads to the liberation and triumph of virtue. This kind of structure could be seen in the first series of *Big Brother*, which quickly developed a selection of character types familiar in the already melodramatic form of television soap opera, most notably 'Nasty Nick' Bateman whose manipulative and deceptive behaviour coded him as the 'villain', and who was confronted, stigmatized by his housemates and finally ejected from the house.

In his work on film melodrama, Thomas Elsaessor (1985) argues that the melodramatic mode is neither subversive nor reactionary in itself, and is instead contingent in its political meaning according to the elevation or devaluation of particular ideological values in a specific textual and historical context. Film melodrama focused primarily on relationships within the family and between familial groups and a broader society. In the Reality TV forms of *Survivor* or *Big Brother* for example, this constraint and domestic space is made public by its reconfiguration

as a specially constructed and artificial domestic space, set up specifically for its relay and representation in the public medium of television
broadcasting. Documentary brings with it the expectation of this public
relevance and discourse directed towards its audience and the conventions of television realism that underlie factual programming. In Reality
TV, the melodramatic mode with its associations with ethics and virtue,
the personal and the domestic, are combined with the apparent surface
denotation of reality and the conventions of television realism. Thus,
the melodramatic and realist modes exist in tension and contradiction,
with each of them predominating alternately or simultaneously within
a given format, programme or individual sequence.

The mode of melodrama imposes restrictions on characters, limiting
their ability to act and creating a sense of claustrophobia and the domination of particular spaces by social and ethical forces that intrude
into them and infuse them. Writing about Hollywood melodramas of
the 1940s and the 1950s, Thomas Elsaessor (1985: 177) describes their
characters as victims: 'The world is closed, and the characters are acted
upon. Melodrama confers on them a negative identity through suffering, and the progressive self-immolation and disillusionment generally
ends in resignation.' In *Big Brother, Survivor* and other created environments there is a similar tension between the resignation of the contestants in their enforced closed space, and the possibility of their ejection
from it, and on the other hand the possibility of escape from this
enclosed world by winning, and gaining access to an alternative world
of celebrity which is characterized by different kinds of enclosure and a
greater breadth of opportunity for self-expression and self-realization.
Both Westerns and crime films represent a melodrama of action, partially determined by their focus on masculinity and male central characters in which conflict is demonstrated and resolved through physical
action. With the reduction of physical actions in Reality TV, this masculine melodramatic mode of expression through action is much less available, and the feminized enclosure and focus on individual pathology is
more evident. The expression of emotion, as David Lusted (1998) notes,
is both a marker of femininity and of working-class culture. While masculine values entail the suppression of emotion in favour of efficiency,
achievement and stoicism, feminine values encourage the display of
emotion as a way of responding to problematic situations. Similarly,
elite class sectors value rational talk and writing as means of expression,
versus emotional release. These distinctions, which are of course cultur-
ally produced rather than biological or natural, have been important to
work in television studies on the relationship between gender and the

different genres of television where news and current affairs are regarded as masculine and melodrama such as soap opera are understood as feminine. Christine Geraghty (1991) and other feminist critics have argued that the world depicted in melodrama is potentially utopian, since the suggestion is always there that it could be reorganized in terms sympathetic to women's desires for community and for openness and honesty of feeling. Thus, Reality TV formats based on enclosure and testing, such as *Big Brother*, represent a combination of appeals based on the expression of emotion and also masculine effectivity.

In relation to the conventions of documentary realism, the temporality of melodrama and realism are significantly different. Documentary realism assumes that the viewer and programme maker do not know what will happen next, thus opening the programme to possibilities that are not determined by the patterns of drama. However, melodrama brings with it powerful conventions of dramatic structure that assume that action will have inevitable and predictable consequences. In this way too, the temporal unfolding of Reality TV programmes exhibits a tension between the assumption of openness deriving from documentary and the constraints of story and morality that characterize melodrama. John Caughie (2000) has noted the paradox evident in drama documentary that arises because of the different forms of mediation adopted in its two component forms. He notes that 'the dramatic look creates its "reality effect" by a process of mediation so conventionalized as to become invisible' (Caughie 2000: 111), referring to those systems of mise en scene and narrative adopted in the majority of television fiction. However, on the other hand, 'the documentary gaze depends on systems of mediation (hand-held camera, loss of focus, awkward framing) so visible as to become immediate, apparently unrehearsed, and hence authentic' (Caughie 2000: 111). The placing of cameras all around the represented space of *Big Brother* and some other Reality TV formats has the effect of connecting spaces to each other. The house or other setting becomes parallel to a machine or an organism that has power and control over the individuals inhabiting it. Because the contestants are spatially close to each other at any given moment, it is possible to represent the allegiances and relationships of contestants with each other. The house also has the effect of both representing and concealing the constraints and possibilities of the space to cause or motivate action as well as simply to supply a location in which it can take place. The house is a machine that predisposes contestants to behave in particular ways and it functions as a mechanism parallel to the control exercised by Big Brother as an institution in that it operates as a power that may be resisted or colluded with. Thus, Reality TV draws on melodrama as a dramatic form but also reconfigures it not only adopting its seculariza-tion and its thematics of 'feminine' characterization but also lacking the dramatic pattern and narrative resolution that mark melodrama as a scripted form.

Dramatizing gender

There was remarkable public fascination with Nadia, a transgender participant in series five of *Big Brother*, and to a lesser extent with previ-ous contestants who seemed to embody unconventional sexual and gender identities. This can be explained by considering the psychoana-lytic theorization of how the human body functions as a projection of cultural anxieties about the relationship between sex and gender identity: between the inner sense of self and the body that is attached to it. The issue revolves around sex and gender as identities that are per-formed rather than simply possessed. As Judith Butler (1990) has argued, gender identity is produced through actions rather than essences, in which the repetition of conventional gender behaviours produce a tem-porarily stable gender identity. Butler has worked extensively on the body as a discursive object, arguing that sexual difference is not a func-tion of bodily differences, for these differences are marked and formed by discourse. Discourses about sex such as those in lifestyle magazines, medical textbooks or Reality TV programmes demarcate and differenti-ate bodies and thus sexed identity 'is not a simple fact or static condition of the body but a process whereby regulatory norms materialize "sex" and achieve this materialization through a forcible reiteration of those norms' (Butler, 1993: 2). The reiteration of norms signifies that sexed identity never conclusively materializes, and that sexual organs will never be sufficient to stabilize sexed identity. Recognizing a sex and a gender involves both identification where a television viewer might measure himself or herself against the person seen on the screen and experience a closeness or distance from that person, and abjection, where some kinds of body are set up as definitively beyond what the viewer can recognize as a comprehensible sexed identity.

The category of abjection incorporates those who are not regarded as individual subjects like the viewer, but who provide 'that site of dread-ful identification against which – and by virtue of which – the domain of the subject will circumscribe its own claim to autonomy and to life. In this sense, then, the subject is constituted through the force of exclu-sion and abjection, one which produces a constitutive outside to the subject, an abjected outside, which is, after all, "inside" the subject as its own founding assumption' (Butler 1993: 3). Recognizing people who are sufficiently alike to help define the viewer's sense of self goes along with identifying some people who are so different that they help to establish the boundaries around what the viewer can perceive as normal and human. Inasmuch as this utterly different kind of abject body is required to establish the boundaries around the viewer's identity, it is itself a necessary part of defining the viewer's identity, by specifying what he or she is not. This complex theoretical framework explains how desires and anxieties can be attached and displaced onto people on television, producing their bodies as others with which to identify and defining the viewer's sense of self through their bodies' perceived similarity and difference to existing norms. Nadia's performance of sex and gender took place without the contestants in the *Big Brother* house or the audience of the programme being offered simple visible evidence about her body. Instead, her playing of a woman's role could take place as a performed and dramatic narrative, and was apparently both convincing and welcome to viewers, who voted for her to win the competition. The play between identification and abjection that was set up by giving and withholding knowledge about Nadia's sex and gender added another level to the drama of *Big Brother* and one that revolved explicitly around the meaning of the body as a determinant of personal identity or as something different from it.

This critical argument about gender as performance is much easier to see in Reality TV programmes that displace recognizably contemporary participants into unfamiliar social environments and was evident in Channel 4's *House* series of historical recreations. Here, gender roles and power relations were each subjected to manipulation, thus producing a powerful combination of opportunities for reflection on them, as Chapter 3 has outlined. Indeed, in some of the programmes in the *House* series, the volunteers act roles specified by the book of rules given to them at the beginning of the series that lays down the expectations for the social type and gender and generational role which they play. In *The Edwardian Country House* the people who struggle most visibly with this role playing are the master of the house, Sir John Oliff-Cooper and the butler. Each of them has responsibility for other members of the household, and the exercise of power without the acceptance of class and occupational restrictions that would be native to the ideologies in the historical period being recreated is difficult for each of them. The audience is invited to wonder whether the exercise of power is a problem deriving from the distance between the contemporary participants and the imagined past or whether it is being used as an excuse for the incapacity of the participants to deal effectively with their own ambitions, desires and self images. The audience is invited to judge their performance in relation to questions of gender and power.

The Edwardian Country House was a history programme, with an accompanying educational aim. But the emphasis on class and gender distinction within the house suggests the conventions of period drama by focusing on a family and the day-to-day problems of running the house. Costume is important to the series, as in period drama, and sequences within the programme dwell on the detail of clothing styles for both men and women. Occasions such as dinners, balls and dances are included to further develop the possibilities for the spectacle of recreation in terms of the roles to be played by each sex. In addition to this, the audience are given access to the confessional video diaries of the participants, counterposing the recreation of an apparently authentic past with the reactions to that past by twentieth-century volunteer participants. This device enables a kind of Brechtian separation between actor and role, where contemporary participants step out of their country house persona to give their opinions on how it feels to be in their situation. The subsequent Reality TV variant in the *House* series, *Regency House Party*, placed an equal number of men and women in an elegant country mansion for the summer. The requirements of historical recreation were given considerable priority, and gender roles were particularly enforced. The constraints of social behaviour, dress, manners and physical confinement had presumably been calculated to create the repressions and frustrations that ultimately erupted into expressions of sexuality. The appeal of the past legitimated eroticism for the contemporary men and women, and thus drew on perceptions of the nineteenth century that could be experienced as both romantic and authentic. The men in the programme were given licence to enjoy the patriarchal authority that literary and television fictional versions of the past have instilled as expectations in the audience and the participants. Similarly, the women were condemned to a largely passive and decorative role that also freed them from significant responsibility.

Like the earlier Channel 4 recreations, the programme had a contradictory attitude towards its project. It was unclear whether it aimed to present the actuality of the past, since it both simulated past circumstances as accurately as possible but also threw thoroughly contemporary participants into this unfamiliar environment. The programme also seemed undecided about whether it aimed to reveal contemporary issues about gender roles, since despite its stress on the resistance and problematic aspects of suffering the constraints of past circumstances, it allowed for nostalgia and for connections with a heritage vision of the past associated with television fiction and especially literary adaptations such as the BBC's *Pride and Prejudice*. The programmes in the *House* series occupied both past and present simultaneously, confusing notions of time, history and the relationship between material circumstances and subjective being. By focusing on the sexual repression in the simulated past, they also perpetuated the mythology found in *Big Brother* and other Reality TV formats that sexuality and its expression is the litmus test of the authenticity of the self. But displacing current social issues such as sexuality functioned effectively as a way to explore them by setting them at a distance and also to cope with the potential resistance that some (older) audiences have to the exploration of these issues in Reality TV formats aimed at younger audiences. The diversity of the audience, in terms of location, age and experience, means that adopting different variations on a similar format can be a way to address audiences with content that is considered relevant and important in ways that deflect questions of taste and value.

Reality TV and the displacement of drama

Each episode of *Wife Swap* lasts one hour, and begins with a voice-over asking: 'What's it like to try out a different spouse for a fortnight? Will the experience alter their views on their own family life?' The content of the programme relies on two weeks of filming where two women exchange households with each other. As well as documenting what happens in this artificially created but actual situation, *Wife Swap* draws attention to three kinds of performance that Helen Piper (2004) has discussed. First, the participants play a social role inasmuch as they do things that may be expected of wives, husbands or children. Each of these roles is infected by questions of class and taste, that establish the playing of the role in terms of distinctions between different class fractions or subcultural groups. Second, the playing out of the role is made concrete by the performance of particular tasks, such as cooking or cleaning, or contributing to the raising of children by undertaking particular responsibilities. Like the first kind of role, this performance can succeed or fail, and is open to evaluation. Finally, these performances are supplemented by the performance of being in a television programme, potentially inflecting each choice, speech or action with the consciousness of its transmission to the television audience and its evaluation by them, as well as by the fellow members of the household.

While *Wife Swap* has been a ratings success and has also been screened outside its British context, in a US version (see Chapter 2), not all such combinations of dramatic conventions with Reality TV have succeeded. *Bedsitcom* (Channel 4, 2003) mixed actors with real people, placing these real people in a shared flat where each week they would be presented with dilemmas created by the programme's writers and played out by the actors. The real participants had been told that they were taking part in an observational Reality TV series (like *The Real World*) so the presence of the cameras was not in itself a clue to the fact that they were being manipulated by a scripted series of incidents. For example, an actor was directed to ask one of the real participants to look after a beloved tropical fish for a relative. The writers decreed that the live fish be replaced by a dead one during the real participant's absence, leaving him with the dilemma of whether to admit his failure to care for it, or to take some more drastic action such as substituting an alternative fish in the hope that no one would notice the difference. By scripting the situation in some detail, *Bedsitcom* generated domestic crises precipitated by the actions of the actors, seeking to provoke dramatic performance from the real person. The writers of the episodes appeared in interposed sequences discussing the narrative unfolding of the situation they had designed and planning the subsequent interventions that would seek to push it in a particular direction. But the extraordinary degree of intervention and the contrived situations presented to the real participants were perhaps some of the reasons why the programme was unsuccessful. It achieved an audience share of only 6 per cent, and was cancelled before its eight-week run was completed.

In playing out the minute details of domestic life within the enclosed space of the house, and especially the kitchen, *Wife Swap* can be argued to perpetuate a naturalistic tradition of family drama that was increasingly displaced by the cinematic forms that television fiction has taken since the 1970s. Helen Piper (2004: 285) suggests that 'one could hypothesize that the appeal of *Wife Swap* rests precisely in its radical development of a territory that television drama abandoned along with the studio play, and the subsequent inflation in series budgets. One might speculate that its evident lack of "onscreen spend" is actually part of its aesthetic appeal, the lack of gloss and "quality" signifiers implying that something far more rare and raw has been recorded.' Although its participants are not actors, have no training for the performances they give and are not provided with a script that will legitimate their actions, they are placed by the constructed situation of the programme in the roles of performers.

If television seems unable to dramatize the ordinary using the available forms of fiction, *Wife Swap* offers the opportunity for documentary to take this on by manipulating the conventions of observational filmmaking in tandem with a premise calculated to generate interpersonal conflict and the revelation of gender difference, and social and cultural difference. In these respects, Reality TV perpetuates the terms of television drama as a mode in which psychological realism is presented as a conduit for audience identification with its subjects. The dominant form of realism in television is a product of the epoch of modern industrial society. It can be seen in the majority of television fiction programmes and also affects the representation of people in television factual programmes and documentary. Individuals' character determines their choices and actions, and human nature is seen as a pattern of character differences. These differences permit the viewer to share the hopes and fears of a wide range of characters. The comparisons and judgements about identifiable human figures represented on television are reliant on a common code of judgement, a notion of 'normality', which is the terrain on which the viewer's relationships with characters can occur. Television's psychological realism represents a world of consistent individual subjects and addresses its viewers as the same kind of rational and psychologically consistent individual. The action of the television text is to establish communication and offer identification with the images it shows. Individual television programmes are constructed as wholes which promise intelligibility and significance. The realist assumption of the match between the television text and a pre-existing reality underlies this process, by posing the image as equivalent to a real perception of recognizable social space. This depends on the equivalence between what and how the viewing subject might see and be seen, and what and how the television point of view might see and be seen. So the category of the rational perceiving subject is the connecting assumption shared by the viewer and television, and by his or her world and the world represented on television. The viewer's varied and ordered pattern of identifications makes narrative crucial to this form of realism, for the different kinds of look, point-of-view, sound and speech in narrative are the means through which this communication between text and audience is produced. *Wife Swap* is premised on a narrative structure consisting of the exchange of spouses and the change in participants' view of themselves across a limited period of time, ending with evaluation of themselves and each other.

Inasmuch as *Wife Swap* belongs to the genre of the 'makeover show' (see Mosely 2000), it seems at first sight to be straightforwardly factual, and shares its emphasis on remodelling the person and personal space with programmes like *Changing Rooms*, *Looking Good* and *Ground Force* where members of the public have their homes, gardens, cooking ingredients, dress style or hair transformed by the intervention of 'experts' introduced by the television programme. But the key moment in these programmes is a dramatic one, a moment of revelation where the newly transformed house, garden or person is exhibited by the programme presenter to the family member, internal audience in the programme (like members of a family) and the television audience. It is the reaction to the change which forms the dramatic climax of the programme, in the same way as *Wife Swap* and *Bedsitcom* are structured around close-ups of participants' reactions to a novel twist in the ongoing narrative. Whereas the improvement of a person's appearance or domestic space is usually a private experience, these programmes make this process public. Indeed, the function of the programme presenter is often to speak directly to the camera and thus to the viewer in his or her own private space and create a bridge between the 'ordinary' person being made-over and the 'ordinary' television viewer, across the public medium of television. This structural transformation of publicizing a private make-over of identity is the premise of *Stars in Their Eyes*, where members of the public transform themselves into facsimiles of celebrities: the private person is transformed into a public figure. Conversely, the BBC comedy-drama *The Royle Family* reverses the same distinctions, being a fictional drama set almost exclusively in the private domestic living-room of the family, where they are always watching television. Since the camera is often positioned in the location of the family's television set, the programme positions the audience at home as gazing at representatives of themselves watching television, making a private experience public. Contemporary television not only mixes dramatic and documentary codes, but extends this into the blurring of the boundary between private experience and public experience, and between being ordinary and not-on-television versus being celebrated and on-television. The motif of transformation, and its bridging of public and private, connects the factual programmes discussed here to examples from television fiction, and the following section elaborates this in relation to the adoption of factual Reality TV conventions in television drama.

From docusoap to drama

Docusoap draws on the conventional documentary shooting techniques of observation, in which shots may be unsteady because of the use of hand-held camera, composition is not always harmonious and the observed action may be captured in movement, or partially obscured by objects or people in the frame. These characteristics that connote the observation of actuality are combined with editing techniques associated with drama. The balance between information and entertainment places greater emphasis on entertaining subjects, like the traffic warden Ray Brown in the BBC's *Clampers* (1998). Having already gathered to itself some of the conventions of drama, docusoap conventions have migrated in the other direction as a way of invigorating scripted, fictional programmes. The conventions of docusoap were used in the BBC situation comedy *The Office*, beginning in 2001, for example, where the camera moves through an office space, witnessing action sometimes through internal windows, or across the barriers of filing cabinets or computer screens. Interview material with the characters includes reflection on events that have just happened, and analysis by the characters of their own and others' behaviour. Docusoap is already a hybrid genre, and its extension into situation comedy means that *The Office* can offer docusoap's blurring of the distinction between observed reality and performance, as well as the scripted performance expected from comedy on television. The characters normally behave as if they are not being filmed, thus making possible the audience's reading of distinctions between what they say and what they mean, and what they think they mean and what the audience may interpret differently. But since the characters sometimes acknowledge the presence of a documentary camera, it is also clear that they are performing for it, acknowledging the process of television production and the presence of the audience in a way that does not normally occur in sitcom.

These possibilities of docusoap performance focused on the character of David Brent, who would like both to be a comedy performer for his audience of workmates, and also an ordinary person who might become a star through his appearance in a docusoap. *The Office* therefore demonstrates awareness of the problems of docusoap as a genre, and its history of producing ordinary people as celebrities, like Jane McDonald in *The Cruise*, and Maureen Rees in *Driving School*. As Brett Mills (2004: 74) states: 'By illustrating how docusoap "characters" are capable of using the camera to their own ends, *The Office* articulates concerns around documentary fakery. And by using the conventions of documentary for humour, *The Office* undermines the distinctions between sitcom and documentary, between seriousness and humour, demonstrating that the outcomes of one can be achieved through the conventions of the other.' As Mills describes, the 1990s witnessed other comic variations on the uses and effects of documentary convention, especially the docusoap and video diary format, such as *Marion and Geoff* and *People Like Us*. As Jon Dovey (2000: 11) has argued, 'documentary and factual television now exist in a space that is neither wholly fictional nor wholly factual, both yet neither'. The imitation of documentary conventions for dramatic and comic purposes (Roscoe and Hight 2001) shows how the confluence of generic components has become increasingly mobile and flexible, but this can have the effect of giving new vitality to the programmes that exploit it, rather than functioning as evidence of contamination or morbidity.

The blurring of the boundaries between fact and fiction in Reality TV (Nicholls 1994) has moved back into fiction as a formal strategy to connote realism in programmes such as the police series *The Cops*, which adopts the visual look of documentary together with an ensemble of fictional characters. In *The Cops* there is a consistent group of main characters who seem at first to be relatively conventional. Indeed, the programme's title is likely to trigger viewers' generic knowledge of other television police series and set up a pattern of expectations. Scenes in *The Cops* were shot with a single camera, always following the police characters into action, rather than establishing a scene before their arrival. The single camera was often hand-held, moving with the police as they moved through the corridors of the police station, through the streets and into houses. Whereas television drama programmes are normally shot using the shot–reverse shot convention familiar from cinema, in which scenes are performed several times with the camera positioned differently each time in order to capture the reactions of one character to another and to provide a coherent sense of fictional space, *The Cops* aimed to give the impression of unrehearsed action occurring in real time. This is of course the camera convention used in television documentary, where a single camera operator tries to catch the action as it occurs, and is often forced to pan quickly between speakers and to carry the camera physically as action moves across a space. The effect of this form in *The Cops* was to generate a sense of realism in following action as it occured. It also had the effect of requiring the audience to observe the police and interpret their actions without the camera providing the movements from wider shots to close-ups and dramatic contrasts which usually offer an interpretive point of view on the action. *The Cops* demanded a more active and interpretive viewer than is usual in television drama, with the camera technique implying observation and investigation as much as identification with the characters. The structural and formal qualities of *The Cops* work together to both signal genre conventions but also to blur them. The ideological consequence of this is that *The Cops* puts into question any easy distinction between us and them, police and perpetrator, and creatively pushed the boundaries of a very established television genre.

In the opening episode, Mel, a young policewoman working with predominantly male colleagues was introduced. Viewers also saw a young Asian policeman and a middle-aged veteran beat constable unhappy with the changes to policing which he regarded with scepticism. These are familiar characters and it is easy to see how storylines familiar in the police genre can develop around them. There could be tensions between Mel and her male colleagues, explorations of racism within the police institution itself and in the community which the Asian police officer deals with, and conflicts between the middle-aged veteran, his younger colleagues and his superiors responsible for carrying out modern police policies. The members of the public with whom the police characters came most into conflict were the inhabitants of a local housing estate, and further storylines involving tensions between the police and the community offered conventional stories in the police genre. Problems of poverty, drugs, street crime and burglary, conflicts between older and younger generations in the community, and the difficult task of sustaining relationships between the police and people they grew up with while also enforcing law and order, form the basis of the action in the episodes. But *The Cops* not only signalled conventional expectations of the police genre for the audience, but also sought to manipulate these. *The Cops* was exciting television because of its negotiation with genre and the audience expectations which it mobilizes. At the opening of the first episode, Mel was introduced in plain clothes, with no indication that she was a policewoman, and was seen snorting cocaine and dancing all night in a nightclub. The distinctions between the upholders of the law and those whose criminal activities make them the object of police attention were being blurred right from the beginning of the series. As the young police officers learned more about the inhabitants of the local housing estate who they were often called upon to search, interrogate and arrest, they developed increasingly caring attitudes to these people and greater understanding of their problems. Again, the distance between the police and the community was reduced, and the easy identification of perpetrators and victims, heroes and villains, was made increasingly difficult for the audience. The television form of the series supported this blurring of genre categories and expectations, scripting a dramatic narrative and shooting it as if it were spontaneous. Like *The Office*, *The Cops* centred this around character, but in common with the realist ambitions of one strand of British television drama tradition, did so as a means to explore the social and political issues around the role of the state's institutions and the people running them or experiencing their intervention. Coming full circle, drama took on the functions that had been the former subject of documentary as a form of social work.

Case Study: *The Cruise*, performance and authenticity

Stella Bruzzi (2001a: 87) argues that 'the substantive quality of docusoaps is their paramount desire to entertain, to replicate in some way the narrative lines of popular drama, to appeal to a mass audience, and to divert rather than just interest and instruct'. Like most docusoaps, *The Cruise* is structured by segmented parallel narratives. In the 1998 episode of *The Cruise* discussed here, for example, the audience sees dancers preparing for a big show and this is juxtaposed with a married couple of cruise workers, Dale and Mary, on a shopping trip. The action moves from one character or group of characters to another, following the development of a temporal sequence that is arranged like the storyline of a dramatic sequence. By editing from one narrative to another and one character to another an impression of breadth and character development is produced, although the individual incidents and length of specific sequences remain very limited. The viewer is drawn into the unfolding drama of these incidents and encouraged to develop a sense that they are getting to know the character and the environment in which each of them coexists. But in fact, the characteristic experience of watching docusoap is of being in a perpetual meanwhile, suspended between storylines in a perpetually unfinished narrative sequence. The sense of knowing that is produced by documentary is blended with the suspension across multiple parallel narratives that is characteristic of soap opera (Kilborn 2003: 110). At the end of each episode, there are brief trails advertising forthcoming episodes, focusing on challenges and arguments among the crew, in a way similar to the way that television soap opera sets up cliff hangers for resolution. However, the satisfactions of each genre are only partial, since the dramatic shape of docusoap cannot match the carefully designed storyline planning of soap opera, and the witnessing of relatively trivial incidents in the lives of the participants does not deliver the revelation or the intellectual engagement of documentary.

The title sequence of *The Cruise* consists of bright colourful shots taken from a helicopter of the cruise ship Galaxy at night, where the ship is covered in golden lights, juxtaposed with daytime shots of the deck of the ship in sunshine as people gather around swimming pools. The music of the sequence is orchestral and operatic, emphasizing the grandeur of the ship and its focus on pleasure and distraction. The images are sensual and allude to the fantasy of television and magazine advertising for cruise holidays, with dolphins leaping around the Galaxy's bows in the title sequence. The main performers in *The Cruise* are introduced in circular graphics that suggest portholes and are captured in head and shoulders poses turning to the camera, with most emphasis given to the 'starring' role of Jane McDonald. The title sequence of *The Cruise* presents aesthetically pleasing images and showing the faces of the main characters in segments of the screen is reminiscent of the prime-time American soaps that were so popular in Britain in the 1980s, such as *Dallas* and *Dynasty*, where melodramatic action was set against a background of affluence and leisure. Alternatively, the focus on the cruise liner itself might recall the 1970s multi-stranded fictional series *The Love Boat*, subsequently re-made and still currently shown. As well as these connections with television fiction, the focus on Jane McDonald and fellow performers on the cruise liner triggers audience awareness of the conventions of the musical as a fictional genre. The programme focuses on putting on a show, not only as a backstage drama with its interpersonal conflicts, ambition and tight deadlines, but also as a format in which the performance of the characters can be evaluated both in the show within the show and also backstage. Each of these elements draws generic expectations from light entertainment into the factual format, offering different kinds of attractions to a range of potential audiences. The programme offers a selection of central characters, each marked with relatively prominent individual characteristics, a focus on the process and behind the scenes story of both the entertainment business and the organization of the leisure industry and the supplementary attractions of the performances put on by the singers and dancers on the ship, which are shown at some length by the camera. The programme therefore combines some of the attractions of variety, a television genre now rarely seen in its own right, with documentary, drama and celebrity. It is a hybrid that updates many of the traditions and conventions of light entertainment and drama, and blends them into television factual programming.

After *The Cruise* was already being screened, its central character Jane McDonald attracted considerable press and public attention which meant that her profile as a celebrity rose. In later episodes and series of the programme, Jane achieved greater centrality as the star, but was also subject to the cycle of celebrity rise and fall that is familiar from other television performers and film stars in the public arena. The representation of Jane changed from being a plucky show performer who was suddenly discovered by television and the popular press and praised for her dedication and achievement as an ordinary person. She subsequently became a signifier of naffness, whose alleged exaggerated sense of her own importance, limited range of talent as a singer and manipulation of others to achieve her own ambitions were extensively criticized.

So the key issue in evaluating docusoap is tone, which determines the balance between actuality and entertainment, narrative and investigation, and crucially, the address to the audience. *The Cruise* both takes itself seriously through its connotations of glamour, pleasure and luxury, and is also mocking in tone since the episodes themselves focus on the trivial detail of the lives of the cruise workers who enable this glamorous world to exist. Richard Kilborn (2003: 100) argues that docusoap is 'a diverting entertainment package in which dialogue and character interaction are always privileged over any attempt to reveal more about the workings of the respective institutions'. The relationship between Dale and Mary is an example of this, since on one level it is an observation of a relationship within a working context. But the relationship is often portrayed through comic sequences. The voice-over in *The Cruise* sometimes adopts a knowing and mocking tone. When Mary becomes ill with measles, the voice-over explains that the illness is the least of her problems, and this statement is followed by a shot of Dale trying to entertain Mary in an idiotic manner. There is no development of this issue about how the married couple will endure one month in quarantine together in their tiny cabin. Some visual sequences seem to have been chosen to present the participants as potentially ridiculous. Jane McDonald is glimpsed in a brief sequence talking about her psychic powers that apparently predicted the outbreak of measles. The show dancers are seen in long shots that emphasize the contortions of their bodies in their tight fitting costumes and potentially eroticize their hard work. This ambivalence of tone can be seen in some of the phrases in the voice-over, such as the description of the dancers as 'hoofers on the high seas'.

Chris Terrill (maker of *The Cruise* for BBC) stated that he wanted to 'make films that were much more about positive aspects of the human condition: endeavour, effort, triumph over adversity, dealing with emotions and coming through comradeship, teamwork' (Bruzzi 2001b: 84). It is significant that the programme focuses on the workers on the ship, rather than the holiday makers, since the focus on work and the difficulty of keeping the cruise liner running has some of the observation and social investigation of conventional documentary. Richard Kilborn (2003: 102) comments that 'series like *The Cruise* did give audiences some sense of the social hierarchies and command structures of organisations or may have revealed some of the harsher realities beneath the superficial glamour of jobs where service workers cater for the ... pleasure seeking multitude'. Viewers are informed about environments they will not have experienced. The hierarchy within the workplace is portrayed through sequences featuring the performers, especially Jane McDonald. The punishing routine of their rehearsals is shown, and the crises that can affect it. In the episode I have been discussing here, the audience witnesses performers preparing a show coping with a shortage of cast members because of illness and the pressure of last minute rehearsals. One dancer breaks his toe during a performance, another injures his back, and finally the principal singer catches a throat infection. We see two dancers rehearsing a sequence to fill in at the last minute for their injured colleague. A caption on the screen informs us that it is 11.41 pm. The next shot shows the rising sun, then cuts back to a shot of the same dancers still rehearsing the sequence the following morning. Among the actuality shots of rehearsals, Jane McDonald speaks to the camera explaining how hard the job is, and the work of performance itself is shown to be only one of the many duties the performers undertake on the ship. They help to usher guests on the ship from area to area, being abused by frustrated holiday makers. The private lives of the cruise ship employees are shown, for example when Dale and Mary discuss how they manage their marriage in the confined space of their accommodation and the ship and how they feel about being far away from home. Jane telephones her mother at home and becomes tearful and upset. The case of *The Cruise* illustrates the combination of television conventions discussed throughout this chapter, and the ways that their components sit sometimes uneasily with each other, because of their different relationships with veracity or authenticity in factual and fictional traditions. The crucial issue of tone is very difficult to evaluate analytically since it is so hard to describe, but the meaning of the combination of television forms in Reality TV is dependent on it.

Conclusion

In the preparation of a conventional documentary, there is a strong relationship between journalism, written evidence, interviews conducted before the making of the programme, and the expectation of argument and the definition of a field of investigation. The preparation of documentary involves a compilation of these different kinds of recorded sound and written material before the programme is structured and assembled. Reality TV has a different kind of temporal structure in terms of its production. There still needs to be a long period of preparation, though this is primarily to identify potential participants and establish the location in which material will be shot and the parameters of the format that will contain the action. So rather than the journalistic enterprise of research and the gathering of evidence that can be expressed in visual form or pursued through a filming process, Reality TV has more in common with the casting of a dramatic programme. Performers, settings, modes of direction and dramatic shaping have a greater importance than the gathering of evidence. Indeed, the performance within the setting is itself the evidence, in the sense that Reality TV documents behaviour under the constraints of setting and format. Reality TV inherits the principles of literary naturalism in its interest in what people do, how they express themselves and how they feel, and the embedding of relationships of identification and empathy with on-screen characters and 'performers' performing themselves in a factual format.

Two of the components that have been argued to characterize television as a medium are its possibility for intimacy and its potential for immediacy. Television is an intimate medium in the sense that it is broadcast into the private space of the home and much of its output promises to reveal the detail of individual action through the alternation of image and sound, with a special emphasis on the ability of the close-up to provide analytical observation of human behaviour. While this capacity is a resource for all television forms, it has been exploited particularly in drama, where psychology, emotion and the expression of each of these has been facilitated by the use of the close-up and the patterning of dramatic forms to emphasise moments of character revelation. As this chapter has argued, Reality TV has adopted these procedures and structural emphases and linked them with the assumption that real people, whether ordinary people or celebrities, are equally as interesting as dramatic characters. The immediacy of television derives historically from the fact that for the first 20 years or so after its invention it was impossible to easily record television footage. This meant that television focused on the live broadcasting of both factual and fictional material, covering events such as football matches or news events, and broadcasting drama that was shot live in the television studio and could not be repeated without assembling its cast of characters and performing the drama again.

In Reality TV, the fascination of seeing something unplanned happen simulates this experience of liveness, and sometimes the events that the camera witnesses are in fact live. The first episode of the UK version of *Survivor* in 2001 emphasizes time immediately through on-screen captions that announce that the audience is watching day one, and that the time is 6.15 am. The viewer is embarking on a journey through the programme that matches the journey of the contestants. The duration of *Survivor* for its participants is 40 days and 40 nights, a resonant period that matches the biblical time span of the temptations of Jesus in the desert. Like Jesus, the participants will have to endure trials and challenges, and may emerge at the end of the period as transformed individuals. Throughout *Survivor* episodes, for example, the fixing of time precisely is emphasized, with captions and narration stating which day in the 40 day period is being witnessed, and the precise time of the day that events take place. By contrast, however, the audience is not told what time of the year the programme takes place, nor what season, month or date. This enables time to be displaced from the present of the audience, since the participants are in an exotic foreign location. By focusing on the details of precise timing, the programme creates an impression of liveness and thus conceals the editing process and also the period of time that has elapsed between the filming of the programme and its transmission. A dislocation of time coexists with an impression of a live present. Both intimacy and immediacy persist as key characteristics of Reality TV. Across the run of a continuing series, participants will become intimate with each other, especially since they are enclosed in a bounded location and are out of contact with their families and friends. Viewers are also encouraged to become intimate with the participants, identifying their characteristic strengths and weaknesses and observing the patterns of their interaction with each other. By using the technology of live broadcasting and video streaming over the Internet in *Big Brother*, the experience of time within the location of some Reality TV programmes can be the same as the temporality of the audience. Cameras are present all the time, offering viewers the opportunity to experience the extreme differences in temporal rhythm between long periods of inactivity and high-points of condensed dramatic interest, for example in the eviction of contestants from the *Big Brother* house. Understanding Reality TV in relation to drama means not only considering how it resembles scripted programmes and acted performance, but also how the dramatic as a mode of audience engagement with an intimate and sometimes immediate temporal process is created and how it is modulated by the tone and address that shapes how its audiences can perceive it.

5
Surveillance

Introduction

A wide variety of Reality TV variants, from the television talk show to 'true crime' programmes, hidden camera series and staged Reality TV formats like *Big Brother* exemplify an uneasy shift in the contemporary ideologies of television from a liberal emphasis on personal empowerment and public service concern with social issues to an aggressive surveillance of the individual subject and the engagement of the audience in a process of stigmatization, social differentiation and risk. From this perspective, Reality TV formats are revealing of the relationships between individuals, and between individuals and the agencies that can see, control and contain them within a physical space. It is appropriate that the participants in the first British series of *Big Brother* were all aged between 22 and 38, and that its audience mainly comprised viewers in the 16–34 age group, of whom 75 per cent watched the programme during its first run. This is also the age group most likely to be perpetrators or victims of violent crime, though men are much more likely to commit such offences or to be assaulted than women. The response to crime against the person across Britain's urban centres has been to deter it by installing video camera systems, operated by remote control. Including surveillance systems operated by local authorities, government agencies and private organizations or individuals, there were approximately 1.5 million security cameras in operation in the United Kingdom in 2002 (Addley 2002: 14). The city of Newcastle had over 300 in locations such as shopping centres, housing estates and industrial zones, while Manchester opened a £1.3 million digital surveillance system using 400 cameras in the same year. The Home Office spent £170 million on surveillance cameras between 1999 and 2003, and local authorities spent the same amount. However, despite widespread public support for video surveillance, Esther Addley (2002: 14) reports official surveys suggesting that improved street lighting may be four times more likely than cameras to deter crime, and despite some initial impact on offences when cameras are installed this effect seems to wear off after a period. She quotes Roy Coleman, lecturer in criminology, who argues that: 'It gives the veneer of a sanitised, clean, healthy public space, and this, says the council, is what investors want. We are turning our cities into glorified consumption zones' (Addley 2002: 16). This context suggests that the observation of others is not necessarily a rational and functional aspect of contemporary culture, but that it does respond to widespread cultural concerns that proceed from the ideologies of the present.

It is, therefore, important to investigate whether Reality TV is a pertinent example of those ideologies and represents those social concerns. This analysis contributes to the project of defining what Reality TV is as a designation for a programme type, since its observation of its participants might amount to the surveillance of them, and thus place questions about the power of looking at others at the centre of its meanings. John Dovey (2001: 135–6) offers the definition that: ' "Reality TV" is now used as a genre description of any factual programme based on an aesthetic style of apparent "zero-degree realism" – in other words a direct, unmediated account of events, often associated with the use of video and surveillance-imaging technologies.' The title of *Big Brother* is an allusion to George Orwell's novel *Nineteen Eighty-four*, in which a future totalitarian society was able to continuously monitor its citizens by video surveillance, summed up in the phrase written on the posters displayed in his dystopian fictional world: 'Big Brother is watching you'. This chapter considers how these connotations of entrapment, restriction and control which the phrase possesses are relevant to the television programme that adopted Orwell's idea of the apparently benevolent but pervasively controlling authority-figure of Big Brother, not only by discussing *Big Brother* itself but also the longer history of programmes based on surveillance footage gathered from public institutions such as the police and reconstructions of actual events.

The prison of the real

Big Brother's title connotes entrapment, restriction and control, and *Big Brother* was marketed at first as an experiment about how human society works, with the contestants like rats trapped in a laboratory maze. As if in a psychological test, the selfishness of desiring the first series' prize of £70,000 conflicted with the contestants' need to gain loyalty from their housemates. Psychologists were on hand to analyze the motivations and feelings of the contestants, establishing them as subjects of a scientific experiment, which the viewing audience was privileged to see, and which required expert commentary to properly understand. However, the prominence of this scientific and psychological discourse waned significantly as each series of *Big Brother* followed its predecessor. Even so, by 2004 and the deliberate pressurization of the housemates by 'Big Brother evil', the motif of the test or experiment conducted on volunteers remained in a modified form. In May 2002, BBC2 screened *The Experiment*, in which 15 men volunteered to take part in a televised version of an experiment conducted by Philip Zimbardo in 1971 at Stanford University. In the original 1971 version, volunteers were divided into two groups comprising prisoners and guards. This degenerated into a tyrranical regime where the guards arbitrarily exercised their authority and the experiment was brought to an early end. The BBC programme included commentary by Alex Haslam and Steve Reicher, two academic psychologists, and participants were able to talk to a clinical psychologist about their problems and the programme was overseen by an ethics committee. *The Experiment* distanced itself from *Big Brother* by being trailed as a social investigation, but clearly the decision to make it in the first place must have been affected by the public attention to *Big Brother* in the media and among television producers and commissioners. Since *Big Brother* had been originally inspired by experiments like these, the television formats of *The Experiment* and *Big Brother* feed off and into each other, developing similar methods and tapping into related interests and fears among their audiences.

The programme producers argued that *The Experiment* was a populist but serious scientific exercise demonstrating that the roles played by the volunteers challenged Zimbardo's original findings. In the BBC programme, the volunteer prisoners and inmates usually cooperated with each other, and did not form into opposing camps who manipulated their power or powerlessness. However, despite the claims made about the scientific purpose of the programme, its outcomes were questioned both by other psychologists and media commentators as the participants had no way of controlling the impact of being on television. The same factor was present in the 1971 version when Zimbardo recorded the events of the Stanford experiment on film. Having completed the shooting of the BBC programme, one of its psychologist advisors Steve Reicher commented: 'There were a lot of bits that would have made good Big Brother drama, which we have left on the cutting room floor as they do not contribute to the science. Likewise, after showing the rough edit to the participants, we have strengthened the voiceover to make clear the psychological motivation behind people's behaviour. The programme will only be a success for the BBC if it is seen as good science' (Crace 2002: 11). What is striking about the comment is Reicher's defensiveness about what he clearly saw as a difference of genre and tone between *The Experiment* and *Big Brother*. Moments that might have been appealing to viewers because of their interpersonal dramatic qualities were excluded from the final cut of the programme, owing to the clear line that the production team supposedly drew between fact and fiction, and between factual scientific television and entertainment. Voice-over, delivered in a sober and informational tone, was used as a means of controlling possible audience responses to the programme, disciplining the audience into certain ways of understanding the programme rather than others. The disciplining of the programme's structure and tone offered a means to discipline the audience about how to understand a programme featuring volunteers undergoing a controlled and disciplined confinement. At each level of these different aspects of the programme text, its format and its available viewing positions, control and a desire for predictability were evident. What is interesting about this situation is how science is used to legitimate these procedures of control, seeking to set up a scientific experiment, to find a tone that would contain some of the undesirable meanings of the programme text and to shape the audience's reactions. Each of these implies that the production and reception of television might be a science itself. But the programme's intertextual relationships with *Big Brother* and the leakage of meanings between it and *The Experiment*, show that this kind of knowledge and predictability about what television means cannot be guaranteed in advance.

The Experiment was made by BBC, according to those who were involved in it, as an informational public service programme, though its range of meanings for its viewers was probably not confined by this. Something similar happened when Channel 4 tried to link the *Big Brother* format to public service aims. *Teen Big Brother* began on 13 October 2003. The programme was commissioned by the educational division of Channel 4, for a school and college audience. Its participants comprised eight 18 year olds, four of each sex, who spent ten days in the *Big Brother* house. Unlike the prime-time version, it was recorded and there was no voting by the public. The teenagers slept in a single bedroom, were denied cigarettes and alcohol and were given tasks that emphasized collaboration and cooperation. These tasks included mending a toilet or simulating the roles of cabin crew on a flight from London to Birmingham. In the same way that the housemates in the adult version were drawn from a range of backgrounds and self-identities, the teen version's participants came from different parts of Britain, different races and represented a range of sexual identities. One housemate was a Muslim, while the Belfast hairdresser Paul was gay, for example. In line with Channel 4's educational agenda, the combination of participants was designed to encourage conversation among them and in their audience about such issues as teenage pregnancy, racism and homophobia. Each participant was expected to teach a skill to one of their colleagues, such as how to cut hair or how to draw.

However, tabloid press coverage of the programme focused immediately on the fact that two of the participants had sex during the series, announced before transmission by headlines in the *Daily Star* and the *Sun*. Although this publicity gave some assistance to Channel 4 in attracting a mainstream audience for the evening broadcast of the series, it represented a tension between the educational and entertainment agenda of Reality TV, as in the case of *The Experiment*. This gave rise to the production of two versions of *Teen Big Brother*, one screened after the 9.00 pm watershed and including the sex scene and another edited version screened on Channel 4 in their morning schedule of educational programmes. The series was accompanied by a website and resource pack for schools and colleges, as Channel 4 attempted to engage 14–19 year olds in line with its public service broadcasting remit. By contrast with the mainstream schools programmes produced by BBC, Channel 4 aimed to focus its educational programmes on life skills that would assist young people in integrating into the workplace and improving their knowledge of sexual health.

Perhaps surprisingly, prime-time Reality TV programmes had already proven that they had an educational component, as *Jamie's Kitchen* and *The Salon* generated thousands of enquiries from viewers interested in careers in catering and hairdressing. Channel 4 commissioned the series *Bollywood Dreams* from the production company Maverick as a version of a *Pop Idol* talent contest leading to the chance to appear in a Bollywood movie. Although this was a prime-time gamedoc, it also aimed to produce a public space for contestants and audiences to consider the role of British Asians and the relationship between British national identity and Asian culture. Channel 4's head of Learning, Heather Rabbatts, explained: 'A programme about cultural diversity might get an audience of half a million people. A show like Bollywood Dreams has all the excitement of a Pop Idol-style contest but is also potentially a really interesting story about what our identity means in modern Britain at a time when it is such a huge topic of debate' (Plunkett 2005b: 9). These Channel 4 offerings attempted to combine attractive entertainment formats and the chance to attract high ratings with the recognition of diversity of audience identities and interests that Channel 4 was tasked by its remit to address. Reality TV provided the opportunity to achieve both of these aims, although in forms that were notably different from the genres and formats in which they had hitherto existed. While being open to criticism for contaminating entertainment with public service messages and contaminating educational programmes with entertainment and thrills, Reality TV has become an important hybrid that can accommodate simultaneous and competing aims. But as these examples of *The Experiment* and *Teen Big Brother* show, it is hard to separate the pro-social sense of responsibility that led in part to their production from the dramatic and entertainment values that they courted and then had to control or repudiate. The motif of surveillance already signals questions of control and discipline, but so too do these programmes' aesthetic forms, scheduling and address to audiences.

Spaces of surveillance

The physical space of *Big Brother* is parallel to the space in which a child might play while overlooked and protected by a parent. Psychoanalytic work on children's play has discussed the playing space as an intermediate zone between the internal psychological world of fantasy and the exterior public space of the adult world. Play space is for learning and for making the transition between fantasy and the constraints of the real world inhabited and known by adults. The fourth series of the British version of *Big Brother* in 2003, for example, set the action in a house with bright colours and simple shapes, often soft and curved ones. It could be described as a play space, or a protected and feminized space where a child might be allowed to wander while its parent was doing something else nearby, like the play areas provided in shopping malls. There were no places of refuge in the *Big Brother* house, and the symbolic divisions between genders and generations were minimized. The lack of a division of bedrooms into separate spaces for men and women and the easy transitions between inside and outside the house brought the whole of the space together as a place for doing whatever the contestants wished, but at the same time a space where they had no opportunity to find their own place. The apparent focus of the environment's design on futuristic or utopian ideas of what a living space might look like, with materials, furnishings and technological equipment that might promise to make living easier and more comfortable, was contradicted by the enclosure and enforced communality that the house required. The removal of constraints on how the contestants might spend their time, since they had little enforced activity to perform, is contradicted by the notion of the house as a space for the acting out of desires and fantasies within a public gaze (Biressi and Nunn 2005: 95–107). As Lynn Spigel (2001) argued, imaginings of the future home figure it as a fetish space that is separate from its surroundings and open to surveillance, for example, through the presence of plate glass windows or the removal of dividing walls. The *Big Brother* house follows the architectural conventions of the modernist machine for living. Its architecture is simple, it has large windows and blurs the boundary between inside and outside. The internal space is not rigidly segmented, and allows multiple possibilities of movement, flow and interaction. It appears to be a functional environment that will stimulate social activity and exchange. But its design is partly the result of the necessity for multiple camera angles across a space that is not bound by physical barriers. Despite the emphasis on light and access from house to garden, the site of the house is cut-off from outside, necessarily, and it makes no attempt to engage in a dialogue with the broader environment of public and social space beyond the high walls that surround it.

The decor of each version of the *Big Brother* house is aggressively modern. It is far from homely by comparison with the visions of home presented in either television commercials or home decor programmes, for example. The *Big Brother* house is more like a set designed for display, perhaps a bachelor pad in which a young, wealthy and independent young person might demonstrate their contemporary taste and modern conveniences. The space outside is mainly a tarmac waiting area in which fans can gather to cheer and boo on eviction days while watching the giant video relay of footage from inside the house. Metal fences and the presence of the burly security guards reference the control of public spaces such as nightclubs in city centres or the policing of light entertainment events such as the Oscars or a Royal Variety Performance. A colourful stage with constructed backdrops, screens, interview area and elaborate lighting sits near the house for Davina to interview evicted participants. The area around the *Big Brother* house is therefore a performance arena, equipped for a large and noisy audience but arranged primarily for the multiple cameras that both share the perspective of the waiting fans but also provide privileged access to Davina and the contestants as they leave and arrive. These settings are especially appropriate for the kinds of contestants who now take part in *Big Brother*, such as Marco and Nadia, who maintain an uneasy balance between being starstruck and vulnerable, but also exhibitionist and camp. It is possible to be lost in the spaces, but also to use them as large stages on which to perform. By designing these spaces, and transitions between them, the *Big Brother* producers manage and discipline the meanings of each of the spaces and the ways in which contestants might perform differently in each of them.

There is still an economy of space which is subject to regulation, then, despite the sense that the contestants can do or say whatever they like. Their possibilities of identity and performance are spatially restrained, so that when these spatial boundaries are breached (when a contestant tries to climb on the roof or fans outside the house invade its space by making too much noise), these transgressions become especially exciting, newsworthy and challenging to the format. The homeliness and attractiveness of the *Big Brother* house exist at the cost of the enforcement of its spatial boundaries, at the same time as these boundaries are reassuring, protective but ultimately a demonstration of spatial meaning as a product of power. The same is true of time in *Big Brother*, which is empty and unmarked by fixed points except when the housemates are given tasks to complete or the eviction votes arrive, and these are points that are fixed by the format rather than by the contestants themselves. Their time seems to consist entirely of leisure, except for artificially imposed work that effectively parodies the reality of work for the audience. The participants have no television, they are allowed only one book for each eight-week period, they cannot use telephones and they cannot write. So they are in a situation of enforced leisure where time can be occupied only with excessive sleeping and desultory conversation. What appears to be a paradise of free time is in fact similar to the almost unbearable ennui of the upper-middle classes of the nineteenth century, for whom the absence of a need to work could at least be exchanged for activities aimed at self-improvement and the charitable improvement of others. It is appropriate that the self-improvement represented by gymnastic exercises, or the improvement of others through caring work such as giving massages or teaching yoga, are among the few things that the contestants can find to do.

I'm a Celebrity and *Survivor* have locations where space has different but similarly contradictory meanings, representing both freedom and confinement, work and leisure. The jungle setting is clearly very significant to *I'm a Celebrity*. It is an exotic location, whose visual appearance is unfamiliar and whose potential danger is emphasized by inserted brief sequences showing apparently dangerous animals such as snakes and spiders. These brief shots of wildlife function as punctuation to cover edit points and transitions between presenters and footage of the participants, but draw attention to the contestants' confinement in a threatening environment. Although Australia is relatively familiar as a destination for British viewers, especially younger viewers for whom it is a common destination in the gap year between school and university or during university vacations, *I'm a Celebrity* emphasizes the particular aspects of its conventional representation that revolve around its significance for adventure and personal challenge. In the jungle location, the celebrities are dressed in the clothing stereotypically worn by explorers, such as khaki shorts and boots, tropical hats, head bands and scarves. In fact the costume is similar to that worn by the film character Indiana Jones or the video game protagonist Lara Croft. The celebrities are framed in a narrative that references adventurous exploration, an exotic holiday or a military exercise. This mixes the different meanings that the programme can actualize by posing tasks that seem to be uncomfortable or dangerous, as well as the daily routines of cooking on a campfire, dealing with mosquitoes and collecting supplies. The homeliness of routine coexists with spatial confinement in an exotic and other location.

The island location of *Survivor* is also presented as a beautiful and exotic place, with lush and green tropical plants, golden sand, sunshine and a calm blue sea. The location is therefore primitive, like the desert island onto which Robinson Crusoe was cast away, thus referencing romantic versions of the exotic tropical other that includes the notion of self-discovery and a return to innocence, at the same time as a gruelling physical challenge to remain alive using only one's own resources. In the first episode of *Survivor*, contestants swam ashore from a picturesque sailing vessel and immediately began to work hard at building a shelter, dividing up immediate tasks such as the collection of materials for roofing, a sleeping platform and the structural components of their beach shelter. The music in *Survivor* emphasizes the exotic by adopting a persistent motif of drumming, such as is used to connote the threat of exotic and primitive locations in film and television adventure narratives. The music is used as an accompaniment to footage of the participants going about their tasks, and more prominently in the credits sequences and in the periodic meetings at which the participants vote to eject each other and undergo challenges. In each of the examples mentioned here, space has contradictory meanings, connoting both discipline and freedom, work and play, the prison and the home. In these respects, space is infused with significance, and opens up the possibility of reading it as a metaphor for society and as a terrain for the testing of what it means to be an individual in a community.

Discipline and confession

The genre of the television talk show has undergone significant changes in the past decade. Talk shows can be regarded as television representations of a public sphere, a conceptual space in which issues of concern to society as a whole can be debated using the shared discourses and assumptions that are necessary to rational debate. As discussed earlier in this book, television provides instances of such debate and constitutes a public sphere, at the same time as contemporary broadcasting atomizes individuals within their homes and fragments society into smaller and smaller niche audiences. Television's public sphere simulates the kind of democratic debate for which the term was first invented, both keeping alive the sense of the public sphere and at the same time substituting for an absent public debate in developed societies. American talk shows which rose to prominence in the 1970s such as the *Oprah Winfrey* show and *Donahue* conventionally focused on individual guests who represented a larger minority constituency that sought a voice. For example, black single mothers, the disabled or people struggling with drug addictions were able to give voice to an under-represented and stigmatized group by individualizing the problems of that group through the confessional and personal discourse of the guests. This ventilation of personal concerns, connected with the concerns of groups, was itself a mechanism of empowerment and resistance to dominant social values. The contributions of experts on the talk show connected the experiences of the guests to institutional discourses such as medicine, psychoanalysis and civil rights. The translation of personal experience into institutional discourses was also a mechanism of empowerment, though of course it also had the effect of incorporating resistance into society's dominant forms and converting anger into some more socially acceptable force.

Beginning in the 1980s, however, the genre of the talk show has modulated into a much less liberal form of television with much less focus on empowerment and the valuation of resistant and excluded voices. The reason for this change in the genre is that broadcasters' research into audience preferences led to the creation of new programmes, and the reshaping of old ones, to gain new and larger audiences. Graeme Turner (Neale and Turner 2001: 6) notes that 'the cumulative effect of repeated tweaking of the format and content amounts to a change in genre' as 'more finely grained, and more readily available, viewing figures have the effect of influencing content, format and, ultimately, genre'. American television talk shows such as the *Jerry Springer* show and the *Morton Downey Junior* show had become, by the 1990s, as internationally successful as Oprah Winfrey had been, but with a very different and much more aggressive attitude to their guests. The hosts of these programmes are much more inclined to make accusations against the opinions and behaviour of their guests than to support them in their resistance to a norm. The most commented-upon feature of these programmes is the prevalence of aggressive physical behaviour when guests confront each other in front of the cameras and the audience. For example, heterosexual couples appear as guests and suddenly, without their knowledge, it is revealed that the secret lover of one of them is also present. The confrontation between guests in this way has given rise to fist fights between them, the throwing of furniture across the set and the necessity for burly security guards to intervene from the edges of the television studio to separate the combatants. The role of the host, who has always functioned both as a representative for social norms represented by the collective audience behind him or her as well as a mediator between the guest, the audience and experts, has become instead that of an orchestrator of confrontation and a ringleader encouraging the audience to vent its condemnation of one or more of the studio guests. The prominence of experts has diminished in parallel with this, so that the conversion of social exclusion and violent emotion into the rational terms of institutional discourses is much less the project of the programmes. A remnant of the liberal discourse of empowerment remains at the end of the *Jerry Springer* show, however, when Jerry delivers his weekly three-minute address direct to camera, containing a more considered homily on the foibles of human nature. Nevertheless the transformation of the talk-show genre demonstrates the erosion of these programmes as a public space in which liberal and democratic ideologies of inclusion, empowerment and personal development are enacted in television form. Instead, their ideology has become increasingly focused on the reinforcement of social norms, where audiences (represented by the studio audience) close their ranks against perceived deviance and thus enact a surveillance of social roles and individuals who represent norms and deviations from those norms.

A further aspect of this development is the controversial centrality of performance to the talk-show genre. There have been celebrated cases (for example in 1999 on the *Vanessa* and *Trisha* shows in Britain) when popular newspapers have revealed that some of the guests have been 'fakes'. Rather than members of the public discovered 'naturally' by programme researchers, these fake guests have been consciously performing their roles in order either simply to appear on television, or to make money from appearance fees and spin-off newspaper and magazine features. The appetite for new guests on programmes sometimes broadcast every day during the week has led to the scavenging of guests from one show by the researchers on another, and the creation of an informal pool of guests who can be relied on to give dramatic and emotional performances. In the context of this emphasis on performance and the importance to programme ratings of guests' extreme emotional responses or violent outbursts it is not surprising that the line between a 'genuine' and a 'fake' guest becomes blurred. The importance of the public display of guilt, shame and rage in the contemporary talk show further contributes to the blurring of the boundaries of the genre. These factors link the talk show to the dramatic fiction genre of soap opera, for example, where these emotions and their exaggerated display are the focus of the narrative. Of course, it is no accident in this respect that both talk shows and soap opera are conventionally associated with, and scheduled to appeal to, a feminine sensibility and a female audience. For in Western societies, it is a conventional attribute of femininity to openly display emotion, and to take an interest in the confessional revelations of others. Indeed the movement of documentary and actuality programmes, as well as talk shows, towards these conventional attributes of femininity is in itself an interesting development in contemporary television. Programme genres, and their assumed audiences, appear to be moving toward a more generalized social dissemination of the confessional discourse formerly attributed to femininity. But while this represents a welcome blurring of the categories of gender conventions, it also shares with other Reality TV forms the use of confessional discourse as a material that can be evaluated and worked on, with the assumption that there is a right to know about the inner life of the individual and an obligation to speak about it.

Rights and regulations

Sam Brenton and Reuben Cohen (2003) argue that Reality TV is preoccupied with the mundane and that its production techniques have aspects in common with torture. Their perhaps surprising alignment of Reality TV with torture arises from their reference to Article 5 of the Universal Declaration of Human Rights, which states that: 'No one shall be subjected to torture or to cruel, inhuman or degrading treatment or punishment.' In *I'm A Celebrity*, for example, one challenge demanded that Catalina Guirado get into crocodile-infested waters. The crocodiles were remote-controlled replicas, but Guirado seemed to be completely panic-stricken and unaware of the trick. Both *I'm A Celebrity* and *Fear Factor* have used challenges of a less exotic but certainly visceral and potentially terrifying nature in which participants are enclosed in spaces occupied by, or their bodies are exposed to, rats, snakes or insects.

For Brenton and Cohen the entertainment context of these challenges (encapsulated in the first *Big Brother*'s catchphrase 'It's only a gameshow') does not automatically separate them from the requirement to uphold the human rights of their contestants. Brenton and Cohen link the argument for Reality TV's social irresponsibility with the charge that the programmes' producers adopt unethical methods to control the participants, specifically paralleling these techniques with military methods of torture and interrogation. For example, the structure of reward and punishment common to Reality TV formats, such as in the giving or withholding of food (about which participants in *I'm a Celebrity* and *Big Brother* frequently complained) and the establishment of apparently random routines for eating or sleeping is aligned with psychological torture that aims to weaken a victim and produce dependency on the interrogators. Contestants in the first British series of *Survivor* lost significant body weight and began to suffer from lethargy because of calorie deprivation. They gave up on their attempts to gather food by fishing or hunting, hoping to save enough energy for the physical challenges set by the producers. The aim to survive these challenges imposed by the format and its human representatives became more significant to them than their bodily health because they placed greatest importance on the competition to win immunity from the upcoming round of evictions from the island.

A different variant of this deprivation technique is one in which the actions of an individual participant can affect the wellbeing of fellow participants and this clearly places a further moral pressure on individuals. One *Big Brother* task required each participant to go and dance on a rostrum in the garden, at any time of day or night, if he or she heard an individual 'signature tune' played in the house. This encouraged them to stay awake so as not miss the signal, and the failure of any of them would be penalized by a reduction in the following week's food budget. Brenton and Cohen argue that the contestants do not feel free to leave this oppressive environment, because they have crossed a psychological boundary once they have entered the *Big Brother* house or arrived in the jungles of *Survivor* and *I'm A Celebrity*. However, Danniella Westbrook did quit *I'm A Celebrity*, and Sandy Cumming left the *Big Brother* house. Reality TV producers have nevertheless subjected participants to treatment that could be called cruel. The second *Big Brother* series in the United States was transmitted at the time of the attacks on the United States by terrorists on 11 September 2001, and the programme makers took the opportunity to call one contestant into the diary room and tell her that her sister and niece (who lived in New York) were unharmed, but that her cousin, whose workplace was in the World Trade Center, was missing. To inform her of this on camera, via Big Brother's unseen and anonymous voice, raised ethical concerns about the public and unsympathetic airing of private feelings that *Big Brother* itself had brought into the closed environment of the house.

Programme producers' guidelines supplied by television institutions have considerable concern for privacy and the requirement for permission to record in particular kinds of space and for permission to broadcast footage or sound featuring members of the public, employees and public figures. These guidelines have most direct relevance to factual programme formats such as news, current affairs and documentary but also affect satire and light entertainment, for example. They are designed for non-scripted programmes, often shot on location, where the presence of people who might appear on the screen cannot always be predicted or controlled. The guidelines have not been significantly adjusted to take account of Reality TV programmes, and this has some effects on the application of the guidelines to programmes involving people who have consented to be filmed or taped, but who may not be entirely happy with the ways in which they are portrayed and the recording of their actions in situations that could be deemed personal or private. The ITC Programme Code (2002), for example, outlines a situation in which permission is received to film or record material in an institution, such as a hospital, factory or department store, which has regular dealings with the public, but where television would not normally have access because the space is privately owned or is controlled by a public body. There is no legal obligation to seek the agreement of subjects who are filmed in this way when they are incidental and anonymous members of the public. Reality TV programmes have more in common with the filming of individuals in their own homes, where broadcasters have clear guidelines that are sensitive about the filming of people in private space without their consent. The ITC Programme Code recognizes the applicability of Article 8(1) of the European Convention on Human Rights: 'Everyone has the right to respect for his private and family life, his home and his correspondence.' Since Reality TV programmes are not normally made for investigative journalistic purposes, they cannot easily claim the 'public interest' defence specified in Article 8(2) of the Convention: 'There shall be no interference by a public authority with the exercise of this right except such as is in accordance with the law and is necessary in a democratic society in the interests of national security, public safety or the economic well-being of the country, for the prevention of disorder or crime, for the protection of health or morals, or for the protection of the rights and freedoms of others.' In effect, people volunteering to take part in Reality TV programmes have signed away their rights.

There is a regulatory distinction between the recording of people's actions when they have consented to be filmed, even by hidden or covert cameras like those installed in the *Big Brother* house, and hidden camera footage used in documentary and current affairs genres. The ITC Programme Code (2002), for example, states that: 'The use of hidden microphones and cameras for the filming or recording of individuals who are unaware of it is acceptable only when it is clear that the material so acquired is essential to establish the credibility and authority of a story.' The fact that these guidelines are shaped for use in journalistic programmes is shown by the use of the word 'story' to refer to the programme's form and structure. The key issues, then are consent by the subject being recorded, the purpose of the recording and its relationship with the public interest. In entertainment programmes, of which Reality TV programmes can be considered a variant, similar constraints are imposed. The ITC Programme Code (2002) states that 'Set-up situations where members of the public or celebrities are featured without their knowledge or without prior warning are an established part of some entertainment programmes. Nevertheless, the use of such situations should always be carefully considered, and safeguards used to prevent unwarranted invasions of privacy. Where material is recorded, the consent of the subjects should be obtained before transmission.' These guidelines are established on the assumption that entertainment programmes are recorded rather than live, but in live programming the Code advises that 'particular care should be taken to avoid offence to the individuals concerned'. It is perhaps more likely, however, that Reality TV formats could be accused of obtaining the consent of participants under false pretences. For example, rather than being a 'serious' look at the working life of a traffic warden, some docusoap and Reality TV programmes could be seen as covertly intended as comedy, entertainment or satire programmes. The 'duping' of people appearing in set-up programmes requires the consent of very senior executives in broadcasting institutions and their consent is required again before transmission. Here the ITC Programme Code has a related set of pieces of advice to producers: 'With unsuspecting members of the public, the use of such material without the subject's permission can only be justified if it is necessary in order to make an important point of public interest. With celebrities and those in the public eye, material should not be used without similar public interest justification if it is likely to result in unjustified public ridicule or personal distress.' The distinction here between the treatment of members of the public and celebrities is interesting. Members of the public might be recorded with an ulterior motive if there is a journalistic motive plausible in some factual programmes such as documentary or current affairs. On the other hand, while the public interest defence is again referred to in relation to celebrities, the issue is the potential damage to an already-existing public reputation. In other words, the protection of a reputation only extends to people who already have one. Thus, for Jade Goody on *Big Brother*, for example, there is no recourse against a programme maker who might portray her in a way that she could consider demeaning or offensive. The power to look, record, edit and transmit in Reality TV does not amount to the wholesale exploitation of its participants and the violation of rights that Brenton and Cohen suggest, but it does manipulate its subjects in ways for which they have little recourse.

Threat and reassurance

The problem-solving structure of some Reality TV variants links apparently different kinds of programme though their structuring in terms of threat and reassurance. ITV's *Pop Idol* and *Fat Club* are in effect versions of the makeover show where what is made-over is the person. BBC has adopted the same format of the makeover for its programme *Would Like to Meet*. In each of these programmes members of the public are advised, but importantly, they are also abused by a team of experts who guide their transformation. In some cases the objective of the transformation is explicitly public fame and recognition, as in *Pop Idol*, and the narrative progress of the serial is from ordinariness to extra-ordinariness, from alignment with the television audience to separation from the audience as the central figure becomes a star. But even in programmes where the objective is simply to become more attractive by losing weight, or to begin a satisfying relationship with a member of the opposite sex, in all cases the focus is on the often aggressive moulding of the subject. The assumption behind these programmes is that the self is a malleable and transformable object, which can be worked upon with the assistance of experts and with personal self-discipline. There is a persistent injunction for the subject to take control of himself or herself and to embark on a potentially infinite programme of self-improvement. As Gareth Palmer (2004) has argued, there is a class dimension to this aspirational project since the people who feature in them seem often to be trying to improve themselves according to expectations about appearance and behaviour that shift them towards middle-class norms. And in many Reality TV programmes, though not all of them, the proof of success in the programme of self-improvement has a sexual dimension. Since sexuality is considered to be the prime location for the expression of personal identity, and sexual activity is a test of the subject's integration into the social norms of (hetero)sexual interaction, this aspect of subjective identity is a readily available demonstration of the integration of the subject.

But integration into a norm of gender or sexual identity is not the only means by which makeover formats discipline the body and the subject. Discussing another kind of Reality TV that is the subject of the case study analysed later, Annette Hill (1999) argues that in the trauma television represented by programmes such as *999* the structure of programmes poses a threat but then contains it through reassurance. Fears about crime, danger to the body or illness are represented by the actuality footage or reconstructions presented in programmes but these offer a resolution in which advice is offered about how to avoid such catastrophes. The expert discourses of psychologists, doctors or policemen provide authoritative information and advice that smoothes over the potential danger producing an uneasy but powerful combination of apparent public service with the thrills of dramatic narrative and entertainment.

It has become commonplace for television not only to rely on found footage supplied by others such as police camera footage or surveillance footage, but also to install covert, hidden surveillance systems in order to generate actuality evidence of wrongdoing and criminality. Programmes such as Granada Television's *Rattrap, Nannies from Hell* and others in the *from Hell* series such as *Neighbours from Hell* or *Plumbers from Hell* have adopted this technique. There is an assumption behind these programmes that they are engaged in a public service so that, for example, the advertisements in *Yellow Pages* and newspapers showing the company names of plumbing companies are shown on screen to inform viewers of exactly which businesses have been exposed as cowboys. Programme narrators provide tips and information on how to spot inferior and overpriced work and give guide prices for what particular common jobs should cost. But there are several questions to ask about programmes like this. If the cowboy workmen exposed by the programme are already known to be operating in dangerous and exorbitant ways, the programme does nothing to change this situation except add evidence. If large numbers of other workmen have been shown doing the same work well, this footage would be undramatic and would not be used, although it may be the case that the vast majority of workmen are both competent and reasonably priced. These programmes feature only the most disturbing and shocking incidents and are necessarily unrepresentative.

The audience for the first programme in the *from Hell* sequence of series, *Neighbours from Hell*, was 11.5 million in 1997. This is a much larger audience than is conventionally gained for documentary programmes in their more traditional forms. The *from Hell* format has been copied by BBC, and sold by Carlton to America in 1999. By contrast, conventional documentary strands such as *World in Action* and *Panorama* have faced declining audiences and schedule positions later and later in the evening. The generic markers of documentary in its conventional form include the journalistic structuring of stories where events are not only denoted but a 'balanced' selection of expert opinion offers opposing views and different contextual frameworks in which to understand them. Conventional documentary narrative hierarchizes these elements so that a hegemonic discourse is established in which an issue is enfolded by the reliable and responsible discourse of the mediator represented both by the presenter and the television institution. The *from Hell* series and other kinds of quasi-documentary factual programmes focus instead on the dramatic and on barely contextualized actuality. One of the interesting consequences of this is the reduced importance of expertise and the discourse of professionals in making sense of the issues denoted in programmes. A different ideological pattern is being established. The discourses of expert professionals tended to value middle-class virtues of specialist knowledge, rational discourse, reasoned debate and discussion and the solution of problems by institutional means. But new documentary and actuality television formats replace this with something else. Risk, unpredictability and danger are represented as endemic to society, and institutions are represented as impossibly distant and too preoccupied with administrative and bureaucratic issues to deal with these problems. Instead, individuals are expected to monitor their own environments (often by using video technology to gather evidence and record deviance since the police and other authorities are too busy to undertake this themselves) and work out their own balance between accepting crime and nuisance and taking independent action against it. In this ideological framework, nothing is certain, individuals are largely on their own, and the future is viewed pessimistically. The shifts in factual television towards these Reality TV formats both represent and encourage shifts in ideology and the perception and meaning of society where surveillance is carried out by individuals and institutions and by television on behalf of each of them.

The grainy images from closed-circuit television which appear in Reality TV programmes carry powerful political and social connotations. The places where closed-circuit television cameras are installed are often places where their job is to police the poor and those who are suspected of being socially deviant (Palmer 2003: 21–43). Closed-circuit television cameras have become a popular means of controlling public space such as shopping malls and railway stations, in the absence of sufficient police manpower to patrol them. The function of these cameras is to police the boundaries between normal and deviant or criminal behaviour, and sequences shot by closed-circuit television cameras appear in television programmes as evidence of deviance. The very visual style of the footage, grainy, in black-and-white, with still cameras, has come to be associated with the visible evidence of deviant behaviour and the identification of deviant people. Whereas documentary has a history of representing and arguing for those in society who are the least privileged, the most vulnerable to exploitation, and the most marginalized, the use of documentary footage from closed-circuit television in Reality TV programmes has the opposite force. It is used to reinforce marginalization, to deprive those perceived as deviant people of the opportunity to explain and provide context for their actions and to remove their actions from larger social and political contexts. It also generates anxiety for the audience and potentially exaggerates social divisions. The television audience are placed in the position of the norm from which deviance departs, and may be encouraged to stigmatize and fear those who appear in the programmes only as the perpetrators of disturbing crimes. In the case of *Nannies from Hell*, for example, the mothers employing nannies who were secretly shot verbally and physically abusing young children vowed to stay at home and care for their own children thus also lending weight to conservative definitions of femininity and motherhood. The ideological action of the programme may have been to imply that mothers who work outside the home are both irresponsible and unnatural.

Reality TV is appropriate to a society that is increasingly under surveillance. One effect of this is to separate the scene of crime and deviant behaviour from the process of dealing with it by enforcing the law. Unfortunately, having camera footage of crimes does not guarantee that the criminals can be caught nor charges against them proved. The evidence that criminal behaviour has occurred is only a first stage in a long and complex process of investigation and prosecution. So the fact that television cameras can gather such apparently incontrovertible evidence has the effect of reassuring the audience that criminals can be identified, yet it does not automatically lead to the capture of criminals or the prevention of crime (Palmer 2003: 111–27). A second effect of Reality TV images like this is that it accustoms the audience to the fact of being seen and potentially having images of oneself broadcast and judged. At any time, especially in a city, anyone's movements can be captured by the many surveillance cameras in operation. The knowledge of being observed may well affect behaviour, not only in the sense that individuals might be persuaded not to commit a crime, but also leading to reflective self-monitoring so that nothing a person might do could be misunderstood as a threatening or criminal activity. Loitering outside a shop, hanging around with a group of strangely dressed young people or approaching strangers to ask them questions, might all be activities that could be misunderstood either as criminal behaviour itself or at least suspicious behaviour. It is footage of activities like these that often appears on reality television programmes as supporting evidence to show that a particular person had been behaving strangely and it identifies him or her as deviant. Knowing this, often unconsciously, affects the ways people act in public space.

Car crash TV

Reality TV accustoms the audience to perpetual surveillance and self-surveillance and contributes to the installation of ideological norms within each subject. Knowing that everyone is potentially being observed by surveillance cameras and therefore taking care to monitor behaviour so that it conforms to the norms expected in the normative culture represented by Reality TV programme discourse amounts to the internalization of surveillance. The self-monitoring and self-policing of behaviour is a powerful way of disciplining and controlling society and eventually might promise that real policemen and real cameras could become no longer necessary. Each person would discipline and police himself or herself. This concept of internalizing norms of behaviour realizes the theoretical concept of ideology as a taken for granted set of norms and assumptions which determines how the subject thinks of himself or herself, his or her relations to others and his or her place in society. There is a danger of a rush to judgment in Reality TV programmes using surveillance footage, and the moment of seeing is simultaneously a moment of judging. The pleasure for the audience is in seeing something hidden, seeing the very moment when something shocking and disturbing is happening, and the provision of this pleasure takes much greater precedence than the investigation and exploration of the behaviour which is portrayed.

The ITV series *Police, Camera, Action* is a factual programme which has connections with both news and police drama. It consists of a collection of extracts from police camera footage linked by the narrating voice of Alastair Stewart. Stewart is a former newsreader, and the programme gains some of its connotations of public service by his association with the values of objectivity, seriousness and reliability which derive from television news programmes. The footage in the programme comprises mainly shots from the cameras installed in police cars, as they follow or chase drivers who are either engaged in criminal activities (such as making a getaway from a robbery) or are committing dangerous driving errors. The rhetoric of this Reality TV form is to present the efficacy of policing, especially through its use of surveillance technology like the cameras installed in police cars and helicopters, as a demonstration of the recuperation of disorder into order. This reassurance is achieved not only through the content of the programme but also by its very structuration as a sequence of mini-narratives orchestrated by its voice-over (Palmer 2003: 43–69).

Programmes using police camera footage sometimes also include closed-circuit television pictures from shops or other premises and footage from police helicopter cameras used to track suspects who are being pursued. The car chase is of course a conventional element of the police drama series, especially American action police drama, where the chase normally occurs in the third quarter of the drama as a prelude to the capture of the criminal. Car-chase sequences in *Police, Camera, Action* do not have the several camera set-ups available to drama programmes, nor the reverse shots showing the drivers of the police car, nor of course shots representing the drivers inside their own cars who are being pursued. The visual quality of the police camera footage is less polished than professional television pictures and there is little alternation between points of view or manipulation of narrative time. But despite these important differences between this police camera footage and television narrative fiction, the function of the chase is still as an action sequence as a prelude to the capture of an offender. Dramatic music is used to underscore this excitement and anticipation, and the voice-over narration by Alastair Stewart adopts a point of view which mediates between the pursuing police's commentary and the anticipated reactions of a normative viewer. Stewart points out the stupidity of errors made by drivers, the recklessness of criminals attempting to escape from a chasing police car, the danger posed to other road users by these drivers and the damage and danger caused to the public by them. Since it is customary for police pursuit drivers to give a running commentary on their actions as they pursue an offender, there is also a diegetic soundtrack running alongside the pictures which helps to explain the action and provides Stewart's narration with a means of access to the police understanding of events. *Police, Camera, Action* draws connotations of public service and authority from news, it draws music, the narrative functions of the car chase and pursuit from the police drama series and the visual conventions of the surveillance camera and found actuality footage from documentary. It is a hybrid composed from the codes of several different television genres. As earlier chapters have shown, genre is a way of drawing boundaries between one kind of programme and another, but the television industry's perpetual search for new combinations of generic elements and the audience's skill in reading genre in complex ways mean that genre boundaries are always being redrawn by viewers and programme makers. Car crash TV and the programmes in Britain and the United States that have relied on footage from emergency services in various ways add to the argument that public space as an arena of risk and contingency requires surveillance at the same time as surveillance does not fulfil the deterrent function that has been claimed for it.

Case Study: witnessing and helping in *Crimewatch UK*

Since the late nineteenth century, photography has been used for collecting criminal evidence, and to record scenes of crime. *Crimewatch* has been broadcast once a month on BBC1 in mid-evening since 1984, and is structured by the witnessing of crime and its reconstruction for the purpose of controlling criminality. In an article on *Crimewatch*, John Sears (1995: 51) discusses how the programme performs 'a social function by helping to solve crime, and drawing on the collective responsibilities, experiences and knowledge of the viewing audience in order to do so'. The aim is to engage with the audience's understanding and experience of crime in their own lives (like witnessing crime, being a victim of crime, experiencing policing or helping to uphold the law).

Crimewatch has a public service function in informing the audience, including the audience in helping to purge crime from society and includes the viewer in a community constructed though the programme discourse in which criminals are other to, or outside of, the community and disrupt it (Palmer 2003: 70–91). The realist aims of *Crimewatch* are based on its denotation of crimes, their victims, evidence about them and policemen, for example, and the viewer's invitation to accept the veracity of its textual world is crucial to the success of the consequent invitation to phone in with information, leading to the audience's connection with the programme, and engagement in a consensual understanding of the realities which are denoted (Jermyn 2004).

Crimewatch often features crimes that have been reported already in television news and newspapers, so the connotations of realism from the news media are carried over into the *Crimewatch* coverage of them, relaying meanings from one medium to another intertextually. The music of *Crimewatch* is brassy and military, sharing connotations with both news and action drama such as *Casualty*. The programme seeks to represent the actuality of crimes by reconstructing them, thus blending the fictionalization associated with entertainment with the uses of dramatization in docudrama. *Crimewatch's* aim to achieve change in the real world by solving crimes involves becoming highly fictionalized, by dramatizing events, emphasizing particular details, sometimes shocking the viewer by reporting violent events and drawing the viewer into the dramatic narrative of how crimes are solved. Involving the audience through drama encourages active audience involvement in solving crimes, and *Crimewatch* has been very successful in assisting police investigations. The realism of *Crimewatch* and its linkage with realities are achieved partly by intertextual borrowings of codes and conventions from other media and other genres of television. Sears argues that *Crimewatch* works by reducing the complexity of its own mixture of codes and conventions, and the complexity of the problems it addresses, to a small number of recognizable and highly coded images and rhetorical devices which can be narrativized in simple ways. This also has the effect of engaging viewer expectations and knowledge derived from other highly coded types of television programme, particularly crime drama and television representations of police procedure. The key status of e-fits (pictures of criminals composed electronically from witnesses' reports), photographs of stolen cars, stills from security camera footage, and physical clues (like weapons or items of clothing) derive from the codes of detective fiction and narratives about solving crimes which revolve around key pieces of evidence. These coded images are metonymic in that the photographs of weapons, cars, clothing and perpetrators are parts of the story of the crime which are associated with each other and which stand in for it. On the other hand, the reconstructions of crimes on *Crimewatch* are metaphors, in that they are parallel to the factual events of the crime but they are fiction. The metaphoric reconstructions substitute for the actual crime and represent it.

The title images used on *Crimewatch* in the 1990s were connected by the signified 'information'. The visual signifiers represented police operating computers, evidence being photographed, police knocking on doors and people telephoning. The fingers telephoning synecdochically represent the dialling hand of a viewer phoning in to the programme, and the police's hands knocking on doors stand for the police as a whole (the 'long arm of the law'). As Sears (1995: 54) points out, 'while the general message of the sequence is one of information-gathering (or, more pertinently, crime-solving) the specific message draws attention to audience participation.' The devices of metonymy and synecdoche are emphasized in the title sequence and connect with the codes used in the rest of the programme. The banks of phone operators seen in the studio connote police procedure and metonymically represent information gathering as a whole. Reports on individual callers' information also metonymically signify all the callers ringing in with information, and the pool of information which has been received. Parts stand for wholes in *Crimewatch*, for example, crucial details will be clues which lead to greater understanding of the crime. This technique of crime-solving by identifying metonymic clues makes intertextual connections with detective fiction, and while elements of the programme are clearly separated out as fact or fiction, *Crimewatch*'s realism sometimes leads to the mixing of the two modes. For example, victims or witnesses sometimes appear in reconstructions playing themselves, since this conforms to the claim of authenticity, rather than contributing by means of interviews inserted into the reconstruction, or appearing as voice-overs during it. The programme has a mixed mode, combining elements of drama and documentary. It uses codes from several genres of television programme, including current affairs, crime drama, documentary and audience-participation programmes. *Crimewatch* is partly live, with live studio presentation including updates on information received from the public who phone into the programme about the crimes featured on it. There is also a live supplementary programme, *Crimewatch Update*, on BBC1 later in the evening which reports progress on solving crimes thanks to the public's help. The effect of *Crimewatch* can be to change the reality which the programme has denoted and which the viewer has experienced, by helping to catch criminals, thus not only forming a mediated public sphere for the representation of crime and policing, but also enacting the change to society that such a public discourse might lead to, though in relatively individualized ways. *Crimewatch* as a surveillance-based Reality TV programme not only disciplines society in the ways that society is represented but also performs that disciplining function.

Like many realist and factually-based programmes, *Crimewatch* has to reduce complex institutional processes (like how policing is carried out) and important relationships between the state, criminality and the public, to smaller-scale personalized relationships. The viewer is asked questions such as 'were you there that day?', 'do you recognize this car?' and 'do you know this man?'. Even though television is a mass medium, broadcast to a collective audience, the viewer is addressed as an individual. It is individual action which is requested from the viewer. The crimes featured on *Crimewatch* are committed by individuals rather than companies or governments, for example, and have emotional and dramatizable effects on their individual victims. Television rarely requests collective action from its viewers and rarely focuses on abstract structural problems like the complex causes of crime. The emphasis on the denotation of particular fragments of actuality in the crime formats of Reality TV, and on narratives of individual experience, militates against representing 'white collar' crimes (like fraud or embezzlement) that concern institutions and are relatively invisible. The result is that society is represented as a collection of separate individuals, rather than groups with common interests and concerns. It is television itself which mediates between viewers and the abstract institutions of the state and the law, connecting viewers to a wider sense of society and community. Television, in a sense, creates community and society by representing that society and linking together its separated individual viewers into a collective audience. The 'reality' of crime for *Crimewatch* is that it is committed by a small group of deviant outsiders against certain unfortunate individuals. The practices of gathering information and solving crimes undertaken by institutions, especially the police force, are not represented either since these are also carried out by collective structures rather than simply by individuals. The consequence of this emphasis on individuation in *Crimewatch*, in common with many other programmes concerned with social problems, is a blindness to the large-scale forces which animate individual action and give it its social meaning. The ways that individual action is determined by factors of social class, economic position and ideologies of gender or race cannot be accommodated in this form of television representation. So the realism of *Crimewatch* uses metonymy to connect the individual viewer into the larger collective television audience, to connect particular individual experiences to a social experience of crime that remains vague and to connect representatives of the law to the unseen institutions of law enforcement. The particular is linked to the general in *Crimewatch* by the form of the programme, through the metonymy that surveys and disciplines microcosmic examples of social space.

Conclusion

Seeing, looking and witnessing are intimately associated with both pleasure and power. In the case of both surveillance video or the images and sound of ordinary people in situations modified for broadcast in Reality TV programmes, the footage changes its meaning once it is put in a broadcast context or has been created so that it can become available for looking at by a television audience. What was private becomes public, or what would be private in ordinary circumstances becomes the focus of public transmission. The fascination of Reality TV programmes derives partly from this contrast between the usually private and intrusive material caught by surveillance or amateur cameras and the very public broadcasting of the material on television. Part of the significance of Reality TV lies in its interaction with existing issues of surveillance and the testing of identity that are found in television but also more broadly in public debate about webcams, police video and the monitoring of public space. Spatial containment or imprisonment are used as concrete demonstrations of the separation of people from each other or the enforced communication between them, as well as simple restriction and control. The imperative for the participants in Reality TV is to find a way of living in the space in which they are found or deliberately placed, so that their attempts to do so can be witnessed by the camera on behalf of the audience. But going along with the despairing isolation between people which this recognizes and responds to, is the sense that all social space is potentially imprisoning.

This contrasts strongly with the freedom to wander in public space and to look at people and objects that writers about the modern city proclaimed in the early twentieth century. The wandering male gazer, the flâneur, could walk the streets of Paris and admire beautiful women and the objects displayed in the newly invented department stores. The freedom of moving in physical space was paralleled by the freedom to look at, and, in a sense, take possession of people and things by gazing distractedly at them. Whereas this kind of pleasure and possession had hitherto been available only to the few, the invention of the mass media, and especially television, brought the ability to enjoy sights and the apparent possession of them through gazing at them, to a mass audience. What happens in modernity, Bauman (1993: 173) argues, is that European capitalism modifies its utopian sense of what the future may bring from one where state institutions will deliver utopia, to one where utopia is privatized into individual consumption, transferring the flâneur's pleasure in modern urban consumerism to everyone in society: 'The right to look gratuitously was to be the *flâneur*'s, tomorrow's customer's reward.' Whereas the flâneur is a figure whose pleasure is contingent on a specificity of time and place, media culture is preoccupied with the construction of systems of media spectatorship and consumption which will deliver the same mobile pleasures of looking to each citizen. With Reality TV, this ability to look, to enjoy the activity of looking, and to weigh the qualities of people and things is made available in a different way. There is still a utopian principle of being able to see everything, and have everything brought into proximity to the one who looks through the technologies of seeing that do the looking on the viewer's behalf. But along with this pleasure comes the disciplining of the things, places and people that can be seen. Gazing easily turns into surveillance, where the power to look turns into an apparent but not always real power to control. Reality TV, inasmuch as it draws on and remodulates surveillance as well the pleasure of appropriation though looking, is a politically ambivalent form.

6
Big Brother Culture

Introduction

In academic studies of television, there has been a shift in the ways audiences are understood. The tradition of mass communications research regarded the audience as a statistical abstraction or a complex market open to manipulation by the forces of regulation, advertising or scheduling. More recently, researchers have been interested in the particularity of audiences in smaller-scale groupings, whether selected by locality, gender, age-group or social class. Similarly, the understanding of the viewer as a textually produced construct hollowed out by the structures of the television programme has been replaced by a more fluid notion of the dynamic interchange between the particular viewer and the flow of television, with attention also to the more diffuse social uses of television, in social talk and cultural processes of self-definition. Uses and gratifications research has described the uses and pleasures which audiences derive from media and genres within a medium, reversing the emphasis in research attempting to determine the effects of media on attitudes and behaviour, by asking how and why people act on and use media. Audiences are considered as active appropriators of meaning, rather than passive recipients of it. In this perspective, research focuses on how television is used instrumentally as an information source, as an entertainment, as a resource for constructing self-identity and/or group identity, and as a way of experiencing social interaction virtually or remotely. However this approach may neglect the specificity of the media text and its particular content, because it emphasizes the different uses and gratifications sought and obtained and their meanings for viewers, thus potentially relegating programmes to the status of cues or resources that prompt these audience responses.

This chapter explores how some of these different strands of work on audiences might address Reality TV, focusing mainly on approaches deriving from the British cultural studies tradition which seeks to find out how audiences make meaning from media texts in a social context. Such a methodology keeps hold of the interest in ideology and the critique of media powers which has marked British studies of media communication since the 1970s, but also stresses the positivity of resistant and particular audience activity, and the pleasures derived from the media by viewers (Morley 1980, 1992). This approach, adopted in studies of television audiences for British and US programmes in the 1980s, has been complemented by more recent studies focusing on audiences outside the US–UK axis. The increasing interest in the specificity of viewer response continues into ethnographic studies, seen by some as a weak form of anthropological ethnography, since it relies on small samples and anecdotal evidence (Lull 1988). The methodological problems of this work revolve around its generalizability, since qualitiative audience studies have to devise the criteria for selecting some data about media, audiences and contexts, while leaving out most of the potential data. Ethnographic research faces a problem of determining what evidence is not relevant. The celebration of the active audience associated with the work of John Fiske (1987, 1994) and with work on fan culture has been critiqued for its lack of empirical evidence, and for its lack of specification of how audience resistance to the apparently preferred meanings of programmes relates to a broader context of political action (Morris 1988), though it was a necessary moment in the emergence of a discourse which could challenge textual interpretive research.

This chapter discusses the media contexts surrounding *Big Brother*, and the culture of 'TV talk' that viewers participated in. Part of this discussion will involve work on the significance of 'new media' such as the Web in this process, and its connections with the predominant audience sectors watching *Big Brother*. Media audiences are regarded as both active and specific either as individuals or temporary subcultures, rather than as spectators passively positioned by textual structures or aggregated as masses by institutional structures or technological apparatuses. *Big Brother* has been the Reality TV series that, in the UK especially, has been most affected by the use of new interactive technologies by its viewers. The cross-media phenomenon of *Big Brother* exemplifies the changing social position of television, and talk about television, in contemporary culture. In this respect, it demonstrates how new directions in television may develop in the twenty-first century as the experience of watching television becomes only one part of a broader interaction with media. While interactive websites, phone services, texting and email were initially seen as supplementary media forms attached to pre-existing television programmes, in *Big Brother* it can be argued that the programme shifts from being the centre of a media ensemble to being one component in a wider mediascape whose title becomes a familiar brand.

Cross-platform and intermedial texts

The issue of audience interaction and spin-off and secondary texts can be illuminated by discussion of the concept of paratextuality, a concept developed by Gérard Genette (1982) which refers to the relationship between what is normally thought of as a text and the paratextual apparatus such as its title, preface, illustrations or footnotes. Paratextuality focuses attention on the boundaries between the text and what is normally considered to be outside it or supplementary to it. This paratextual material is on the margins of the text, and appears to be an additional supplement to it, but because of this, it leads to the notion that the text is itself incomplete because it requires this supplementary material. On one hand, paratexts are regarded as inferior because of their marginal status, added to the text and unnecessary to its essential meaning. But although these paratexts seem to be marginal and relatively unimportant compared to the main text itself, they also have the status of completing and framing devices that shape the text or elements of it by providing further information. While the main body of the text is considered to be a whole, the power of paratextual material is to confer a greater, prior or subsequent wholeness that renders the conventional text incomplete. Thus paratextuality raises the question of textual propriety and the issue of what is central and marginal. An attention to paratextual material makes the text seem incomplete, whereas an attention to the conventional whole text itself makes the paratext seem secondary and supplementary. Text and paratext cancel out each other's claims to unity and closure.

However, in the case of *Big Brother*, the relationship between the programme and its website is no longer one of an 'original' text and a supplement that enhances the programme or perpetuates audience interest in it beyond transmission. The two are integrated, planned at the same time and interdependent. This makes *Big Brother* an important facet and example of convergence in media culture. The interactive services associated with *Big Brother* were created by the Victoria Real agency. Endemol owned a 50 per cent stake in the agency and bought it outright in 2003 (Gibson 2003). *Big Brother* is sponsored by the telephone company 02, which offers text updates and seeks to associate itself with the programme and enhance the value of its own brand. The new media community expects that convergence between media will not mean that programmes are made for broadcasting by Internet, but that convergence will provide vehicles for consumers to flow between media such as the Internet, mobile telephones and television. Programme brands will be able to perpetuate their life beyond the run of an individual series, by encouraging their audiences to interact with programmes after they have finished, and also draw audiences to programmes when they begin since those programmes will already have a presence in other media.

For the 2004 series of *Big Brother*, Channel 4 changed its offerings on the Internet to give greater priority to interactive services. In 2003, interest from Internet users dropped by half after the first week of screening, but in 2004 hits on the *Big Brother* site placed the programme second only to the BBC's weather information pages (Clapperton 2004). The managers in charge of interactivity at the production company Endemol speculated that the revival in the use of interaction was a result of the casting of *Big Brother* where more conflict and more titillation was on offer. For the first time, the 2004 version of the website carried content that could only be seen there and had to be paid for by users. The content included behind the scenes documentaries and extended footage. The free streaming of coverage that marked the first series of *Big Brother* was no longer available. With its access to the families and friends of the contestants, the official website was able to present webchats and brief written reports that could extend the information available to users. The material on the programme site aimed also to divert its users to other services offered by Channel 4, such as its pages on cars and property.

Audience composition and modes of address

The audience composition of Reality TV viewers is markedly different from the family audience imagined previously by both television institutions and theorists of television. In the 1980s, Jane Feuer (1986) argued that television programmes are based on an opposition between the inside of the family and the outside of the family. Social and individual situations refer back to the family as a structure where problems and tensions are assumed to be solvable. Feuer argues that television ideologically positions its subjects, assuming that the audience is a family group with constructed gender and family roles that are reinforced by television programmes. Television's ideological effect is therefore to reinforce and contain the family values on which capitalism is based. Inasmuch as television audiences are regarded as domestic and members of a family, television is also a feminized medium in that it adopts this domestic tone and form. What Reality TV programmes have achieved, however, is to find a mode of address that includes the audience in a viewer community that is not familial (like a family) at the same time as it adopts a very familiar (informal) register.

The discourse of narration in Reality TV moves interestingly between poles of formality and informality. Conventional documentary narration is presented in well-formed sentences, using standard English. Voices speak in a calm and measured manner, adopting the literate codes of journalism in quality newspapers and the class authority of official documents and reports. In Reality TV, voice over adopts different variations which blend these conventional expectations with demotic forms and produce a compromise discourse. The narration of *Big Brother* is delivered in a Newcastle accent, thus connecting it to representations of the popular and the ordinary, in that it is distanced from the received pronunciation of Southern English which has connotations of institutional authority and middle class expertise. However, by contrast, the sentences spoken by the narrator are grammatically complete and correct, normally adopting the form of the statement, like: 'All the housemates are in the garden, discussing how to complete the task'. There is little slang, few broken sentences, few prominent adjectives or metaphors, and a consistent and measured tone of voice. The delivery of the narration balances the sobriety and coolness of conventional documentary narration with regional specificity that marks itself as different from documentary conventions.

The delivery in *I'm a Celebrity* pushes this balance more towards the ordinary and further away from documentary convention. Because it is coded as a conversational mode in which Ant and Dec exchange apparently unscripted comments as well as presenting the viewer with information, there is a much greater presence of slang, metaphor and adjectival colour. Much of the linking material in *I'm a Celebrity*, especially at the opening and closing moments in the segments of the programme, consists of direct appeals to the viewer by Ant and Dec to phone in and vote. The personal address has three functions. First, voting by telephone to eject a celebrity or to keep them in the programme is important for generating income. A proportion of the cost of telephone calls goes to the programme producers. The second reason is simply to encourage audience participation. Viewer loyalty to the programme and the likelihood of watching forthcoming episodes is much increased by the action of voting rather than simply taking the position of a passive viewer. Interactivity is a mechanism for positioning the audience and encouraging involved viewing. The third reason is to provide a direct illustration of the power of the audience over the celebrities. This enacts a power reversal in which the celebrities in the jungle are subject to the whims of the audience, which can make them do something or evict them. The ordinary viewer is able to exercise power over personalities who are more usually seen as part of a removed and bounded world of fame in which audiences have little opportunity to modify their behaviour. This power to create change within the programme has an other side, however. The threat that Ant and Dec repeatedly emphasize is that if individual viewers do not bother to vote then their favourite celebrity may well be evicted by other audience members. So there is also an internal competition among the audience, though one that cannot be directly witnessed but only represented through the on-screen presenters, to direct the programme towards a resolution favoured by the individual viewer.

Audience perceptions of Reality TV

Academic audience research has shown that audiences believe Reality TV is there so that viewers can see for themselves, and gain an unmediated insight into some aspect of life and behaviour (Hill 2002, 2005). However, audiences are cynical about the truth claims of Reality TV programmes, place programmes along a continuum between fact and fiction, and give the greatest respect to what they perceive as the most factual programmes. The BBC's real-life trauma series *999* is regarded as factual, whereas docusoap is seen as more like fiction. Audiences expect less factual information from docusoaps and programmes that they align with fiction, and believe that factual programming that borrows fiction conventions or style contributes less to their social learning. The self-critical attitude that audiences have to their own viewing of Reality TV and to the programmes themselves is informed by public discourses that have stigmatized Reality TV as trash TV, such as the much-publicized complaint by news presenter John Humphrys at the Edinburgh Television Festival in 2004 that Reality TV is vulgar and demeaning to its participants and audiences. The presence of large numbers of Reality TV programmes in the schedules has not increased viewing hours, so audiences evidently do not value Reality TV any more than the programmes that they have replaced. If Reality TV had a special status among audiences, the viewing of Reality TV would be an addition to other viewing time and total viewing hours would increase. So although in the television industry Reality TV is seen as the latest significant trend, the commissioning of such programmes may have more to do with competition over audience share and the branding of channels and audiences, than with a decisive shift in habits of television viewing.

In detailed work on audience perceptions of Reality TV, Annette Hill (2002) used audience research data gathered as part of a project funded by the Economic and Social Research Council, the Independent Television Commission, and Channel 4. She conducted a survey in August 2000 that included over 8000 people, comprising both adults and children, and gathered sample statistics adjusted for age, sex and class variables to match the national population. This audience sampling method is the one used by the broadcasters' own organization that gathers ratings and data about viewers' preferences, the Broadcasters Audience Research Board. Further detail about audience reactions to factual television came from focus group discussions. Hill found that *Big Brother* belongs to one of the least popular factual television formats, which she described as 'documentary as diversion', meaning a kind of factual documentary programme that offers itself as entertainment. But by contrast, *Big Brother* was also perceived as one of the most popular examples of the 'gamedoc': 'Viewers prefer informative, behind the scenes factual entertainment, preferably concerning law and order, or homes and gardens, and are skeptical of the more "performative" entertainment programs about real people. Thus, in the factual programming market, BB is not an all-round entertainer, but rather an extraordinary "media event" whose life span may be short-lived' (Hill 2002: 324). As subsequent series of *Big Brother* and a raft of other Reality TV formats have shown, its status as an event remains significant, but its distinctiveness as an event has diminished. Clearly, this makes Hill's detailed conclusions about why audiences choose to watch *Big Brother* more important than simply as a commentary on the first series of the programme.

The appeal of *Big Brother* was found to rest on two factors. Viewers watched it because everyone else was watching it and it enabled them to join social groups and conversations, especially among young people or when older adults wished to connect with younger adults and children. Second, the content that audiences most prized was the moment of revelation of the self: 'audiences look for the moment of authenticity when real people are "really" themselves in an unreal environment' (Hill 2002: 324). Many respondents mentioned 'Nasty' Nick and Mel in *Big Brother* series 1 in relation to this, and especially the moment when Nick cried when confronted by the fact that he had been cheating. But different categories of viewers interpreted the signs of performance versus authenticity differently: 'Young boys thought no adult would cry on camera unless they were genuinely upset, while some more cynical adults believed that crying to camera was a clear sign of performance. Thus, viewers judge the moment of authenticity in a gamedoc such as BB by referring to their knowledge of the contestants coupled with knowledge of themselves, and how they would react in a similar situation.' (Hill 2002: 335). Hill suggests briefly that viewers are probably drawing on their understanding of 'emotional realism' in soap operas (Ang 1989) and how the actions of fictional characters are regarded both within the context of the form and genre of a programme and also in relation to the experiences of the viewers themselves.

She also notes that the saturation of factual entertainment and viewers' distrust of its artifice may mean that viewers are sceptical in their evaluation of authenticity. Hill asked the sample whether they trusted the veracity of factual programmes that included factual reconstruction. Over 70 per cent of the sample distrusted the programmes, thinking that stories were either exaggerated or made up (Hill 2002: 328). Of the sample 45 per cent were not sure whether they could tell the difference between a real story being filmed and a recreation specially for a programme. Seventy per cent of the sample thought people acted up for the camera (Hill 2002: 328–9). She points out that most viewers of factual entertainment do not watch traditional observational documentary, so they are unfamiliar with how *Big Brother* might represent a slippage from, or betrayal of, a former mode of factual television. So it is probably not the case that viewers think the contestants are performers because they do not match up with some kind of authentic representation of ordinary people in another part of the factual television landscape: 'Audience attraction to judging levels of authenticity in BB is primarily based on whether contestants stay true to themselves, rather than whether the program is truthful in its depiction of contestants' (Hill 2002: 336). Furthermore, Hill suggests briefly that an important attraction of *Big Brother* is that it is about the transformation of the self, and how contestants manage themselves and improve their self-knowledge. They often talked in these terms about the experience of being on the show as one of self-improvement, whether they are winners or losers, and for losers they can claim they have got something out of it for themselves personally on this level. So *Big Brother* is a privileged example of the general pervasiveness of makeovers and self-improvement formats in factual television.

Hill adopts the terms 'use value' and 'exchange value' to mean respectively the programme's use value for audiences, describing what gratifications they get out of the programme, and its exchange value as the economic and institutional value of programmes to their makers and broadcasters. Statistical information about audience size and composition demonstrates the exchange value whereby television institutions gain advertising and sponsorship revenue on the basis of who is watching, while audience members' comments to Hill about their enjoyment relate to *Big Brother*'s use value as a resource for audiences to gain pleasure and information. Factual entertainment was watched at least occasionally by 72 per cent of children aged 4–15, 80 per cent of children aged 10–15, and by 70 per cent of adults (Hill 2002: 327). Hill divided factual entertainment into the three most popular programme types: 'police/crime programs' like ITV's *Police, Camera, Action* which were watched occasionally or regularly by 72 per cent of adults and 71 per cent of children, then ' "places" programs' like BBC's *Airport* that were watched by 71 per cent of adults and 75 per cent of children, and finally 'home/garden shows' like the BBC's *Changing Rooms* which were watched by 67 per cent of adults and 84 per cent of children.

Hill produced three further categories of factual entertainment, which she separated according to how much they are staged or designed, as opposed to how much they conform to the observational mode of conventional television documentary. The three categories were 'observation' programmes where ordinary people are followed around in ordinary places (like *Airport*); 'information' programmes where true stories illustrate an argument or provide information about something deemed to be of interest like learning to drive, first aid or pets (like *Animal Hospital*); and finally 'created for TV' programmes like *Big Brother* where people are put in a specially created situation. The respondents said that the programmes they liked most were observation and information programmes, at 67 per cent and 64 per cent of the sample, with created for TV programmes preferred by only 28 percent of those questioned (Hill 2002: 328). But very significantly, the preference figures among younger viewers were much higher for 'created for TV' programmes: 48 per cent of 16–24 year olds and 69 per cent of 13–15 year olds said they liked this kind of factual entertainment (Hill 2002: 328). Although Hill points out that the aspect of factual programmes that people liked most was 'information' and least liked was 'intrusive cameras' these aspects scored similarly. In Hill's sample 30 per cent of the males watched 'real people programs' like *Big Brother* either regularly or occasionally, as did 48 per cent of females. She notes that: 'occasional viewers ... were more likely to watch factual entertainment about real people if the viewers were female, sixteen to thirty-four years old, ABC1 social grade, college or university students, with children in the household, and with access to the internet' (Hill 2002: 328). So although *Big Brother* might not be appealing to the whole of the potential television audience since a majority of viewers preferred observational programmes, it does appeal to Channel 4's target audience of young upwardly-mobile people, with an emphasis on women.

The viewing of *Big Brother* was significantly different across the run of the first series. During August 2000, 30 per cent of the UK population watched it at least once, and although this is a high figure it is not nearly as high as the 67 per cent of the population who watched at least once during the series (Hill 2002: 330–1). It is very likely that many occasional viewers only watched near the end of the series in September, when the narrative drama of who would win, the massive media profile of the series during the summer, and the degree of social talk about the programme had all arrived at a peak. The spread and composition of the *Big Brother* audience was very similar to Hill's figures for 'created for TV' programmes in general. It was twice as likely that 16–34-year-olds rather than older viewers would watch it. Adults were twice as likely to watch if they had children in their households, so adults watched with their children, who were on school holidays at the time.

This focus on younger viewers requires an explanation of the traditions in television studies that have discussed youth audiences and valued their resistant attitudes to programmes. The movement from a model of the audience as a collective resistant subject to a more nuanced and problematic object of research can be seen in the development of work on youth subcultures in British Cultural Studies over the last 30 years. This research takes its bearings from the work of the Birmingham Centre for Contemporary Cultural Studies, and in particular the books written in the 1970s by Stuart Hall and Tony Jefferson (1976), Paul Willis (1977), and Dick Hebdige (1979). Their emphasis on class as a determinant of different modes of youth experience challenged earlier accounts of youth culture as largely univalent, and showed that youth subcultures existed in relation to parental class-inflected culture. Thus youth subcultures, especially those of the working class, were seen as spaces of resistance to dominant culture where the evidence for resistance was found in attitudes to schooling, and in codes of taste, behaviour and appearance. The valuation of these subcultures as actively produced (as opposed to passively reproduced dominant commercial culture), authentic (rather than imposed by the culture industries), and resistant (rather than conforming to the dominant ideology), forms the basis of the positive value given to the same traits in studies of a whole range of cultural practices. But youth subcultures were regarded in masculine terms, and the dominant which they opposed was discursively constructed as feminine. The resistance which the researchers had discerned at one level could be characterized as complicit at another level with conventional patterns of gender power. The attention to gender which feminist concerns brought to this issue had the effect of bringing the agency of young women to the fore, so that resistance would then appear progressive in its gendering as well as being both active and authentic. Angela McRobbie (1994) showed how girls negotiate their own feminine identities, under the constraints of family duties and behavioural controls which affect them more than boys. Girls, she argued, continued or challenged preexisting models of teenage girlhood, in collusion with or in opposition to a sense of their future roles as wives and mothers. This process of negotiation was conducted by using and remodelling mass-produced commercial cultural products, thus refusing the characterization of mass media culture as univalent by showing how its resources were adapted for resistant activity.

The viewers of *Big Brother* may not have been the same people as the visitors to the programme website. Hill found that although 50 per cent of 16–24-year-olds have access to the Internet, 82 per cent said that they did not access websites connected to factual entertainment programmes (Hill 2002: 332); they watched the first *Big Brother* series so they could join in with conversations about the programme. Hill asked about this in the focus groups, and the reasons for not accessing websites were that people found them too difficult to download (perhaps because of the slow and unreliable dial-up connections common in the UK at the time). This problem has been resolved to some extent by E4 streaming live footage of *Big Brother* in the second series, allowing interaction via the digital TV handset at the same time as watching the programme. Hill asked adults which aspects of *Big Brother* they liked the most, and Internet interaction scored very low. The top four aspects were: seeing people live without modern comforts; watching group conflict; seeing contestants visit the Diary Room; and seeing people do tasks set by the programme-makers and viewers. The least liked aspects of *Big Brother* were: watching people do private things; media coverage of the programme; visiting the website; and talking about the programme in chat rooms (Hill 2002: 332). These preferences are predicated on watching the programme and talking about it before the broadcast, during and after it. People wanted to experience the *Big Brother* media event at first hand themselves, often with others, rather than reading about it or interacting with it. However, Hill correctly predicted more preference for interaction when, from series two onwards, E4 enabled interaction more easily by using live digital TV coverage.

Television institutions and Reality TV audiences

The creation of television programme brands, personalities and gossip have been important for a long time. Once competition between BBC and ITV began in 1955, both channels used popular formats like quiz shows, variety and adventure series to keep their hold on their audiences. In response to ITV's gradual success with these popular television forms, the BBC audience fell, and it responded by increasing its broadcast hours and introducing the first television soap opera *The Grove Family*, resulting in consistently high ratings for the programme and massive press coverage. The increased fragmentation of the television audiences resulting from the current five terrestrial channels and dozens of digital ones means that broadcasters are even keener to anchor schedules and capture audiences with must-see programmes. The threatened effect on current ways of organizing television is that it would cease to consist of must-see programmes when mass audiences view the same live broadcast at the same time, except perhaps in rare times of crisis such as the terrorist attack on the World Trade Center in New York in 2001. The heritage of liveness and the conception of the audience as a mass or series of masses would cease to apply. Live (or nearly-live) shows like *Big Brother* are partly a response to this, to create must-see programmes, or 'event TV'. The consequence is that Channel 4 is keen to make the most of its branded formats like *Big Brother* in the face of increased competition and falling terrestrial audiences. In a newspaper article about Channel 4's financial prospects, Maggie Brown (2004b) reported that the channel expects to lose 20 per cent of its audience by 2012 as the number of channel increases and grabs some of its audience and advertising revenue. Text messaging and interactive services brought in the relatively small amount of £2 million in 2004, including *Big Brother*. In 2004 Channel 4 had a 13 per cent share of terrestrial viewing, an 11 per cent share in Freeview homes and a 6 per cent share in Sky homes. It expected its share to fall to 8 per cent when terrestrial is switched off. In this context, maximizing the revenue from interactive services associated with programmes, and especially strong brands like *Big Brother*, may be crucial to the channel's continuing health.

Having a valuable and successful programme brand like *Big Brother* is also important because it is perceived as British and it compensates for the problems emerging in scheduling the US programmes that hitherto gave Channel 4 big audiences. In a newspaper article about US programmes in the Channel 4 schedule, Jason Deans (2004b) reported that the scheduling of *The West Wing* at 7.35 on Friday evenings against the ITV soap opera *Coronation Street* suggested Channel 4 had decided it would not be a mass-audience hit, and the channel shifted US HBO imports *Six Feet Under* and *The Sopranos* to slots at 11 pm or later because they had not drawn big audiences at 10 pm. Channel 4 banked on *The Simpsons*, poached from BBC2 at great expense, to draw audiences in its 9.00 pm Friday slot, with repeats at 6.00 pm stripped across other weekday evenings in the same slot it had on BBC2.

Like *Big Brother* for Channel 4, Reality TV gamedoc formats have been crucial to gaining large audiences for terrestrial channels seeking to attract younger viewers. The audience of BBC1's *Pop Idol* peaked at 13.1 million viewers, with a 56 per cent share of the audience, and 8.7 million viewers voted on the final night when Will Young beat Gareth Gates (Hughes 2002: 38). *Popstars* began its second series on ITV1 on Saturday 7 September 2002. The first series (beginning in January 2001) produced the pop bands Hear'Say and Liberty X, and had an initial audience of 7 million and a peak audience of 12 million (Cassy 2002: 7). The second series was titled *Popstars: The Rivals* and involved a boy band and a girl band competing to get a Christmas number one single, releasing one record each. *Popstars: The Rivals* began with 10,000 hopeful contestants being reduced to 10 male and 10 female contestants, reduced again by viewer voting to a girl band and a boy band of five members each. The series was produced by Granada, whose income derived partly from a share of the phone calls, the records, music tours and merchandizing. In *Big Brother* series three, 6 million people voted for the evictions using their remote controls, generating 25 per cent of the total £20 million that Channel 4 gained from the programme.

Television talk and gossip

Big Brother unexpectedly became an integral part of many people's conversation, and viewer involvement was not only with the programme and the website but also with the commentary on the programme among other viewers and in the media. Gossip was an important pleasure for viewers of *Big Brother*, and it became a ready-made topic for conversation about people who viewers felt they knew. The production of viewer talk is encouraged and mirrored by talk in Reality TV programmes themselves. Television programmes are dominated much more than cinema, for example, by people talking and interacting in familiar situations, just as life for viewers at home is often centred on these activities. *Big Brother* consists largely of sequences of conversation between the participants, representing familiar interaction and conversation which could then be talked about by viewers. The frequent use of close-up shots of faces in *Big Brother*, and on television in general, reinforces this sense of intimacy between the viewer and what is shown on television, and contributes to a perception of equivalence between the audience's ordinary world and the constructed worlds of the format. This way of using and experiencing television gives the illusion of physical closeness, and invokes rules of social interaction which demand attention and create social proximity. Soap opera has been discussed in these terms for a long time, and as Chapter 4 has shown, press coverage of *Big Brother* built up a selection of character-types, and the producers' selection of outgoing and dominant contestants provoked dramatic conflict and performance comparable to soap opera fiction.

Some of the social circumstances surrounding television viewing support television involvement like this. The television set is usually placed in the familiar domestic space of the home. It is physically embedded in audiences' domestic routines, which decreases the sense that activity on television is 'other'. The private space of the *Big Brother* house becomes public (even more so on the Internet, where real time footage is screened), promising access to private space and the opportunity of interaction by phone-in voting. Media use is strongly influenced by habits and routines, since cultural commodities are not used in a vacuum, but in the context of other forms of appropriation and use which form the fabric of everyday life. New developments in technology are more likely to be adopted when they enhance a service that already exists, or offer services that are linked to an established brand or property. When Channel 4 planned its second series of *Big Brother* in 2001, it introduced interactive services accessible through its digital television channel E4, as well as on the Internet. Since the programme already had an established brand identity, and viewers of the first series had already been able to interact with the programme, Channel 4 was able to enhance the second series in ways that audiences already understood.

Big Brother has a large audience among the 18–34 audience, and this group is more likely than others to have access to interactive television and the Internet. Viewers are able to take part in interactive games using their remote control handsets, and can also vote for the exclusion of contestants, take part in quizzes and gain access to additional information and video coverage. *Big Brother 2* had numerous benefits for Channel 4 in attracting and maintaining a valuable youth audience, stimulating the use of and demand for digital interactive services, and promoting the brand identity of a programme closely identified with the channel. The establishment of brand identity can also be assisted by the production of tie-in products such as books, videos and DVDs, and merchandize such as tee-shirts. Commercial broadcasters are permitted to advertise programme-related products like books, CDs or videos, though only briefly, factually and at the end of programmes. Significantly, however, the ITC Programme Code (2002) reminds producers that, 'The unacceptability of a promotion of a product or service within programme time does not prevent the use of paid for advertising as an alternative, including advertising carried on interactive programme enhancements.' Products produced by third parties can be advertised on programme websites or in paid commercials inserted between programme segments. The sponsorship of programmes by third parties is of course permitted, and many Reality TV programmes (including *Big Brother*) have been sponsored in this way, indicated by short on-screen segments preceding the opening titles of the programme and more briefly as introductory segments before the programme resumes after a commercial break. Programme-related websites must predominantly concern the programme itself, rather than being used as locations for advertising of programme-related products or products offered by third parties, and broadcasters are responsible for maintaining websites like these and the interactive services that they often contain. But the use of tie-ins, products and advertising in programme websites are a further attraction for programme-makers in investing in Reality TV formats if they seem likely to be popular and thus commercially lucrative. While Reality TV programmes are not significantly different in principle from any other programme in their usefulness in income generation and the creation of public profile for products, broadcasters or programme brands themselves, they do have a special relationship to commercial culture and its connection with audience cultures. This is because of the shared emphasis on commodification as a cultural process that exists between consumer culture in general and the commodification of identity and personality in Reality TV. Since Reality TV is itself part of celebrity culture, it is especially open to the transfer of brand values, ideologies and the reciprocity of meanings between programmes and audiences. As Marx argued, in a commodity culture people become understood as things, and things are given life.

For the production companies of Reality TV programmes, such as Endemol, *Big Brother* is not a television programme. For the producers, television is not about creating the identity of a programme or even a channel identity, but creating an audience which identifies with a brand whose value and meaning depend on that audience itself. The branded audience community experience the *Big Brother* event in many different ways either simultaneously in time or not. The *Big Brother* audience identifies with itself, in watching what appears to be the same thing either live or recorded or webcast. *Big Brother* suggests that audiences interpret more differently and unpredictably because *Big Brother* is live. The assumption of liveness allows the audience to distinguish moment by moment between an image and a real person supposedly underneath as the authentic self. So in *I'm a Celebrity Get Me Out of Here*, series three, there were moments when Jordan seemed to oscillate between a persona of Jordan or her reality as Cathy Price. *Big Brother* was almost live so that there was an opportunity in the 15 minute delay for the production team to cut material that might be legally dangerous, such as libellous statements, the advertising of product names, or the singing of copyrighted song lyrics, for example. But it is these trappings of contemporary life, that have to do with the circulation of public information and gossip, branded clothes, and identification with musical styles and subcultures identified with products, that create the identities of people today.

The appearance of new media formats seem to proclaim a realignment between the audience and the text, and *Big Brother* has been at the forefront of the exploitation of young audiences' familiarity with technology, such as the Internet and interactive technologies where the users are able to prompt new textual configurations. When interactive users are able to influence and reconfigure texts, this can have the effect of producing a greater sense of authenticity and belief in the liveness of the material. Research by Janet Jones (2004) suggests that these interactive formats reduce the suspicion of the mediation of information by conventional textual means, building on the convergence of new media with the old media, in order to produce a sense of the immediate by drawing on the apparent authenticity of live and interactive material. Authenticity is often produced by the relationship between the live and the mediated, which exist in a dialectical tension and symbiosis. Jones's research on how people remember actuality after experiencing a text through different levels of mediation offered by different media platforms, shows that the first encounter with a textual event creates a frame for subsequent memories of that moment. In *Big Brother*, the media platforms were the broadcast television signal, either live or edited, broadcasting over the Web, broadcasting over interactive television channels, and automatic messaging systems that sent notification of significant events to the user's mobile telephone. Where there is less mediation because of a live broadcasting context such as the E4 channel or a web broadcast, this produces a more detailed memory of a moment than in a more highly mediated form. Audiences for less mediated material show a greater diversity of remembered moments, and more personalized recollection of those moments.

There are significant differences between the technological platforms in which viewers encounter Reality TV programmes that may be broadcast live, broadcast in the form of recorded highlights, streamed over the Web, or disseminated by short messages to mobile phones. The live broadcast on E4 has low mediation in that although there is some editing for taste, decency and legality, it is marked as live despite its 15 minute delay, with a caption 'live' on the screen, and the material itself is visual, audio and graphic. The relatively unmediated live broadcast gives the opportunity for the viewer to actively interpret the material and create meanings for himself or herself. The messages broadcast to mobile phones have comparatively high mediation, since they consist only of short text similar to newspaper headlines, and very brief descriptions of events. The messages are sent within 20 minutes of the occurrence of an event, so despite their high mediation they are close to the temporality of live broadcasting. These messages provide viewers with only a limited set of interpretive possibilities. The input is restricted to the written form of verbal messages. The broadcasts of recorded highlights in the evening Channel 4 schedule exhibit a high degree of mediation, since any event is enfolded in a complex of voice over, editing of visual material, using graphics on the screen and also music. The recorded programmes have much less temporal closeness to the events, since programmes usually refer to events that occurred in the *Big Brother* house in the previous day. Viewers are provided with primarily visual information, which frames events using a very varied range of points of view mixed with information presented in graphical or caption form. These evening broadcasts restrict the opportunities for viewer interpretation, though less so than for mobile-phone messages. This recent work by Jones (2004) suggests that the viewer's emotional engagement is restricted by a high degree of mediation. Overall, the watching of live broadcast appears to present opportunities for interaction with the narrative that are not present in the recorded programmes.

Poaching and fandom

Viewers, and especially fans, 'poach' programmes for their own ends. This throws light on practices of television spectatorship and audience activity, as well as the core narrative images of the programmes that fans rework. There is a distance between the programmes as produced and the ways programmes are 'remade' in various ways by fans. This distance illuminates the tension between the supervision and institutional control of programmes by their makers and the celebratory and critical ways that fans take control over them. The newer technologies of Internet chat and email have offered much greater scope for interaction with television and also viewers' appropriation of its meanings. Interactive culture has been evaluated both as a positive, even utopian realignment of the relations between people which media enable and produce, but it has also been regarded as a perpetuation of politically regressive structures of domination and inequality. What is at stake, therefore, are questions of determination by technologies and by socio-political structures, questions of agency, empowerment and access, and questions of discursive effectivity in shaping the terms in which media culture is understood.

Habermasian notions of the public sphere (see Chapter 3) reappear both explicitly and implicitly in analyses and popularizations of computer-mediated communications, because one of the supposed advantages of this media culture is the possibility of communication at a distance between users of the technology. This communication, assuming that it can take place between rational subjects, can be argued to be the basis of a radically extended democratic and participative culture. However, the actual uses of computer-mediated communication can be much more problematic than this abstract account suggests. For example, as well as through conventional media outlets, the popularity of Reality TV programmes among young and technologically literate viewers has led to advertising by means of subviral marketing. This describes the emailing of photographic images (often manipulated by image editing software) or video clips to colleagues or friends, and is done both by amateurs and also anonymously by PR companies. They can be more potentially offensive than conventional ads and thus potentially have more impact. During the run of *Big Brother* series three, one of these ads showed Jade from the house on one side of the image, and on the right hand side a digital composite showing Jade with the face of Miss Piggy from *The Muppet Show*. Ian Harris (2002) reports: 'Sources claim Endemol pioneered subviral emails over the summer in an effort to keep Big Brother 3 the talk of the office. "Many of the Big Brother stills that came out over the summer – Jabba the Hutt with Jade's face Photoshopped on – were actually done by Endemol or their PR agency," says Jonathan Gabay, marketing consultant and author of several books on cybermarketing. "And why not? They made people laugh, they're were [sic] good fun, and it kept them in our face." ' In this example, computer users seemed to be appropriating *Big Brother* content in an ironic and critical way, though the evident sexism and cruelty of the images referred to by Harris and Gabay should prompt reflection on the assumption that such appropriation is in itself progressive. Furthermore, Gabay's suggestion that Endemol or its public relations agency was behind the emails in the first place demonstrates the duplicity and complicity of the institutions that stand to benefit from the circulation of talk and gossip about Reality TV programmes.

There is a tension between a rhetoric which refers to computer-mediated communication as a community, and the solitariness of the time of the interaction and its dependence on a relation between the user's individual body and the computer itself. Indeed these public and private forms of cultural engagement fold into each other on the basis of their dependency on each other. For participation in a virtual community or computer-mediated environment provides the possibility of separation from bodily surveillance in the 'real' world, precisely in order that a virtual identity can be publicly performed in virtual computer space. It is significant that Mark Lajoie (1996: 85) has described the Internet as a 'spectacular hall of mirrors', for the attraction of a hall of mirrors is to see oneself differently, as a virtual mirror image, but also to allow this distorted image to be seen by others in a public space.

Case Study: *The Osbournes*, celebrity and multi-accentuality

The final case study in this book uses close analysis of the aesthetics of one Reality TV series to develop the ideas about *Big Brother* and other programmes that have been discussed in this chapter. I have chosen to discuss *The Osbournes* because it offers multiple ways for audiences to engage with its format and characters, demonstrating how a single programme can be read multi-accentually (in different ways by different audiences) according to the particular viewer's knowledge and enthusiasms. Produced by the youth-oriented music channel MTV, *The Osbournes* was marketed as a Reality TV sitcom, framed as an ironic take on Reality TV forms that could attract a media-literate audience. In its opening episodes, for example, *The Osbournes* explicitly references the house tour genre represented by *Through the Keyhole* and the MTV programme *Cribs* where a celebrity leads the viewer on a tour of their home. By the time it reached its fifth episode it was MTV's highest rated series ever, with over six million viewers per week (Kompare 2004: 97). The series was first aired on MTV in March 2002, rapidly became a hit, and was then purchased by Channel 4 where it was screened in evening prime-time at 9.00 pm. *The Osbournes* combines the melodrama of soap opera, the actuality footage of documentary, the voyeurism of the celebrity house tour, the drama of competing personalities, and the themes, issues and framing of a sitcom.

The opening sequence of *The Osbournes'* first episode establishes character identities and possible patterns of relationship. The sequence begins with a photographic family portrait, identified as the perfect American family, and reminiscent of the opening or closing shot of a sitcom title sequence, or a fly on the wall documentary such as *The Family* or *An American Family*. It provides a normative image against which the subsequent drama can react, setting up the tension between generic expectations and the confusion of conventions deriving from different historical periods. The family members are sitting together, smiling, looking happy in a posed and very conventional portrait composition. The harmonious qualities of the pictorial composition reinforce the expectations of the audience about family relationships in a stereotypical suburban environment. But immediately, this is contrasted with a shot of Kelly Osbourne shouting and swearing at her brother Jack, throwing something at his groin. Sharon as the mother might be expected to stop the children fighting with each other and to adopt the role of the peacemaker. She does tell them to shut up and go to bed, but her speech is also interrupted by expletives, and she says that she is not Mother Teresa, thus establishing herself as 'other' to the conventional role of caring matriarch. Ozzy steps back from the conventional role as head of the household, saying that he loves them all but they are all mad. He seems overwhelmed by his family. There follows a sequence of shots showing him performing as a rock and roll star, and across the sequence he is established as father and rock star, but not the embodiment of the conventions offered by these roles. In this opening sequence, Jack walks around with a large knife in Army camouflage, suggesting the conventional situation comedy role of the troubled teenager. Similarly, Kelly is established as a rebellious daughter, dyeing her hair, staying out late, and acting in the way which she knows will offend both her parents and adults in general. But Sharon does not respond in a critical way, thus disturbing the patterns of conflict that might be established between generations. The conflict between parents and children, between male and female, and between insiders and outsiders, is established in the series as a base on which unconventional manipulations of these conflicts can be played out, as viewers bring to bear different combinations of generic extra-textual knowledge to make sense of the programme's multiple components.

In the opening credits, each family member is introduced singly, with live action frozen into black and white stills suggesting a typical role. The credits introduce the characters using the word 'starring', drawing attention to the notion of performance and the centrality of performance to sitcom. In the first episode's credit sequence, Ozzy is presented as 'the Dad', counterposing his rock star role with his familial role. Ozzy was the lead singer of the group Black Sabbath in the 1970s, and different audiences will have different levels of knowledge about the programme and its participants that affect their reading of its meanings. At the start of the series, only Ozzy had a public profile, so stressing his role as the Dad and his role as the rock star enables the audience to distinguish their knowledge beyond the text and place it in relation to the roles established by the series. In the credit sequence, moving shots of the family members suddenly freeze into characteristic roles, creating a narrative image that condenses characters visually. They fade to black and white from colour, referencing the documentary conventions of photography and its relationship with newspaper journalism as a factual form. The credit sequence is otherwise very colourful, using greens and reds prominently. The graphic style of the lettering in the titles sequence is self-consciously elaborate and kooky, suggesting the upbeat tone of situation comedy. The lettering and the vignettes framing the characters reference the opening sequences of 1950s American television sitcom and comedy films such as those starring Rock Hudson and Doris Day. The retro style of the programme emphasizes its self-consciousness as television and its generic positioning as entertainment. The textual reading of the credits as referencing sitcom is confirmed by MTV's official website, which proclaims: 'Forget the Bradys. Screw the Cosbys. ... The Osbournes are television's most infamous family, plus they're real and almost too raw for broadcast. Foul mouths, erratic behavior and pets aplenty return for the new season.'

Since the programme takes place in domestic space most of the time, the meanings of stardom are troubled in an interesting way. The audience is invited to witness stars being ordinary, but also to witness the exaggerated performance of ordinariness that these people enact in their apparently normal lives. Celebrity and ordinariness turn into each other. The focus of the programme therefore becomes the pleasure commonly associated with Reality TV of deciding whether these people are acting or being. The opening sequence shows Ozzy performing on stage with his band, but also walking the dogs and watching television. The music accompanying this sequence is one of Ozzy's songs which contains the lyric, 'I'm not the kind of person/You think I am', drawing attention to this contest of roles. These confusions introduced the idea that these are real people who are the self-conscious stars of their own real lives, thus confusing reality and acting with each other. The characters might be either acting or being, and each turns into the other. For example, Kelly sticks out her tongue, connoting the cheeky rebellion of a teenager. An establishing shot locates their house and is followed by a series of tracking shots showing the large and luxurious rooms inside. The brief moving sequences and still images that follow illustrate expectations of family life that derive from the sitcom, with each character finally frozen into a characteristic pose. The family sitcom not only features the most central ideological grouping that bridges private and public, but also ventilates anxieties about gender roles and the power relations within the nuclear family.

In the subsequent episodes, the family talk about drugs, alcohol and sex, and we hear Ozzy warning his children: 'don't get drunk, don't do drugs tonight and if you have sex, wear a condom'. Ozzy's role as a normal father is combined with his role as an example of the dangers about which he warns his children. Ozzy performs characteristic rock star behaviour, most notably in the opening episode pretending to have sex with his dog. His trembling body, slurred speech and slow reactions are the results of his years of abuse. Rock and roll is linked to sex, drugs and rebellion, issues associated particularly with Ozzy but largely contained in the past mythology of his character rather than in his current behaviour during the filming of the series. The baggage attaching to the characters was particularly demonstrated in material form in the first episode as the Osbournes move into a new house. The camera lingers on the removal boxes containing their possessions, whose labels initially denote conventional domestic possessions such as 'Jack's stuff' and 'kitchen things'. But then the camera tilts down the pile of boxes to labels that say 'devil heads' and 'dead things'.

The family sitcom in its traditional form in Britain is familiar to current audiences through the popular BBC sitcom *My Family*, as well as its repeated versions from the 1970s and imported American variations on the format. The dysfunctional nature of the family draws *The Osbournes* away from the optimism about the family displayed in 1950s sitcom and towards later and more cynical variations on the genre such as *Married ... with Children* and *Roseanne* from the 1980s. In the Fox network's *Married ... with Children*, for example, the comic tone is cynical and based on conflict. There are conflicts between the brother and sister (Bud and Kelly), the family and their neighbours, between the regular characters and outsiders, between husband and wife (Al and Peggy), between parents and children. The family relationship is not loving or affectionate, but it relies on the strength of the stereotype of the nuclear family in order for its comedy to be comprehensible. Although Al and Peggy love each other, a running joke in the series is that they no longer have sex. They mock each other and seem to have little sexual attraction. The children treat their parents as a resource for pocket money, and storylines revolve around the manipulation of one generation by another, or one sex by another. There is a restricted repertoire of character positions, in which, for example, the son and the daughter switch between being 'the naughty one' or 'the good one'. Patterns of solidarity and conflict emerge in which loyalties and antagonism switch between genders and generations, or cross the boundary between family members and outsiders.

The Osbournes has to connect with these genre conventions and the expectations of its viewers about television representations of the family in order to be comprehensible. Variations on the family sitcom revolve around conflict between siblings and parents, and also the boundaries that unite the family in distinction to outsiders. There are horizontal relationships between family members of the same generation, vertical relationships between characters of different generations, relationships based on gender. The patterning of relationships produces storylines in the sitcom, and allows for multiple variations of union and conflict. In *Married ... with Children*, for example, the opening sequence shows Al Bundy resigned to the perpetual demands of his wife and children, and even his dog, for money and he is positioned simultaneously as a static figure, occupying the central role in the centre of the screen on the family sofa, but also having no possibility of refusing the responsibilities that he tries to evade. The Bundy family are riven by conflict but periodically come together to demonstrate their unity, especially against outsiders, by doing the Bundy family cheer. In *The Osbournes*, conflict between family members is also put aside in conflict with outsiders. Each of the family members becomes involved in a feud against their neighbours and takes the rivalry to extremes. Sharon, for example, throws a ham into the neighbours' garden, and Jack raises the volume on his powerful stereo system up to maximum to drown out the noise from next door with the consent and aid of his parents. However, the hand-held shooting of *The Osbournes* distances it significantly from sitcom tradition. The format of sitcom is designed for taping in the studio, using three primary camera positions with the performance directed outward from a box set towards a studio audience. Scripts are designed to include short scenes in standing sets, with one-liners and physical, gestural comedy interrupting the narrative frequently to allow for moments of audience laughter. So despite its allusions to sitcom, the visual aesthetic of *The Osbournes* relies on the conventions of observation that suggest veracity.

These conflicts between aesthetic and generic forms support conflicting relationships with the audience. The family are paralleled with their imagined audiences in some of their conventional bickering and role playing, but are distinctly different to the audience's likely self-image in the excess of their behaviour and the lavishness of their possessions. For the audience, the family are offered for identification but also they are there to be made fun of. As Kompare shows (2004: 110), 'Ozzy is most often the subject of comic sequences as he struggles with new technology (a state of the art home theater system) animals (the unruly Osbourne pets) and the rest of the family (trying to restore order during an argument).' The viewer can simultaneously experience aspiration for their wealth and freedom, but also stigmatize them as selfish, ridiculous and eccentric. *The Osbournes* represent an aspirational ideal of living the American dream by achieving wealth and fame through the talent of Ozzy as a rock star, whereas the Bundy family from *Married ... with Children* and the Connor family from *Roseanne* partially critique this idea as an ideological fiction. Jennifer Gillan (2004: 58) argues of *The Osbournes*: 'It tackles the same familiar terrain as the classic sitcom, exploring the same issues (e.g. sibling rivalry), problems (e.g. balance of power between husband and wife), and questions (e.g. what impact will women's entrance into the public sphere have on the private sphere?).' Kelly gets tattooed to the disappointment of her parents, and dyes her hair in shocking colours. Jack comments 'a teenager's brain doesn't wake up until after 10.30'. Sharon is not stereotypical, however, in that she dyes her hair shocking colours too, and is the person responsible for household finances, so that she combines the roles of rebel and homemaker. Finally, however, *The Osbournes* makes an irony of these issues by its focus on the family members as celebrities.

The fact that the series producers have chosen to focus on a family led by an entertainer, whose family members also have celebrity status and burgeoning careers as media personalities, foregrounds the importance of performance in the format and in the behaviour of its characters. The celebrity status of the family members was enhanced by the production of the show itself. Sharon hosted her own talk show, and appeared as a judge on *The X Factor*. Kelly launched a singing career and gained a role in a US television series. Thus *The Osbournes* opens up questions for the audience about possible falsification and fictionalization. As an observational Reality TV programme, *The Osbournes* refuses the assumption that it will observe and document a reality which could exist independently of the making of the series. The family are often placed in constructed situations which would alter their behaviour. Editing of the single camera footage is used to create the meanwhile effect of parallel montage, condensing time and counterposing storylines. In the opening episode, Jack and Kelly appear in a series of short sequences, but their hair changes rapidly as it continues, demonstrating how ellipsis has been introduced. The section titles dividing sequences of the episode are also humorous and often reflexively reference the programme as a fictional construct by alluding to other media texts and the production of television, as in the sequence titles 'Fight Club' or 'Lights, Camera, Ozzy'. Episodes do not address public concerns or make an argument in the manner of conventional documentary. However, across the series, continuing domestic conflicts revolved around Kelly and Jack, but also included Sharon's battle with cancer and Jack's problems with drugs.

The second series focused particularly on these more conventional documentary subjects. The end of the first series took account of critiques of the programme that had emerged during its run. It was criticized for not reflecting an observable reality, and the producers were accused of scripting and rerecording parts of episodes. The response to these criticisms was to produce a bizarre season finale. Jack claimed he had been acting violently in his sleep, so cameras were placed in his bedroom to record him over several nights. One night, he was shot killing Sharon's beloved dog Mimi. Sharon left the house, Jack ran away, Kelly moved out, and Ozzy was left alone. The storyline revolving around Jack was integrated with others developing from previous episodes, such as the saga of Kelly's problems with her boyfriend. The reaction of the family to the dog's death was emotional, and there were few cues for the audience to disbelieve the storyline about Jack's violent murder of the dog. But at the end of the episode, the storyline was revealed to be a construction. There were shots of the production team shouting 'It's a wrap' at the end, and the family, with the dog Mimi, enter the living room at the end of the episode cheering, as they might do in the final closing shot of a sitcom where the family's unity is reinforced. In these closing moments of the episode at the end of season one, a series of takes showed Ozzy repeating the line 'I love you but you're all fucking mad' until he got it right. This line was the one strongly featured in the first episode of the first series, and which was used in many of the trailers advertising the programme. The effect of screening an apparent series of rehearsals for this line undercut the assumption of belief in observational filmmaking throughout the series. In contrast, the second series began with Sharon's discovery that she had cancer, and the reactions of the family to this news. By introducing this 'serious' storyline in series two, the continuing debate about the real or performed quality of the series continued. By focusing on illness, the body, and the intimacy associated with cancer especially, series two continued the complex negotiations in *The Osbournes* with observational documentary and performance comedy.

Conclusion

The confidence to state general principles about media reception, use and effects has increasingly given way to work on particular media involvements and the specifics of agency by media audiences. Audience identity is itself fragmented into a complex of determinations, including class, region, age, gender, race, or occupation, and studies of Reality TV have begun to show that its lack of coherence as a television form is parallel to a lack of homogeneity in who watches it and in what ways. The discourse of media theory has moved from discussing the structural determinants of culture (for example, theories of television as a mechanism for transmitting ideology) to theories of subjective agency (choice, the search for negotiated individual identities, micro-analyses of agency and empowerment). The danger here is that rather than exploring how cultural representations encode and debate ideologies originating in economic and productive relations, the analysis remains at the level of culture alone, comparing and contrasting different representations and cultural expressions at a great distance from their determining factors in terms of production. In other words, media theory can idealize and reify particular aspects of media culture, which are divorced from systematic and structural determinations. This chapter has moved between discussing work on programme texts like *Big Brother* or *The Osbournes* to the media technologies that carry them and the institutions that make and broadcast them, in order to bring these questions together. The effacement of production which the media theory of an earlier generation discerned in media texts, for example the naturalization of cultural relations in television programmes, commercials and films, might reappear at another level. Media theory now emphasizes individual choices and negotiations within culture, with an uncertainty over how these specific choices, actions and beliefs can be related to an understanding of social forces, institutions, and possibilities for change. Reality TV as a heterogeneous form and one that has been merged with media other than television broadcasting is a fertile ground for considering these questions, but as with studies of other television phenomena, there seems little consensus on how to connect descriptive understandings of Reality TV with evaluative critique. In this respect, the study of audience cultures looks less illuminating than the textual analyses that have been less favoured in television studies in recent years.

Conclusion

Some years before Reality TV had become an established term for a kind of television programme, Jim Collins (1989: 2) wrote that: 'Culture is no longer a unitary, fixed category, but a decentred, fragmentary assemblage of conflicting voices and institutions', and argued that it is no longer clear how to evaluate one discourse as more true, worthwhile or effective than another. The claim that Reality TV has both assisted in, and is an effect of, the disintegration of culture is clearly an aspect of a larger problem that has been diagnosed for some time. There is general agreement among both academic theorists and media producers that new kinds of private and public social formation are forming, deforming and reforming at the start of the twenty-first century. Like Collins, I have argued in this book that Reality TV is a nodal point at which different discourses within and outside television culture have temporarily come together in an unstable conjunction. Rather than producing coherence, the label 'Reality TV' and the programmes and practices that it describes are engaged in processes of self-definition and self-legitimation necessitated by the reduced purchase of an orchestrating hierarchy of value which could assign them to specific and secure places in culture. This brief concluding chapter therefore returns to the questions raised in the Introduction about how the study of Reality TV can judge the significance of what it addresses.

Reality TV opens questions of categorization and evaluation. The foregoing chapters have considered what genres these programmes belong to and how the placing of them in different contexts or the bringing to bear of different critical approaches will affect judgements of them. The book has outlined the instability and methodological challenges of this apparently monolithic television form. When I was invited by Palgrave to write this book, it was suggested that I focus on *Big Brother* because it seems the paradigmatic example of Reality TV. The advantage would have been that I could locate arguments in the context of an example that readers would probably all know. But I have decided not to do that, and to risk discussing Reality TV more broadly, and with a greater emphasis on abstract and methodological points, because the whole purpose of this book is to question what is at the centre of Reality TV, and to question what we mean by the term at all. It is too big an assumption to suggest that the significance of Reality TV can be gauged by discussing *Big Brother* in particular, despite the excellent work done by other writers who have adopted that focus (Mathijs and Jones 2004). The editor who commissioned this book wanted it to be about how *Big Brother* represents the Orwellian idea of a surveilled society as a prison. *Big Brother*, that argument would go, has a special privilege as a representation in coded form of what reality now is like and is therefore more central and matters more than other programme examples. However, the book has become much more complex than that and a lot harder to finish, because I began asking myself what Reality TV means and why it matters.

This is partly an issue about the definition of a genre and the relationship between Reality TV and existing genres of programme. This book has argued that Reality TV is not a genre, but an attitude to the functions of television, its audiences and its subjects (both its subject-matter and the individuals who are represented on it and who make it). But it is worth considering the activity of defining television genre, which is to locate programmes in genre categories, and the functions that genre performs in both addressing and also missing out on important features of Reality TV. This leads into wider questions about the purchase of Television Studies on its subjects. The connections between Reality TV and other genres suggest that it opens questions of categorization and evaluation. As this book has shown, Reality TV shares features with documentary, as a factual genre based on observation of non-actors. It also has links with access programmes featuring 'ordinary' people, with game shows where there are prizes and tests, and with soap opera where there are continuing storylines, exhaustive press coverage and stereotyped or melodramatic characterizations. Like talk shows and some kinds of television drama (Bignell 2004b), *Big Brother* relies on personal confession and the centrality of the body and sexuality as the key to the expression of identity. This combination is a strategy to enable a multi-accentual address to the audience, and, connected with this, as a matter of generic negotiation with other television forms. The point is for people to reveal themselves to each other and to the audience, to establish a 'structure of feeling' that the television audience can share and adduce to understand the foibles, embarrassments and triumphs of the participants, who are most often presented as familiar and ordinary. Although *I'm a Celebrity* featured millionaire television personalities, it was peopled by characters who were treated like ordinary contestants and sometimes resented it.

These similarities and differences between Reality TV and programmes from existing genres negotiate new positions for their audiences and their makers. Television institutions and audiences need novelty, so they extend and mix genres and formats. Television focuses on the present and the new, but any programme's offer to the audience must be understood in terms of previous ones. The confessional talk show has a persistent interest in personal issues with a public dimension, particularly associated with sexual politics. The genre depends on the dissemination of expertise and the offer of self-improvement. Interestingly, the debut of *Big Brother* in the late 1990s coincided with the shift to prominence of confessional talk shows addressed to a more youthful audience. The focus on improvement and individualism was supplemented by a greater emphasis on interpersonal conflict, sexuality and emotion, and the staging of aggression. *The Jerry Springer Show* (1991–) and *Ricki Lake* (1993–) are notable internationally syndicated examples of this format, and it has significant similarities to the confessional forms in Reality TV. The off-screen interviewer in *The Cruise*, the video diary in *The 1940s House* and the Diary Room in *Big Brother* are there for that confessional purpose.

This rapidly evolving cross-generic product responds to contemporary television culture. So whereas talking about genre seems to lead towards disciplining the boundaries between one type of programme and another, by contrast, instead of discipline, genre is about transgression. But if the boundaries between one programme form and another are uncertain, because of the leakage between genres and the continual mixing between them, perhaps the critical response should be to substitute the industry term 'format' instead. The format consists of the elements of the programme that can be abstracted and sold, such as the game structure, the house setting, the elimination process and branding concept for *Big Brother*. Formats are stable, unlike genres, because they have to be as intellectual property and objects of trade. Cheaper formats allow rapid bandwagon-jumping to pursue newly identified audiences who may be attractive to advertisers and channel controllers anxious about ratings and share. In these programmes, the time from pitching to shooting can be very short, and they use a small crew, no script, no stars and minimal post-production facilities. But more expensive competition formats like *Pop Idol* create ranges of licensed branded products, not only attracting audiences but also launching lucrative spin-offs. The buyer of the format is responsible for capital costs and production costs but gets income from merchandising, tie-ins and advertising. The seller of the format profits from selling the future profitability of a brand idea. The adoption of a focus on format simplifies the issues around Reality TV to some degree, by specifying predominant programme types according to their aims, functions and production methods rather than their content.

But there are two problems with this approach that remain. There are severe difficulties for television institutions in defining the uniqueness of a format as a stable property, as the legal contest over *Big Brother*'s possible infringement of *Survivor*'s format parameters illustrated. The boundaries of a format need to be policed by their owners precisely because they are not definitive. Second and more conceptually, any commodity and thus any television format has different relational meanings for the people who create, participate in or watch it. *Big Brother* might look the same but it does not mean the same in different television territories and for different audiences. If the solid centre of Reality TV in Britain is *Big Brother*, in the United States it is *Survivor*. If it is *The Osbournes* for some of my students, it is *Operatunity* for my wife. Like genre, format as a general term will not prescribe the objects of analysis since they are particular because they are commodities, as well as being comparable because they are commodities. It is important to recognize how similar and different three kinds of facet of a television phenomenon may be. These are, first, the brand values that define the programme format as a property and economic enterprise (such as the swapping format of *Wife Swap*, the gamedoc enclosure of *Big Brother* or the historical recreation of the *House* series). The second facet is the key signifier of the programme as a textual object, in the ways that it might be understood by academic critics but also identified by trailers, excerpts and highlights, and they include for example the eviction dramas of *Big Brother*, the tribal bonding of *Survivor* or the elegant posing of *The Edwardian Country House*. These are narrative images of the programmes that differ from the parameters of the format by being specifically textual objects shaped by features of characterization or mise-en-scene or dramatic form that cannot be predicted by the format, though they are enabled by it. Third, these former two facets are made possible by the features of the television medium and how they emphasize some of its possibilities and exclude others, for example the role of liveness, intimacy and

Bignell, J. (2002a) *'Don't Look Back*: documentary and the mythologisation of Bob Dylan', *la licorne*, 13, 237–52.

Bignell, J. (2002b) *Media Semiotics: An Introduction, Second edition* (Manchester: Manchester University Press).

Bignell, J. (2004a) *An Introduction to Television Studies* (London: Routledge).

Bignell, J. (2004b) 'Sex, confession and witness', in K. Akass and J. McCabe (eds) *Reading 'Sex and the City'* (London: I.B. Tauris), 161–76.

Bignell, J. (2005) 'Exemplarity, pedagogy and television history', *New Review of Film and Television Studies*, 3: 1, 15–32.

Biltereyst, D. (2004) 'Reality TV, troublesome pictures and panics: reappraising the public controversy around Reality TV in Europe', in S. Holmes and D. Jermyn (eds) *Understanding Reality Television* (London: Routledge), 91–110.

Biressi, A. and H. Nunn (2005) *Reality TV: Realism and Revelation* (London: Wallflower).

Bondabjerg, I. (1996) 'Public discourse/private fascination: hybridization in "True-Life-Story" genres', *Media, Culture and Society*, 18: 1, 27–45.

Bourdieu, P. (1998) *On Television and Journalism* (London: Pluto).

Brenton, S. and R. Cohen (2003) *Shooting People: Adventures in Reality TV* (London: Verso).

Brooks, P. (1985) *The Melodramatic Imagination* (New York: Columbia University Press).

Brown, M. (2003) 'Why I can't wait for Kevin', *The Guardian*, Media section, 15 September, 2–3.

Brown, M. (2004a) 'Swapping success', *The Guardian*, Media section, 4 October, 10.

Brown, M. (2004b) 'The £100m crisis at Channel 4', *The Guardian*, Media section, 11 November, 8–9.

Brown, M. (2005) 'The knives are out', *The Guardian*, Media section, 18 April, 10–11.

Brunsdon, C. (1981) 'Crossroads-notes on soap opera', *Screen*, 22: 4, 32–7.

Bruzzi, S. (2001a) 'Docusoaps', in G. Creeber (ed.) *The Television Genre Book* (London: Routledge), 132–4.

Bruzzi, S. (2001b) *The New Documentary: A Critical Introduction* (London: Routledge).

Bulkley, K. (2003) 'Vocal goldmine', *The Guardian*, New media section, 11 August, 30.

Burton, G. (2000), *Talking Television: An Introduction to the Study of Television* (London: Arnold).

Butler, J. (1990) *Gender Trouble: Feminism and the Subversion of Identity* (London: Routledge).

Butler, J. (1993) *Bodies that Matter: On the Discursive Limits of Sex* (London: Routledge.

Caldwell, J. (1995) *Televisuality: Style, Crisis, and Authority in American Television* (New Brunswick, NJ: Rutgers University Press).

Cassy, J. (2002) 'Hopes high as popstar show returns', *The Guardian*, 7 September, 7.

Caughie, J. (1986) 'Popular culture: notes and revisions', in C. MacCabe (ed.) *High Theory/Low Culture* (Manchester: Manchester University Press), 156–71.

Caughie, J. (2000) *Television Drama: Realism, Modernism and British Culture* (Oxford: Oxford University Press).

Cavender, G. (2004) 'In search of community on Reality TV: *America's Most Wanted* and *Survivor*', in S. Holmes and D. Jermyn (eds) *Understanding Reality Television* (London: Routledge), 154–72.

Clapperton, G. (2004) 'Hitting on Big Brother', *The Guardian*, New media section, 14 June, 42.

Clarke, N. (2003) 'Get a grip on reality', *The Guardian*, Media section, 26 May, 2–3.

Collins, J. (1989) *Uncommon Cultures: Popular Culture and Post-Modernism* (London: Routledge).

Corner, J. (1992) 'Presumption as theory: "realism" in television studies', *Screen*, 33: 1, 97–102.

Corner, J. (1995) *Television Form and Public Address* (London: Edward Arnold).

Corner, J. (1996) *The Art of Record: A Critical Introduction to Documentary*, (Manchester: Manchester University Press).

Corner, J. (2004) 'Afterword: framing the new', in S. Holmes and D. Jermyn (eds) *Understanding Reality Television* (London: Routledge), 290–9.

Crace, J. (2002) 'The prison of TV', *The Guardian*, Education section, 14 May, 10–11.

Creeber, G. (2001) (ed.) *The Television Genre Book* (London: BFI).

Cummings, D. (2002) (ed.) *Reality TV: How Real is Real?* (London: Hodder and Stoughton).

Deans, J. (2004a) 'Reality bites', *The Guardian*, Media section, 23 February, 4.

Deans, J. (2004b) 'American high', *The Guardian*, Media section, 4 November, 13.

Deans, J. (2005a) 'The last laugh', *The Guardian*, Media section, 17 January, 2–3.

Deans, J. (2005b) 'Sugar and splice in the editing suite', *The Guardian*, Media section, 14 February, 11.

Derrida, J. (1996) 'Demeure. fiction et témoignage', in M. Lisse (ed.) *Passions de la litérature. Avec Jacques Derrida* (Paris: Galilée), 13–73.

Dovey, J. (2000) *Freakshow: First Person Media and Factual Television* (London: Pluto).

Dovey, J. (2001) 'Reality TV', in G. Creeber (ed.) *The Television Genre Book* (London: BFI), 134–7.

Dunkley, S. (2002) 'It's not new, and it's not clever', in D. Cummings (ed.) *Reality TV: How Real is Real?* (London: Hodder and Stoughton), 35–46.

Eco, U. (1984) 'A guide to the neo-television of the 1980s', *Framework*, 25 18–25.

Ellis, J. (1982) *Visible Fictions: Cinema, Television, Video* (London: Routledge & Kegan Paul.

Ellis, J. (1999a) *Seeing Things: Television in the Age of Uncertainty* (London: I. B. Tauris).

Ellis, J. (1999b) 'Television as working through', in J. Gripsrud (ed.) *Television and Common Knowledge* (London: Routledge), 55–7.

Ellis, J. (2005) 'Documentary and truth on television: the crisis of 1999', in A. Rosenthal and J. Corner (eds) *New Challenges for Documentary*, second edition (Manchester: Manchester University Press), 342–60.

Elsaessor, T. (1985) 'Tales of sound and fury: observations on the family melodrama', in B. Nichols (ed.) *Movies and Methods*, vol. 2 (Berkeley, CA: University of California Press).

Featherstone, M. (1991) *Consumer Culture and Postmodernism* (London: Sage).

Feuer, J. (1986) 'Narrative form in American network television', in C. MacCabe (ed.) *High Theory/Low Culture* (Manchester: Manchester University Press), 101–14.

Fiske, J. (1987) *Television Culture* (London: Routledge).

Fiske, J. (1994) *Media Matters* (Minneapolis, MN: University of Minnesota Press.

Flitterman-Lewis, S. (1992) 'Psychoanalysis, film and television', in R. Allen (ed.) *Channels of Discourse, Reassembled* (London: Routledge), 203–46.

Foster, D. (2004) ' "Jump in the pool": The competitive culture of *Survivor* fan networks', in S. Holmes and D. Jermyn (eds) *Understanding Reality Television* (London: Routledge), 270–89.

Friedberg, A. (1993) *Window Shopping: Cinema and the Postmodern* (Berkeley, CA: University of California Press).

Fukuyama, F. (1989) 'The end of history?', *The National Interest*, 16, 3–18.

Fukuyama, F. (1992) *The End of History and the Last Man* (New York: Free Press).

Gardiner, A. (2004) 'Why I know it's a jungle out there', *The Guardian*, Media section, 8 November, 4.

Geertz, C. (1967) *The Interpretation of Cultures: Selected Essays* (London: Fontana).

Genette, G. (1982) *Palimpsests: La littérature au second dégrée* (Paris: Seuil).

Geraghty, C. (1998) 'Audiences and "ethnography": questions of practice', in C. Geraghty and D. Lusted (eds) *The Television Studies Book* (London: Arnold), 141–57.

Geraghty, C. (1991) *Women and Soap Opera: A Study of Prime Time Soaps* (Cambridge: Polity).

Gibson, O. (2003) 'Let's get interactive', *The Guardian*, Media section, 16 June, 47.

Giddens, A. (1995) *The Consequences of Modernity* (Cambridge: Polity).

Gillan, J. (2004) 'From Ozzie Nelson to Ozzy Osbourne: the genesis and development of the reality (star) sitcom', in S. Holmes and D. Jermyn (eds) *Understanding Reality Television* (London: Routledge), 54–70.

Gripsrud, J. (1998) 'Television, broadcasting, flow: key metaphors in TV theory', in C. Geraghty and D. Lusted (eds) *The Television Studies Book* (London: Arnold), 17–32.

Grossberg, L. (1987) 'The in-difference of television', *Screen*, 28:2, 28–45.

Habermas, J. (1987) *The Theory of Communicative Action*, vol. 2, *Lifeworld and System: A Critique of Functionalist Reason* (Cambridge: Polity).

Habermas, J. (1989a) 'The public sphere: an encyclopaedia article', in S. Brunner and D. Kellner (eds) *Critical Theory and Society* (London: Routledge), 136.

Habermas, J. (1989b) *The Structural Transformation of the Public Sphere* (Cambridge, MA: MIT Press).

Hall, S. and T. Jefferson (eds) (1976) *Resistance through Rituals: Youth Subcultures in Postwar Britain* (London: Hutchinson).

Haque, S. (2003) 'Oh brother', *Midweek*, 5 November, 1.

Harris, I. (2002) 'Fwd: have you seen this?', *The Guardian*, New Media section, 4 November, 34.

Hebdidge, D. (1979) *Subculture: The Meaning of Style* (London: Methuen).

Hegel, G.W.F. (1956) *The Philosophy of History*, trans J. Silbee (New York: Dover).

Hill, A. (1999) 'Crime and crisis: British Reality TV in action', in E. Buscombe (ed.) *British Television: A Reader* (Oxford: Oxford University Press), 218–34.

Hill, A. (2002) '*Big Brother*: the real audience', *Television and New Media*, 3: 3, 323–41.

Hill, A. (2005) *Reality TV: Audiences and Popular Factual Television* (London: Routledge).

Holmes, S. (2004) ' "All you've got to worry about is the task, having a cup of tea, and doing a bit of sunbathing": approaching celebrity in *Big Brother*', in

S. Holmes and D. Jermyn (eds) *Understanding Reality Television* (London: Routledge), 111–35.

Holmes, S. and D. Jermyn (2004) (eds) *Understanding Reality Television* (London: Routledge).

Hughes, J. (2002) 'A future full of wizardry', *The Guardian*, New Media section, 21 October, 38.

Independent Television Commission (2002) *Programme Code* (London: ITC).

Innis, H. (1951) *The Bias of Communication* (Toronto, ON: University of Toronto Press).

Innis, H. (1972) *Empire and Communications*, rev. M. Innis (Toronto, ON: Toronto University Press).

Jameson, F. (1984) 'Postmodernism, or the cultural logic of late capitalism', *New Left Review* 146, 53–92.

Jameson, F. (1991) *Postmodernism, or the Cultural Logic of Late Capitalism* (London: Verso).

Jameson, F. (1992) *Signatures of the Visible* (London: Routledge).

Jermyn, D. (2004) ' "This *is* about real people": video technologies, actuality and affect in the television crime appeal', in S. Holmes and D. Jermyn (eds) *Understanding Reality Television* (London: Routledge), 71–90.

Jones, A. (2003) 'British hits in America', *The Guardian*, Media section, 11 August, 2.

Jones, J. (2004) 'Emerging platform identities: *Big Brother* UK and interactive multi-platform usage', in E. Mathijs and J. Jones (eds) *Big Brother International: Formats, Critics and Publics* (London: Wallflower), 210–31.

Kavka, M. and A. West (2004) 'Temporalities of the real: conceptualising time in Reality TV', in S. Holmes and D. Jermyn (eds) *Understanding Reality Television* (London: Routledge), 136–53.

Keveney, B. and G. Levin (2002) 'Starmakers heat up TV series plans', *USA Today*, 23 July, 3D.

Kilborn, R. (2003) *Staging the Real: Factual TV Programming in the Age of Big Brother* (Manchester: Manchester University Press).

Kilborn, R. and J. Izod (1997) *An Introduction to Television Documentary: Confronting Reality* (Manchester: Manchester University Press).

Kompare, D. (2004) 'Extraordinary ordinary: *The Osbournes* as "An American Family" ', in S. Murray and L. Ouellette (eds) *Reality TV: Remaking Television Culture* (New York: New York University Press), 97–116.

Lacan, J. (1977) 'The mirror stage', in *Ecrits: A Selection*, trans. A. Sheridan (London: Tavistock), 1–7.

Laing, S. (1991) 'Raymond Williams and the cultural analysis of television', *Media, Culture and Society*, 13: 2, 153–69.

Lajoie, M. (1996) 'Psychoanalysis and cyberspace', in R. Shields (ed.) *Cultures of the Internet* (London: Sage), 70–98.

Lamont, D. (2003) 'Could they be related?', *The Guardian*, Media section, 20 January, 10.

Lash, S. (1990) *The Sociology of Postmodernism* (London: Routledge).

Los Angeles Times (2002) television ratings for 9–15 December 2002, Wednesday 18 December, E17.

Lull, J. (1988) 'Critical response: the audience as nuisance', *Critical Studies in Mass Communication*, 5, 239–43.

Lusted, D. (1998) 'The popular culture debate and light entertainment on television', in C. Geraghty and D. Lusted (eds) *The Television Studies Book* (London: Arnold), 175–90.

Lyon, D. (1994) *The Electronic Eye: The Rise of Surveillance Society* (Minneapolis, MN: Minnesota University Press).

Lyon, D. (2001) *Surveillance Society: Monitoring Everyday Life* (Buckingham: Open University Press).

Lyotard, J-F. (1991) *The Inhuman*, trans. G. Bennington (Cambridge: Polity).

Macdonald, D. (1994) 'A theory of mass culture', in J. Storey (ed.) *Cultural Theory and Popular Culture: A Reader* (Hemel Hempstead: Harvester Wheatsheaf), 29–43.

Macgragor Wise, J. (2002) 'Mapping the culture of control: seeing through *The Truman Show'*, *Television and New Media*, 3:1, 29–47.

Mathijs, E. and J. Jones (2004) (eds) *Big Brother International: Formats, Critics and Publics* (London: Wallflower).

McLuhan, M. (1987) *Understanding Media: The Extensions of Man* (London: Ark).

McRobbie, A. (1994) *Postmodernism and Popular Culture* (London: Routledge).

Metz, C. (1982) *The Imaginary Signifier: Psychoanalysis and the Cinema*, trans. B. Brewster (Bloomington, IN: Indiana University Press).

Mills, B. (2004) 'Comedy verite: contemporary sitcom form', *Screen*, 45: 1, 63–78.

Modleski, T. (1986) (ed.) *Studies in Entertainment: Critical Approaches to Mass Culture* (Bloomington, IN: Indiana University Press).

Morley, D. (1980) *The 'Nationwide' Audience* (London: BFI).

Morley, D. (1992) *Television, Audiences and Cultural Studies* (London: Routledge).

Morris, M. (1988) 'Banality in cultural studies', *Block*, 14, 15–25.

Morse, M. (1990) 'An ontology of everyday distraction: the freeway, the mall, and television', in P. Mellencamp (ed.) *Logics of Television* (London: BFI), 193–221.

Mosely, R. (2000) 'Makeover takeover on British television', *Screen*, 41: 3, 299–314.

Neal, A. (2003) 'Dealing in illusions: television through the film lens', unpublished MPhil dissertation, University of Newcastle.

Neale, S. and G. Turner (2001) 'Introduction: what is genre?', in G. Creeber (ed.) *The Television Genre Book* (London: BFI), 1–7.

Nichols, B. (1991) *Representing Reality: Issues and Concepts in Documentary* (Bloomington, IN: Indiana University Press).

Nichols, B. (1994) *Blurred Boundaries: Questions of Meaning in Contemporary Culture* (Bloomington, IN: Indiana University Press).

Paget, D. (1998) *No Other Way to Tell It: Dramadoc/Docudrama on Television* (Manchester, Manchester University Press).

Palmer, G. (2003) *Discipline and Liberty: Television and Governance* (Manchester: Manchester University Press).

Palmer, G. (2004) ' "The new you": class and transformation in lifestyle television', in S. Holmes and D. Jermyn (eds) *Understanding Reality Television* (London: Routledge), 173–90.

Piper, H. (2004) 'Reality TV, *Wife Swap* and the drama of banality', *Screen*, 54: 4, 273–86.

Plunkett, J. (2005a) 'The wizard of Ozzy', *The Guardian*, Media section, 11 April, 4.

Plunkett, J. (2005b) 'When TV sex is "educational" ', *The Guardian*, Media section, 13 October, 8–9.

Rogers, Z. (2005) 'Variety is the spice of life in Los Angeles', *The Guardian*, Media section, 11 April, 9.

Roscoe, J. (2004) *'Big Brother* Australia: performing the "real" twenty-four-seven', in R. Allen and A. Hill (eds) *The Television Studies Reader* (London: Routledge), 311–21.

Roscoe, J. and C. Hight (2001) *Faking It: Mock-documentary and the Subversion of Factuality* (Manchester: Manchester University Press).

Rosenthal, A. and J. Corner (2005) (eds) *New Challenges for Documentary*, second edition (Manchester: Manchester University Press).

Schiller, H. (1969) *Mass Communications and American Empire* (New York: Augustus M Kelly).

Schiller, H. (1976) *Communication and Cultural Domination* (New York: Sharpe M. E.).

Scott, A. (1997) 'Introduction', in A. Scott (ed.) *The Limits of Globalisation: Cases and Arguments* (London: Routledge), 1–22.

Sears, J. (1995) *'Crimewatch* and the rhetoric of verisimilitude', *Critical Survery*, 7: 1, 51–8.

Shattuc, J. (1997) *The Talking Cure: TV Talk Shows and Women* (London: Routledge).

Siune, K. and O. Hulten (1998) 'Does public broadcasting have a future?', in D. McQuail and K. Siune (eds) *Media Policy: Convergence, Concentration, Commerce* (London: Sage), 23–37.

Spigel, L. (2001) *Welcome to the Dreamhouse: Popular Media and Postwar Suburbs* (Durham: Duke University Press).

Thompson, J. (1994) 'Social theory and the media', in D. Crowley and D. Mitchell (eds) *Communication Theory Today* (Cambridge: Polity), 27–49.

Thompson, J. (1995) *The Media and Modernity* (Cambridge: Polity).

Tincknell, E. and P. Raghuram (2004) *'Big Brother:* reconfiguring the "active" audience of cultural studies?', in S. Holmes and D. Jermyn (eds) *Understanding Reality Television* (London: Routledge), 252–69.

Wells, M. (2003) 'Top of the heap', *The Guardian*, Media section, 11 August, 2.

Williams, R. (1976) *Keywords: A Vocabulary of Culture and Society* (London: Fontana).

Williams, R. (1977) 'A lecture on realism', *Screen*, 18: 1, 61–74.

Williams, R. (1990) *Television, Technology and Cultural Form* (London: Routledge).

Willis, P. (1977) *Learning to Labour: How Working Class Kids Get Working Class Jobs* (Aldershot: Saxon House).

Winston, B. (1995) *Claiming the Real: The Documentary Film Revisited* (London: BFI, 1995).

Index